From Exorcism to Ecstasy

From Exorcism to Ecstasy

Eight Views of Baptism

Russell Haitch

Westminster John Knox Press

LOUISVILLE • LONDON

Book design by Sharon Adams
Cover design by Alfred Moreschi

First edition
Published by Westminster John Knox Press
Louisville, Kentucky

This book is printed on acid-free paper that meets the American National Standards Institute Z39.48 standard. ∞

PRINTED IN THE UNITED STATES OF AMERICA

07 08 09 10 11 12 13 14 15 16 — 10 9 8 7 6 5 4 3 2 1

Library of Congress Cataloging-in-Publication Data is on file at the Library of Congress, Washington, D.C.

ISBN-13: 978-0-664-23000-5
ISBN-10: 0-664-22958-1

Contents

Introduction

If the cross is the universally recognized Christian symbol, then baptism is the universal Christian act. Most Christians reading this book have been baptized, whether as infants or adults, whether in water or with the Spirit. Around the world and down through the ages, Christians have undergone baptism.

But what is baptism?

People attending a wedding have a fairly good sense of what is happening when vows are said and rings are given. People coming to a baptism may or may not bring this same degree of clarity, but quite likely they also bring a hazy sense of troubled history. They may think to themselves, "Our beliefs about baptism differ from those of some other churches."

They may go on to think, "What do those other churches believe anyhow?" Or even, "What do *we* believe?"

Many volumes have been written on baptism, but this is the first to give readers a scholarly yet accessible overview of eight important positions, from the Eastern Orthodox with its attention to exorcism, to the Pentecostal with its concern for ecstatic utterance. Like a journalist, I have tried to report each position accurately. Like a portrait painter, I have tried to set each position in the best possible light. Like a family therapist, I have tried to help each voice be heard, despite some history of antagonism.

For all the writers represented here, baptism is important, even crucial, but for none is baptism a thing unto itself. Rather, the reality of baptism takes place in relation to Jesus Christ. In writing about baptism each theologian is attempting to illuminate what it means to be a Christian.

Therefore my intention was not to pit one position against the others. Baptism is not primarily an argument to be won but a mystery to be embraced. As such, it is more than can be put into words. Thus I am not suggesting that you must read every word of this book before going to a baptism, or undergoing baptism, or even baptizing someone else. However, I can highlight some ways this book can help pastors, church leaders, seminary students, and other thoughtful Christians.

First, we live in an age of denominational mobility. People come to a church with different backgrounds (or maybe no background) and with questions. Sometimes the questions are specifically about baptism. At other times, baptism can be a concrete way to explore a host of related issues.

Second, there is movement not only between but *within* denominations. Perhaps in recent years the lines of doctrine on baptism have become less hard and fast. I know a Baptist pastor who allowed infant baptism after reading Calvin, and a Presbyterian pastor who would not baptize her baby after reading Barth. People moving more deeply into their faith tradition also ask questions. One could point to Pentecostals who wonder what others believe about Spirit Baptism, Methodists who wonder whether Wesley contradicts himself, Lutherans who wonder what Luther believed, and many in the West who wonder what the Eastern Orthodox believe. Answering such questions, as this book aims to do, can help readers to modify, or else solidify, their own views.

Third, as we are painfully aware, we live in a time of divisions. The issues dividing some churches may not be resolved any time soon. Can we find a place of deeper unity? Many churches have officially stated that baptism is a ground for Christian unity, following a meeting of the Faith and Order Commission of the World Council of Churches in Lima, Peru, in 1982. The Letter to the Ephesians also speaks of "one faith, one Baptism . . ." If baptism is to be a place of unity, we should endeavor to understand it better. Are different people referring to the same thing when they speak of baptism?

In reading the views in this book you may find one that lines up exactly with yours. But if not, knowing these different views can still help for the three reasons just named. There is a fourth reason as well, which I discovered in writing my doctoral thesis. There are two kinds of dissertations, my advisor told me: those you finish and that is the end of it, and those that turn into lifelong passions. Let me do the first kind, I said. So I chose to research baptism, since it appeared to be a concrete activity, not some nebulous philosophy that could go on and on.

Little did I anticipate the outcome. It is true, there is something simple about baptism. But it is the kind of simplicity that masters a range of complexity, like the formula "$E = mc^2$," or the statement "Jesus is Lord." Thus I came to see, in writing and subsequent teaching, how baptism is an excellent way to introduce people to theology. Each view of baptism gives us a beautiful window into a different branch of the church. Through each view the reader can see an entire worldview and frame of mind.

In seminary settings I have found that baptism helps students bring into focus a number of scriptural, dogmatic, and practical concerns. For the same reasons, I think baptism is a good topic for a church Bible study or discussion group. The questions swirling around baptism can become a source of deeper unity, rather than division, when they are treated as topics for discussion, not just as edicts delivered by authorities from on high.

Perhaps every church can benefit from hearing the range of voices in the wider church. As you read these chapters, you will see that my procedure has been to say how each theologian answers the question, what is baptism? The answer in each case is summed up in a single sentence. Baptism is death and resurrection. Baptism is the act of washing. Baptism is God's Word with water. Baptism is sign and seal. Baptism is, and is not, the new birth. Baptism is the new humanity. Baptism is power. Baptism is prayer. My editor, Don McKim, has called these short sentences "bumper stickers," and we all know the danger here. Yet a bumper sticker at least is easy to read and remember, which can be a good thing. But it would be a very bad thing if I did not state at the outset, and ask you to underline, certain qualifications.

First, in saying that for a particular writer baptism is x, I am not claiming that it is *only* x for this writer—or that it is x for this writer alone. Second, I have connected each view to a verse or two of Scripture, but obviously I am not saying that this verse is the only verse that applies to the position. Third, I have also connected each view to a contemporary concern, in order to show how baptism matters for everyday Christian living. The concern may be timely, or timeless, or both—as in the case of Alexander Schmemann, whose Orthodox view of Baptism addresses the issue of consumerism, but also the question of death. In each case the concern I highlight is meant to be suggestive, not exclusive. By saying that Calvin is concerned with the family (both nuclear and ecclesial), I do not imply that other writers care less about the family, or that Calvin's sole concern is for the family. (By now I have made basically the same point three times, because scholars must do all we can to avoid charges of reductionism.)

The writers represented in this book do not speak for entire denominations. At the same time, their views are widely recognized as being important and influential. Almost as a consequence, seven of the eight writers are white males of European descent. This fact means what it means. It means no doubt that historically certain voices have been overrepresented; it means perhaps that the best voices have yet to be heard. This book does not try to redress the balance so much as pave the way for newer voices by providing valuable background. I asked people in each denomination (both women and men, and of diverse ethnicities) which voices have been most influential in their branch of the church. The views here show the results of my poll, but the views are still a sample, and the whole book only part of a well-rounded curriculum.

The eight views are not in chronological sequence. Because we make assumptions of progress, a chronological sequence can imply a movement from the more primitive to the more refined, and I did not want to imply any such movement. Instead the chapters are arranged to prompt interesting comparisons. By reading Luther and Aquinas side by side, you can see how both seek to base their view of baptism in Scripture, and the careful reader can see how (contrary to popular stereotypes) Aquinas is concerned with justification by faith, while Luther admonishes people to strive against sin. By reading Karl Barth and Aimee Semple McPherson side by side, you can see they both care intensely about the Baptism of the Holy Spirit, though they differ considerably on what it means. By reading Alexander Schmemann and John Howard Yoder side by side, you can see not just how one favors infant Baptism, the other believers' Baptism, or how one is "high church" and the other "low church," but also how both are in some sense "sacramental realists." For both the question is not what do the sacraments signify, or what reality do they mediate, but rather, what are they in fact and in truth and in lived experience? While it could be said that Yoder focuses more on the world and Schmemann more on worship, each in his own way wants to remove the gap between the two, making the life of worship normative for life in the world.

We could continue making such connections. However, just as I have not intended to champion one position as being superior, so I have not tried to unify them all into one grand scheme. My wife Judi has grown weary (or wary) of the term *postmodernism*, but it was she who observed that this project has a postmodernist aspect. Its aim is not to propose one objective and universal position, but to allow diverse voices to be mutually illuminating and mutually correcting.

Though baptism is an exciting topic, the reader may decide not to read all eight chapters at once. Would you listen to eight sermons on the Prodigal Son in the same week? I might, but I tend to like intensity. At any rate, the comparison to sermons is instructive. Just as we can listen to the same text preached over and over, and our appreciation grows deeper and deeper, so it is with meditating on baptism. There is great depth to baptism. The questions are deep: "Or do you not know that all of us who have been baptized into Christ Jesus were baptized into his death?" (Rom. 6:3). The first chapter offers one magnificent—for me, life-changing—reading of this verse. The views of subsequent chapters can take us back to other portions of Scripture with fresh interest.

My summaries of these views may be too short for some, too long for others. I tried to make sure that each chapter could withstand scholarly scrutiny.

I also tried to keep in mind a favorite quote of my mother's, which comes from a child's thank-you note: "Dear Aunt Martha, Thank you for the book on elephants. It told me more about elephants than I wanted to know."

Both my parents were journalists; my mother taught me to think and my father especially taught me to write. His writing for me always exemplified clarity and accuracy with a touch of wit. He also taught me that the first rule of newspaper writing is to make your deadline. With that in mind, I will stop here, with this prayer:

May all our thinking and teaching on baptism glorify God and edify the church.

Russell Haitch
Richmond, Indiana

1

Alexander Schmemann

Baptism Is Death and Resurrection

Do you not know that all of us who have been baptized into Christ
Jesus were baptized into his death?

Rom. 6:3

COUNTERING CONSUMERISM—
BY CONFRONTING DEATH

Though Jesus warned that life does not consist in the abundance of possessions (Luke 12:15), consumerism is a well-known problem today. For Alexander Schmemann (1921–1983), the depth of this problem can be seen in the way
it has affected Christianity. People treat the Church as if it were a consumer
good or service; they shop around for a religion that will satisfy their personal
desires or help them to cope with life.

All the while people, even pastors, try to ignore the intractable fact of death,
because death is not "helpful," and pastors have joined the ranks of the helping professions. But ignoring death only fuels the problem of consumerism.
For consumerism, and many other "isms," manifest the power of death at work
in daily life.

Baptism is a different sort of "ism" entirely. Schmemann says Baptism[1] provides a way out of consumerism. It does so by not ignoring but directly confronting death—and not just figuratively but actually. How can Baptism
counter consumerism? And how could it possibly conquer death?

---

1. Baptism is capitalized in some chapters and not others, depending on the usual
style of the represented theologians and their denominations.

To grasp this view of Baptism, we need to ask three basic questions:

- What are "life" and "death" *actually?* In what do they consist?
- How does Christ's death destroy death and its power?
- Precisely how does Baptism unite people with Christ in his death-destroying death?

Answering this last question will be especially important for tackling the problem of consumerism, for when Baptism unites people with Christ, it also transforms the entire material world, starting with water. Further, Baptism transforms how people relate to the material world, restoring these relations to their God-intended form. The world is then no longer a *commodity* to be consumed or exploited, but rather all creation becomes once more a means of *communion* with God.

To understand these large claims and answer the three large questions just posed, we can start with an equally large context, namely Schmemann's history of civilization. His historical narrative juxtaposes "old religion" with new "secularism," then distinguishes Christianity from both. Even if one takes issue with his narrative, it raises compelling issues.

OLD RELIGION AND NEW SECULARISM

We begin with ancient religions. They were death centered in that one of their main functions was to help people die, by reconciling them to the fact of death. "What pains Plato took in his *Phaedo* to make death desirable and even good," observes Schmemann.[2] Religions before and after Plato also tried to console people with various ideas: that God made death, that death is part of life's normal pattern, or that even when people die at least their soul is immortal.

These attempts to normalize death are futile in that they fly in the face of everyday experience. People sense, when they have lost someone they love, that death is wrong and somehow not meant to be, even though it is the universal fact. The Orthodox Christian message declares death to be "*abnormal* . . . and truly horrible. At the grave of Lazarus Christ wept."[3]

Old religion tried to reconcile people to death by proclaiming death as an escape from this world. Christianity aims to reconcile people to God, proclaiming that Christ has overcome death for the life of the world. This is the gospel message of Baptism that has been lost and needs to be reclaimed.

2. Alexander Schmemann, *For the Life of the World* (Crestwood, NY: St. Vladimir's Seminary Press, 1965), 97.
3. *For the Life of the World*, 100.

But why was the message lost? In part it was lost because Christianity adopted the ancient pagan song that said, "death to the body, immortality for the soul." This is not a Christian doctrine, for it posits an opposition between the spiritual and the material.[4] The Christian message said there will be a resurrection for the body as well as the soul. Yet too often Christianity adopted Neoplatonic thinking, starting with Baptism. After Augustine, many theologians called the visible, material water of Baptism a "means" to obtain an invisible, spiritual thing called "grace." This way of thinking bifurcates the material from the spiritual, then denigrates the material. It can even turn grace into a kind of commodity that one obtains by means of the sacrament.

Then too the true message of Baptism was lost due to the triumph of secularism. Modern secularism is actually an outgrowth of Christianity, says Schmemann. It is a phenomenon found only within the "Christian world." The Christian message offering "fullness of life" liberated people to be less fearful and more active in relation to the world, giving rise to secular enterprises.[5] Secularism, however, is also a religion—not the absence of religion. It is not the old religion, but the new religion. It is the religion of those who say that the only world and the only life we can know are here and now. Hence it is up to us to be busy, to be happy, to be useful. Secularism does not deal with death but rather tries to ignore it.

The word that best sums up the secular frame of mind is *consumer*. The whole world is a bazaar or shopping mall of experiences, and the goal is to pack as much in or squeeze as much out of life as you can, before the inevitable arrival of death. Getting the most out of life can also mean giving—the secular mind-set can engender a charitable dedication to building a better world or a more just society. But all the while the fact is overlooked that society is situated in a "cosmic cemetery."[6] There are additional ironies of secularism. Overconsumption can fuel feelings of emptiness. A culture that is death-denying can also become necrophilic when what is repressed reemerges as an attraction to violence or evil.

Often Christian pastors have carved out a place for themselves by being alternately pagan and secular, but not Christian. When asked to officiate at a funeral, they may draw upon ancient pagan doctrines to portray this world as a place of suffering and death as liberation for the soul. But when called to join the ranks of the helping professions, they may give homilies on coping with life's difficulties or expanding human potential, all the while ignoring the fact

4. *For the Life of the World*, 97.
5. *For the Life of the World*, 100.
6. *For the Life of the World*, 100.

OLD RELIGION

Aim—To reconcile people to death
Message—Death is escape from this world
Irony—Attempts to "normalize" death are futile

NEW SECULARISM

Aim—To avoid and deny death
Message—Maximize consumption and activity
Irony—This consumption leads to emptiness

CHRISTIANITY

Aim—To reconcile people to God
Message—Jesus died for the life of the world
Irony—His death is "deathless"

of death, because it is not helpful. In both cases, whether ignoring death (like a secularist) or calling it liberation (like a pagan), pastors have forgotten how to teach an Orthodox Christian understanding of death. Baptism would provide the perfect opportunity to do this teaching, but pastors have also forgotten, if they ever knew, the Orthodox understanding of Baptism.

To recap, a Neoplatonic understanding of Baptism fuels consumerism by separating the physical and spiritual realms, thus turning grace into a kind of spiritual commodity. A secular denial of death also fuels consumerism by turning the world into a cosmic shopping mall. To arrive at the Orthodox Christian understanding of both Baptism and death, let us focus on the first question named above: What are "life" and "death" actually? In what do they consist? Here I will draw mainly on Schmemann but also other Orthodox sources.

THE MEANING OF "LIFE" AND "DEATH"

A flat line on the heart monitor points to death but does not tell the whole story. For we know that life is more than physical breathing, and death is more than expiration. Whenever people say, "I don't want merely to exist but truly *to live*," they refer to the fact that life and death are more than physical. When the Fourth Gospel says of Jesus that "in him was life" (John 1:4), this "life" refers to a relationality with God, and thence with people and the world. This relationality is one of love, joy, peace, goodness—all these betoken life.

This life in Jesus is both spiritual and physical; the two realms are distinct yet united. In the beginning, God creates the world, breathing Spirit into matter. God creates the man and woman to have communion with God and with each other, a communion that takes place in and through the material world. They are invited to take and eat from the Garden—consuming it not as a commodity apart from God, but as part of their communion with God. Overall the Lord's intent for humanity is that they will be like God (Gen. 1:26), participating in God's creative energies (though not essence), for they have been created in the image and likeness of their Creator.

Into the Garden comes the tempter, the ancient enemy, who says: You don't need God to be like God. You can be like God on your own, apart from God: "For God knows that when you eat of it . . . you will be like God, knowing good and evil" (Gen. 3:5). The woman and man thus come to know about evil by doing it, and having done it, they lose the power of choosing otherwise. They also become the first consumers in the modern secular sense—consuming the world apart from obedient relationship with God. God's purpose is for humanity to be like God in relationship to God, but primordial sin and death consist in this desire to be like God apart from God.

For the first consumers, Eve and Adam, sin as separation from God spells death, first spiritual then physical. Sin leads to death, theologically speaking. But empirically speaking, death in turn leads to sin. Death drives people toward sin because they experience life as a limited commodity, in terms of scarcity rather than abundance. Death says you only go around once, so you have to grab for all the gusto you can, even when it means grabbing from other people or strip-mining the world. Therefore, as James says, people covet and kill, quarrel and fight to obtain what they do not have.

When Paul says in Romans 5:12 that death has spread to all people, he could be saying that sin leads to death, or that death leads to sin. Eastern Orthodox theologians have often chosen the latter tack. They translate the Greek phrase of this verse, *ep ho pantes hemarton*, in a way that is grammatically correct though not contained in most Western Bibles: Death came through sin, *and because of death all sinned*. This translation identifies death as the enemy. It is one reason Orthodox doctrines of atonement usually stress victory over death more than payment for sin.

To understand the Orthodox frame of mind, one must apprehend this power of death, as well as God's intent for fullness of life. Even in everyday understanding, people who doubt they are sinners still know that they are going to die. The thought of death may be repressed. However, when the fear of death does crop up, it is mainly the fear of physical death. For physical death appears to be what causes separation from "life"; it appears to be the most severe event imaginable. This appearance, however, is somewhat deceiving, on two counts: because spiritual death first instigates separation from life, and because Baptism, theologically speaking, is an even more severe event.

HOW THE DEATH OF CHRIST DESTROYS DEATH

To grasp the magnitude of Baptism from an Orthodox perspective, we turn to the second question posed at the start: *How does Christ's death destroy the power of death?* To the previous question—In what do life and death consist?—the short answer is that life consists in God and death in separation from God. Thus "eternal life" entails not just duration, but quality of life in God. *In him was life*—this life speaks of the way Jesus lived. From the start his earthly existence is the apotheosis of life. It consists entirely in love for God and thus love for people. It consists entirely in obedience to God and therefore in the desire to save the world and liberate people from whatever enslaves them.

Nor did his death differ from how he lived. His desire to "drink this cup" and be plunged into the "baptism" of crucifixion (Mark 10:38; Luke 12:50) was an extension of his life, the ultimate expression of its love and obedience. But—here is the crucial juncture—if death is really the absence of this love and obedience, then this death, *his* death, is actually "deathless." Jesus takes death into himself and undoes it. Certainly his death is not painless; it is undertaken with agony and full participation in suffering humanity. But because there is pure *life* in his death, pure love and obedience in his willingness to die, therefore *this* death, his death, conquers death.

Furthermore, his resurrection is consistent with how he lived and died. Not just a bizarre occurrence, this resurrection is rather the logical outcome of his conquering spiritual death. Since the spiritual is joined to the physical, one can say that it is not impossible for Jesus to rise physically from the dead. Instead, as Peter says in Acts, "it was impossible for him to be held in death's power" (Acts 2:24). Jesus not only overcomes death, he destroys its power, and not only for himself, but for all who are united with him. In the Orthodox liturgy for Easter, originally the time of Baptism, the Church sings repeatedly: "Christ has risen from the dead, trampling down death by death, and upon those in the tombs bestowing life."

Christ's death defeats death, it brings about the resurrection, and it transforms the very nature of death. Thus to "die" with Christ through Baptism becomes a good thing, even the best thing possible. Here the central text is Romans 6:3–5:

> Do you not know that all of us who have been baptized into Christ Jesus were baptized into his death? Therefore we have been buried with him by baptism into death, so that, just as Christ was raised from the dead by the glory of the Father, so we too might walk in newness of life. For if we have been united with him in a death like his, we will certainly be united with him in a resurrection like his.

To summarize, "death" has at least three meanings beyond physical expiration.

- There is the death of humanity that spells separation from God. This death, foremost a spiritual reality, is something of which one can partake while walking down the street, or by the same token, from which one can be free while lying in the grave.
- There is the death of Jesus Christ. This death conquers spiritual death and even transforms physical death into resurrection—a "passover" to fuller life and communion with God.
- There is the death of Baptism. This death enacts union with Christ in *his* life-giving death. Baptism is participation in Christ's once-for-all death. At the same time, Baptism is also a co-death. Following Romans 6, the baptized person both becomes included in Christ's death and also undergoes a "death like his." Both dimensions are important.

How is Baptism a death "like his"? It is not like his only because going under the water is somehow like his crucifixion or burial, though from the patristic period until now this analogy has been a preaching point when churches practice immersion. But more truly, baptismal death is like Christ's death because it is *voluntary*. This death does not come about as a consequence of sin, but rather this death by Baptism, like Christ's voluntary death by crucifixion, is chosen out of love for God and in obedience to God. Schmemann's view of Baptism as voluntary death includes a vigorous defense of infant Baptism, as we shall see momentarily. But first, we can review some of the preceding points by reading an excerpt of his book, *Of Water and the Spirit*:

> Christ's life is made up entirely, totally, exclusively of His desire to save man, to free him from that death into which man transformed his life, to restore him to that life which he lost in sin. His desire to save is the very movement, the very power of that perfect *love* for God and man, of that total obedience to God's will, the rejection of which led man to sin and death. And thus His whole life is truly "deathless." There is no death in it because there is no "desire" to have anything but God, because His whole life is in God and in God's love. And because His desire to die is but the ultimate expression and expression of that love and obedience—because His death is nothing but love, nothing but the desire to destroy the solitude, the separation from life, the darkness and the despair of death, nothing but love for those who are dead—*there is no "death" in His death*. His death, being the ultimate manifestation of love as life and of life as love, removes from death its "sting" of sin and truly destroys death as the power of Satan and sin over the world.
>
> He does not "abolish" or "destroy" the physical death because He does not "abolish" this world of which physical death is not only a "part" but the principle of life and even growth. But He does infinitely more. By removing the sting of sin from death, by abolishing death as a spiritual reality, by filling it with Himself, with His love and life,

He makes death—which was the very reality of separation and corruption of life—into a shining and joyful "passage"—passover—into fuller life, fuller communion, fuller love. "For to me to live is Christ," says St. Paul, "and to die is gain" (Phil. 1:21). It is not of the immortality of his soul that he speaks, but of the new, the totally new meaning and power of death—of death as "being in Christ," of death as having become, in this mortal world, the sign and the power of Christ's victory. For those who believe in Christ and live in Him, "death is no more," "death is swallowed up in victory" (1 Cor. 15:54) and each grave is filled not with death, but with life.[7]

HOW BAPTISM IS DEATH AND RESURRECTION

We turn now to the third question: How does Baptism unite people with Christ in his death-destroying death? Also, how does Baptism unite spirit with matter so that human relations with the world (starting with water) are restored to their God-intended form?

If we somehow grasp that life is in Christ and that his life-filled death destroys death, we may still wonder how Baptism lets people be included in his death. In general, Orthodox theology is more concerned with the what and why of Baptism than the when and how. God has given Baptism as a reality to enter into, not a mechanical operation to be explained. At the same time, Baptism is clearly an event, a decisive event, and how it happens is through a synergy of divine and human activity. God's energy acts in, with, through, and beyond the human action. In that basic sense Baptism is clearly "sacramental." Prayer is especially vital to Baptism; the prayers of exorcism are crucial preparation, and the *epiclesis*, or invocation of the Holy Spirit, is a central moment in both Baptism and the Eucharist.

Though a decisive event, Baptism is not an isolated event. The Baptism is connected to a person's whole life, the person is connected to the whole Church, and the Church is connected to Jesus Christ and related to the whole cosmos. All these connections are involved in Baptism being death and resurrection.

Schmemann implies that even Orthodox Christians have trouble embracing this wholistic frame of mind, because they have been influenced by Western sacramental views. Western sacramental theology has often named seven sacraments; for the Orthodox there are those seven, but really there is *one* ultimate sacrament—the Church in relation to Jesus Christ. Western sacramen-

7. Alexander Schmemann, *Of Water and the Spirit* (Crestwood, NY: St. Vladimir's Seminary Press, 1974), 64.

tal theology has often spoken of Baptism as a visible means of invisible grace. For the Orthodox, says Schmemann, that view is too Neoplatonic. Baptism does not mediate grace; it *is* grace—God's presence and activity in creation. Likewise Baptism does not signify or point to death and resurrection; it *is* death and resurrection.

Western sacramental theology has often made a distinction between *ex opere operato* and *ex opere operantis.* In the former case the sacrament is made valid "by the work worked" (by its proper administration), while in the latter it is valid "by the work of the worker" (by the disposition of the ones giving and receiving it). For the Orthodox frame of mind it may be both, or neither. For the real question, says Schmemann, is not one of "validity" but rather "fulfillment." The Baptism of Stalin, for example, was probably perfectly "valid" in its administration, but it was not fulfilled in his subsequent life. Fulfillment is more the issue than validity.[8]

The rhythm of preparation and fulfillment is central to Baptism; indeed Schmemann believes "it constitutes the very essence of the liturgical life of the Church."[9] He urges churches to reclaim this rhythm. In the early church, catechumens underwent a time of preparation lasting one to three years. Since Baptism took place at Pascha (Easter), the entire church prepared for it during the period of Lent. Baptism fulfilled this Lenten preparation and in turn prepared those baptized for the ensuing Christian life.

Even within the baptismal liturgy itself there is preparation and fulfillment. For example, the exorcism prepares the candidate to renounce Satan. This renunciation fulfills exorcism and in turn prepares a person to swear allegiance to Christ, and the pattern is repeated throughout the liturgy. Baptism, being plunged into water, fulfills all these steps—and it prepares for Chrismation, the anointing with oil to receive the Holy Spirit. Chrismation fulfills Baptism and in turn prepares for the Eucharist, which is given even to baptized infants. Every fulfillment is again a new preparation. The entire Church is herself the fulfillment of Christ's coming and the preparation for life eternal.

---

8. See Alexander Schmemann, *The Eucharist: Sacrament of the Kingdom* (Crestwood, NY: St. Vladimir's Seminary Press, 1988): "For (and we most strongly stress this) both the Latin reduction of the sacraments to *ex opere operato* . . . and their reduction to *ex opere operantis* . . . are equally foreign to Orthodoxy. For Orthodoxy this is a false dilemma, one of those impasses to which theological rationalism inevitably leads. In the Orthodox perception of the Church, both the absolute non-dependence of the gift that God has given on any earthly, human 'causality' whatsoever, and the personal character of this gift, whose reception depends, consequently, on the person to whom it is given, are equally self-evident" (116).

9. *Of Water and the Spirit*, 17. Subsequent citations to this work appear in the text as page numbers in parentheses.

This coherence of events is paralleled by a coherence of people and elements. In Baptism, the infant stands for the whole church that is being redeemed. The water stands for the whole creation that is being reclaimed from the enemy and restored to its rightful purpose. Baptism thus has cosmic proportions.

Schmemann's defense of infant Baptism relies on this connection between the infant and the Church, and between the Church and Jesus Christ. It is quite true, he acknowledges, that faith is needed for Baptism. But what faith is truly adequate? The only sufficient faith is that of Jesus Christ, his faithfulness, which is imparted to his body, the Church. Baptism is still voluntary, in that the Church freely requests Baptism on behalf of the infant that is connected to her.

This Orthodox way of thinking eschews any division of labor that says grace is what God does, while faith is what humans bring to the table of salvation. Rather faith becomes a kind of divine gift imparted to infants and the Church, even while grace entails human activity. For grace is not just unmerited favor, but God's presence and power, which is at work within people. Grace involves both divine and human activity, just as faith involves both divine and human activity.

Hence the central concept for grasping the Orthodox frame of mind is that of participation. Divine participation in human life and human participation in the divine life is the recurring theme. In Jesus, God participates in human life and death, so that through Jesus humanity may participate in divine life. From the start, God's intent for people is that they become "like God" (Gen. 1:26). This divinization or *theosis*—this participation in the divine nature (2 Pet. 1:3)—is a continual focus of Orthodox life and the ultimate purpose of Baptism. This purpose becomes more apparent in looking now at some specific aspects of the liturgy for Baptism.

EXORCISM: PERSONAL AND COSMIC

In the early church catechumenate, baptismal candidates often underwent daily instruction that included daily exorcisms. Then, in the liturgy of Baptism itself, there were further prayers of exorcism. Much changed with the rise of infant Baptism, but present-day liturgies still include exorcisms. What is exorcism and why is it done? It is speaking to the devil and other demonic powers. It is done because the devil is the first person one meets after deciding to follow Christ. "The exorcisms come first," says Schmemann, "because on our path to the baptismal font we unavoidably 'hit' the dark and powerful figure that obstructs this path" (23).

This understanding of evil has seemed antiquated to many educated people in the West, though it may be regaining acceptance amid postmodern critiques of modern rationality. Certainly the majority of the world's people has always lived in a world populated with evil spirits.

Exorcism says at least three things about evil. First, evil is an irrational power that cannot be understood or overcome by reason alone. The early catechumenate included much instruction, but it never presumed that education could accomplish salvation. The Church saw evil as an irrational power, and even today, says Schmemann, "all those who try, be it only a little, to 'better' themselves" will encounter "something which truly takes possession of us and directs our acts" (22).

Second, this power of evil is personal: "For just as there can be no love outside the 'lover,' i.e. a person that loves, there can be no hatred outside the 'hater,' i.e. a person that hates" (22).[10] Evil is a personal presence, not just an absence of goodness. The "personal world of those who have chosen to hate God" (22) is a spiritual world containing creatures who use their God-given freedom to separate themselves from God, which leads to their enslavement and their desire to enslave others.

Third, exorcism says that evil must be confronted. The extent of this personal desire to destroy God's love and light cannot be minimized. The devil cannot be placated, circumvented, or explained away, but must be dealt with, and the best way to do so is by praying—by speaking words with God-given authority:

> The Lord lays thee under ban, O Devil!
> He who came into the world and made His abode among men,
> that He might overthrow thy tyranny and deliver man;
> who also upon the Tree did triumph over adverse powers,
> . . . by death has annihilated Death,
> and overthrew him who exercised the dominion of Death,
> that is thee, O Devil.
> I adjure thee by God. . . . Be thou under ban! . . .
> Fear, begone and depart from this creature,
> and return not again;
> neither hide thyself in him either by night or by day;
> either in the morning or at noonday;
> But depart thence to thine own Tartarus
> until the great day of Judgment which is ordained. . . .
> Begone and depart from this sealed, this newly enlisted warrior of God;
> . . . Begone, and depart from this creature with all thy powers and thine
>   angels!

(24–25)

10. See also John Meyendorff, *Byzantine Theology* (New York: Fordham University Press, 1979).

The baptismal exorcism, much longer than the portion quoted here, evinces an entire worldview. It also implies something about the nature of words and prayer. In a "desacralized and secularized worldview," speech is "reduced to its rational meaning." But words are first and foremost power. "God created the world with His Word," and human words also have power to create or destroy. Schmemann calls exorcism "a *poem* in the deepest sense of this word, which in Greek means *creation*" (25). The exorcism is a poem because it creates the reality of which it speaks.

After addressing the devil, the exorcist makes supplication on behalf of the one to be baptized, typically an infant:

> Look upon thy servant;
> Prove him and search him;
> And root out of him every operation of the Devil.
> Rebuke the unclean spirits and expel them;
> And purify the works of Thy hands.
> And exerting Thy trenchant might,
> Speedily crush Satan under his feet;
> And give him victory over the same. . . .
> Open the eyes of his understanding,
> That the light of Thy gospel may shine brightly in him.
>   (26)

Here there is a clear connection between first being liberated from demonic power and then receiving enlightened "eyes of understanding." This sequence provides an additional motive for infant Baptism. Says Schmemann, "The Orthodox Church, radically different from some 'rationalistic' sects, has never posited 'understanding' as the condition for Baptism. She would rather say that true 'understanding' is made possible by Baptism, is its result and fruit, rather than its condition" (18). Thus all the baptismal prayers apply to infants, though parents or sponsors speak when a response is needed.

Exorcism is a personal act with cosmic dimensions. In exorcising a baptismal candidate, the priest, according to the rubrics, "breathes thrice upon his mouth, brow and breast." The devil is, so to speak, blown away. The material and spiritual worlds are united here, since this breathing also purifies the physical element of air. The world, both spiritual and material, is polluted with sin, evil, and death. The acts of Baptism are intent upon reclaiming the world from the enemy. "The act of liberation therefore is not only 'spiritual' but also 'physical': it is the purification of the very air we breathe" (26).

Later in the liturgy, something similar and even more extensive happens with the element of water. Before Baptism, the water is blessed and consecrated at length. It is also exorcised and even anointed with oil. The priest signs the water thrice with the sign of the cross, dipping his finger into it, breathing upon it, and saying three times, "Let all adverse powers be crushed beneath the sign of the image of the cross!" And then:

> We pray Thee, O God, that every aerial and obscure phantom may withdraw itself from us; and that no demon of darkness may conceal himself in this water; and that no evil spirit which instilleth darkening of intentions and rebelliousness of thought may descend into it with him who is about to be baptized. (48)

In this worldview, there is nothing in the material realm that is not also spiritual. "Matter is never neutral," says Schmemann. "If it is not 'referred to God,' i.e., viewed and used as a means of communion with Him, of life in Him, it becomes the very bearer and locus of the demonic" (48).

Since the material world is spiritually charged, there is no separating it from the spiritual world. Schmemann thus opposes both the materialism of a secular world that rejects God and the spiritualism of a religion that rejects matter. Matter as God's creation is essentially good, but it has become the vehicle of human enslavement. In the cosmic battle of Baptism, Christ liberates matter, taking back ground, air, and water from the enemy and restoring them to their God-created goodness. No longer simply a commodity to be consumed, the world is consecrated to "become again the symbol of God's glory and presence, the sacrament of His action and communion" with humanity (49).

BAPTISM: CONTOURS AND CONTENT
OF THE LITURGY

Preparation for Baptism in the early church entailed a long, often intense period of instruction and exorcisms. But even then, and still today, the liturgy itself contains further preparation, including exorcisms, renouncing Satan, swearing allegiance to Christ, and confessing one's faith. The confession of faith is that of the Niceo-Constantinopolitan Creed adopted in 325 and completed in 381. The Creed summed up the catechumens' previous instruction, and after reciting it they would bow and say, "I bow down before the Father, and the Son, and the Holy Spirit, the Trinity, one in essence and undivided" (33). Physical acts are important. Spitting is how one seals the renunciation of Satan, and this bowing down before the Holy Trinity seals the allegiance to Christ.

Baptism took place on the eve of Easter, called Pascha, which means literally "passover" or "passage." The connection between Baptism and Pascha, says Schmemann, "remains the key not only to Baptism but to the totality of the Christian faith itself." For Baptism is a "participation in the decisive events of Christ's Death and Resurrection," and as such it is a "*passage—Pascha*—from 'this world' into the Kingdom of God" (37, 38). The connection between Baptism and Pascha is "the starting point of all liturgical renewal and revival." While Schmemann anticipates that Orthodox churches will continue to baptize people at different times throughout the year, still he wants them to know that "whenever and wherever Baptism is celebrated, we find ourselves—spiritually at least!—on the eve of Pascha" (38).

If exorcisms and reciting the Creed are preparation, then Baptism proper begins with blessing the water. This rite is "relatively lengthy," but priests ought not omit it, for it alone reveals the "truly cosmical content and depth" of Baptism. As the "most ancient and universal of all religious symbols," water represents the whole material world. It symbolizes life, for there can be no life without water ("In the beginning . . . the Spirit of God was moving over the face of the waters" [Gen. 1:1–2, RSV]). Water symbolizes death too; in the flood and in the destruction of Pharaoh's army, it brings God's wrath and judgment. Water also symbolizes purification and cleansing: "It washes away stains, it re-creates the pristine purity of the earth" (38, 39).

Whatever is symbolic here is also real. To contemporary ears, *symbol* may connote a lesser reality, but for Schmemann symbols are quintessential reality. Thus within Baptism the elements *are* and the actions *do* the very things they symbolize.

Though lengthy, the blessing of the water is redolent with meaning, which Schmemann finds even in its short opening doxology: "Blessed is the Kingdom of the Father, and of the Son, and of the Holy Spirit, now and ever, and unto ages of ages." This doxology announces the end at the start, for the kingdom of God is the destination of Baptism and every sacrament. All sacraments are "a participation in and pilgrimage toward the Kingdom of God" (41). The doxology heralds the journey's outcome at its outset.

The blessing of water also hearkens back to water's history in Christ's life. Jesus went to the Jordan to be baptized by John, and this event was "the first epiphany of the Trinity in the cosmos" (42).[11] Thus the cosmic import of baptismal water is seen in several ways: it is the principle of both life and death, it is the place where the Trinity first appears, and it is the procedure for liberating the material world from demonic powers. Not only are people purified through this material substance; contra consumerism, matter itself is purified and restored to become once more "a means of God's presence" (42).

---

11. In the early church, a common name for the baptismal font was simply "the Jordan." See Kilian McDonnell, *The Baptism of Jesus in the Jordan: The Trinitarian and Cosmic Order of Salvation* (Collegeville, MN: Liturgical Press, 1996), 77.

In the blessing and consecration of water, the priest prays that "this water may be to [the baptized person] a laver of regeneration unto the remission of sins." How can water regenerate a person? Not naturally or magically, says Schmemann. Water regenerates "only inasmuch as the one who is to be baptized wants—in faith, hope and love—to die with Christ and to rise with Him from the dead, inasmuch as Christ's Death and Resurrection have become for him the decisive event of his own life" (43).

The priest needs washing too. In blessing and consecrating the water, he asks God to "wash away the vileness of my body, and the pollution of my soul" (44). This prayer demonstrates the communal nature and continual nature of Baptism. The entire church prepares for Baptism, because though one person may be going under the water, everyone needs to participate in the baptismal process of "spiritual growth and fulfillment." Baptism involves a person's whole lifetime and the whole church community (45).

The blessing and consecration of water resemble in structure the eucharistic prayer over Bread and Wine. There is a *preface*; an *anamnesis*, or remembrance of God's saving acts; an *epiclesis*, or invocation of the Holy Spirit, "Who alone fills with power and reality that which we hope and ask for"; and a *consecration*, by which the elements are restored to their ultimate purpose (48). This consecration, says Schmemann, does not "*replace* 'natural' matter with some 'supernatural' and sacred matter." Rather it *restores* natural matter to its God-intended status "as a means of communion with God" (49). And "thus consecration is always the manifestation, the epiphany of that End, of that ultimate Reality for which the world was created." It reveals the end but is not an end in itself. Hence "in the Orthodox Church there is no 'adoration' of the Holy Gifts in themselves or for themselves." Rather the gifts are meant to be "that which all matter is meant to be: a means to an end, which is man's deification—knowledge of God and communion with God" (50).

After the water is blessed, it is anointed with oil, with a similar structure of prayer. Even the oil is exorcised, just like the person and water. Liberated from the demonic realm, oil is restored to the purpose of aiding humanity's deification. The priest uses oil to make three signs of the cross in the water, then anoints the person to be baptized, making the sign of the cross with two fingers upon the brow, the breast, between the shoulders, and then on the ears (saying, "unto the hearing of faith"), the hands ("Thy hands have made me and fashioned me"), and the feet ("that he [or *she*] may walk in the way of Thy commandments").

The climax of the baptismal liturgy is immersion or Baptism itself (53). After the body is anointed, the priest immerses it in the water, "looking toward the east, as he says: *The servant of God is baptized in the Name of the Father, Amen. And of the Son, Amen. And of the Holy Spirit, Amen.*" The body is immersed and raised three times, once at the invocation of each name. Schmemann calls this sacrament "the gift of Christ's Death and Resurrection to each one of us" (70). He depicts this dying in terms of desire:

> It is faith that desires Baptism; it is faith that knows it to be truly dying and truly rising with Christ. Only God can respond to this desire and fulfill it. . . . Where there is no faith and no desire there can be no fulfillment. Yet the fulfillment is always a free gift from God: *grace* in the deepest sense of this word. This sacrament then is precisely this: *the decisive encounter of faith and the Divine response to it, the fulfillment of the one by the other.* Faith, by being desire, makes the sacrament *possible,* for without faith it would have been "magic"—a totally extrinsic and arbitrary act destroying man's freedom. But only God, by responding to faith, fulfills this "possibility," makes it truly that which faith desires: dying with Christ, rising again with Him. Only through God's free and sovereign grace do we know, in the words of St. Gregory of Nyssa, "this water truly to be for us both tomb and mother." (66–67)

CHRISMATION: THE SACRAMENT OF THE HOLY SPIRIT

Traditionally the candidate undresses and goes naked into the water of Baptism. After being immersed three times, the neophyte is vested in white garments, then anointed with Holy Chrism. This Chrismation differs from anointings before Baptism, for it entails receiving the gift of the Holy Spirit.

Several scriptural passages, including the account of Pentecost in Acts, distinguish Baptism with water from being baptized with the Holy Spirit, which raises the question of how the latter happens. For Orthodox Christians the answer has been Chrismation, sometimes called the sacrament of the Holy Spirit. Schmemann even calls Chrismation a "personal Pentecost" (79).

In the West, confirmation became the rite for imparting the Holy Spirit. Confirmation was logically connected with Baptism but separated by a span of years in a person's life. But in the East, Baptism and Chrismation and the Eucharist remained organic parts of one another. Typically a person, even an infant, receives all three on the same day.

Chrismation follows and fulfills Baptism. Baptism restores people to their true nature by freeing them from "the sting of sin" and reconciling them "with God and God's creation." But Chrismation goes even further than that, by drawing them to a higher place than Adam and Eve. Chrismation, says Schmemann, "takes man beyond Baptism, beyond 'salvation': by making him 'christ' in Christ, by anointing him with the Anointment of the Anointed One, it opens to man the door of *theosis*, of *deification*" (80). Following Athanasius (ca. 293–373), the

Orthodox have said that God became human in order that humanity could become like God. Chrismation inaugurates this process of *theosis*.

More specifically, Schmemann connects Chrismation to the three "offices" of Christ: the royal, the priestly, and the prophetic. Christ is king, priest, and prophet, and Christians can be so too. They can, in the words of John Chrysostom, "abundantly possess not one but all three of these dignities." These dignities or offices are what Schmemann calls the "three essential dimensions of genuine Christian 'spirituality.'" Quoting Revelation, he says that "Christ 'has made us kings and priests unto God and His Father' (Rev. 1:6)" (81).

This view of humanity is "anthropological maximalism" (82). To be truly human is to be royal and priestly and prophetic. In this threefold vocation there is in each case a movement from God's original design, to humanity's fallenness, to Christ's restoration. We can detect this movement in the following descriptions.

How People Become Royals

Kingship or royalty entails having God-given power and authority. God gives humans dominion over the earth (Gen. 1:27–28) in order to be "the *benefactor* of the earth." Separated from God, humans become fallen royals. Instead of leading creation to its fulfillment, they seek "to benefit from it, to have and to possess it" in self-centered ways (82, 83).

But behind these deviations we can detect the via. People misuse their vocation of kingship, but the vocation itself is good. We misuse power, but power itself is good; we worship idols, but worship is good (85). Likewise creation itself is essentially good. As opposed to "escapist spiritualities," this view does not sever human relations with the world. Rather in Christ we are restored to being rightly and royally a part of creation. Christ is Savior *of* the world, not *from* it (84).

Here we come to the concept of the crucified king. Two different reductions need to be avoided: first, to say that restored kingship is for this world only; second, to say that it applies only to the kingdom to come. The first is the materialist reduction, the second the spiritualist reduction, and both, says Schmemann, are rejections of the cross, making it "emptied of its power" (1 Cor. 1:17). A third way is to love the world that God has created, but also, as 1 John says, not to "love the world [as it has degenerated] or the things in the world" (1 John 2:15). Schmemann thus juxtaposes John 3:16 and 1 John 2:15.[12]

---

12. Cf. "Liturgy and Eschatalogy," in *Liturgy and Tradition: Theological Reflections of Alexander Schmemann*, ed. Thomas Fisch (Crestwood: St. Vladimir's Seminary Press, 1990), 93.

This third way is the way of the Cross. What does the Cross show and do? First, it reveals this world as fallen. In crucifying Christ, the world shows itself; it shows its false colors. The crucifixion is the all-encompassing expression of the world rejecting God. Every sin is a rejection of God and surrender to evil, and the ultimate expression of evil is the rejection and crucifixion of Christ.

Second, the Cross reveals this evil in order to condemn it. "This world" is condemned, because in crucifying Christ the world condemns itself.

Third, the Cross becomes the start of salvation and inauguration of the kingdom, for the Cross becomes the enthronement of Christ as King and the epiphany of his glorification: "Now the Son of Man has been glorified, and God has been glorified in him" (John 13:31) (89). The Cross becomes the way to enthronement for Christians too (see Gal. 6:14).

Thus the Cross reveals evil, then condemns evil, then commences God's reign. This reign summons people to kingship, and this kingship transcends an "either/or" mentality that makes faith either this-worldly activism or other-worldly escapism. For the Cross means the rejection of the world as the site of human enslavement and death, as well as the rejection of the world as those powers that create consumerism, including "the desire of the flesh, the desire of the eyes, the pride in riches" (1 John 2:16). But the Cross also makes possible the acceptance of the true world as God's creation.

In some sense, therefore, the entire world undergoes a death and resurrection because of Christ. As Schmemann portrays the Orthodox view, there is this constant rejection of the world as self-sufficient—but constant acceptance of the world as God's gift to us, and continual embrace of the world as a means of communion with God. Sin consists in the fact that people love the world for its own sake and try to make even God into a servant of it. To restore people to royalty is not merely to equip them with some supernatural power but to liberate them from worldly activity, in the sense that this activity is no longer the source of ultimate meaning and value. When the taste of the kingdom is on their lips, then people can say again that the world is a sign, a promise, a thirst and hunger for God. Those who have tasted of the kingdom—its joy, peace, and righteousness—can overcome the world by the power of the Cross and can then offer the world to God and thus truly transform it.

How People Become Priests

This offering of the world to God takes us to the "second dignity" bestowed on each Christian or anointed one, that of being a *priest*. If the vocation of a king is to have power and dominion, then that of a priest is to offer sacrifice and so to be a mediator between God and creation. The king receives dominion over the world from God. The priest offers the world back to God. When something of creation is offered to God, it becomes sanctified. The priest has the power to sanctify the world by sacrificing it to God, thus "making" the world into a communion with God.

No word better expresses humanity's fall from proper priesthood than the word "consumer." After having glorified themselves as *homo faber*, then as *homo sapiens*, humans seem to have found their ultimate vocation as *consumer*, Schmemann says ironically. Adam and Eve were the first consumers. Eventually "the most tragical fruit of that original sin is that it made religion itself into a 'consumer good' meant to satisfy our 'religious needs,' to serve as a security blanket or therapy, to supply us with cheap self-righteousness and equally cheap self-centered and self-serving 'spiritualities' . . . in a society and culture which otherwise do not have the slightest interest in the divine calling of man and the whole of creation" (96–97).

Christ restores us to priesthood, to the power of presenting our bodies "as a living sacrifice, holy and acceptable to God" (Rom. 12:1). As we are transformed, we become priests who transform creation by witnessing to Christ's truth and being bearers of sacrificial love. This royal priesthood belongs to all believers.

The early church, notes Schmemann, affirmed both the royal priesthood *of* the Church and the institutional priesthood *in* the Church. The two are complementary, and both rely on Christ, since Christ himself is the Church's one true Priest, Shepherd, and Teacher. He makes possible the royal priesthood of all believers, and he also chooses and sends people to make his priesthood incarnate within the Church. People appointed to Church offices are really the underpriest, or undershepherd (to use the imagery of 1 Pet. 5:4). They are supposed to embody the priesthood of Christ.

How People Become Prophets

The third dignity given to humanity through Chrismation is the vocation of being prophet. Again, Christ is *the* Prophet and fulfillment of all prophecies. He restores to humanity the gift of prophecy that has been lost.

What is prophecy? Not merely the ability to foretell the future, prophecy is instead a certain power to hear and to see. The prophet hears God's voice and discerns God's will. The prophet "reads" events and situations with God's eyes. The prophet relates what is human and temporal to what is divine and eternal. In other words, the prophet is one "for whom the world is transparent to God" (100). This power, part of true human nature, is now largely lost. In pride, people thought they could know and possess the world apart from God and without prophecy, and this nonprophetic knowledge people have come to call "objective."

Schmemann issues a mordant critique of any "objective" knowledge that seeks to know the world apart from God. In education, he says, one generation after another "leaves the dreams and visions of childhood" for schools and universities where people become "blind worshippers of 'objectivity.'" Yet this objective knowledge and the techniques based on it have failed to prevent Western civilization from becoming "one all-embracing crisis—social, political, ecological, energetic, etc." In fact, it increasingly seems to be the case that this knowledge and these techniques are a main cause of crisis. Purporting to liberate us, this knowledge has led instead to feelings of enslavement and loneliness. A "horrible feeling of a total vacuum permeates the very air we breathe and cannot be dispelled by the superficial euphoria of our 'consumer society.'" Meanwhile, within our "technological and rational" society there is a surge in "such phenomena as astrology, magic, esotericism and occult interest of all kinds." This attraction shows how the prophetic vocation, severed from its "God-given essence, reappears as a fallen, dark and demonic obsession" (101).

Christ restores the gift of true prophecy. It is included in the gift of Holy Spirit, which is, says Schmemann, received through the chrismation that completes Baptism. Prophecy may actually be defined as "the gift of sobriety," for sobriety is the essential foundation of spirituality in Christian ascetical literature. Sobriety in turn may be defined as openness to God; or as Schmemann puts it, "Sobriety is that inner *wholeness* and *integrity*, that harmony between soul and body, reason and heart, which alone can *discern* and therefore *understand* and therefore *possess* reality in its totality, *as it is*, to lead people to the only true 'objectivity'" (102).

Hence discerning and understanding are key activities of the prophet. "To discern and to understand does not mean to *know* everything," cautions Schmemann. One does not suddenly become a "miraculous expert" of all things. Also, the Orthodox Church affirms that human reason is "the highest of God-given faculties," and so there is no contempt for knowledge, science, and wisdom. But to be a prophet means one's human reason is reconnected to its "*vertical* dimension." This vertical dimension pertains, explicitly or implicitly, "in all conditions and situations, in all professions and vocations, in the use of all our human gifts" (103). In all these things a person knows Christ, in whom all things cohere (Col. 1:17), and thus in all these ways one can bear witness to Christ.

Chrismation is more than the sum of these three offices—the royal, priestly, and prophetic—large as they are, for "in the sacrament of anointment we receive the Holy Spirit Himself, and not merely 'grace.' . . . It is the Holy Spirit, and not some divine power, that descended on the apostles on the day of Pentecost" (104). Christ, by giving his life, gives us the Holy Spirit; and the Holy Spirit, by descending upon us and abiding in us, gives us the life of Christ.

This new life means that we are united with Christ, are part of his Body, and partake of his kingship, priesthood, and prophecy. The new life does not obliterate our personality but reveals "our *true personality*" and thus becomes "our only self-fulfillment" (107). The new life does not split life into "spiritual" and "material," but restores them to a wholeness.

This new life, because it is the Life of Christ, conquers death. It replaces the cravings of consumerism with the fullness of God's Presence.

2

John Howard Yoder

Baptism Is the New Humanity

Baptized into Christ, you are clothed in Christ, and there is neither slave nor free, neither male nor female; you are all one in
Christ Jesus.

Gal. 3:27–28, Yoder's translation from Body Politics

THE PATH TO PEACE

If death is one universal problem, so too is *living together*. The world's population has expanded while distances between people have shrunk. People are
more "together" than ever, connected by international commerce, satellite
communications, and other features of the "global community."

But a smaller and closer world has not been a more peaceful one. There has
been no end to the violence people of different nations, ethnic groups, and
religions have inflicted against each other; and no limit, in this age of technology, to the extent of violence imaginable.

Baptism, says John Howard Yoder, lets us imagine a different way—and it
also has power to commence this new way of life. In the section of Galatians
quoted above, Paul is not laying out a systematic theology of the sacraments.
Rather he is describing a new social reality where Jesus Christ is the ruler and
his reign of peace prevails. Peace is central to the gospel and to the meaning
of baptism.

Baptism does not bring about peace by establishing a Christian state. Yoder
rejects that theocratic or Constantinian option, along with its corresponding
infant baptism. Neither does baptism bring about peace solely on an individ-
ualistic level. Yoder likewise eschews the "spiritualist" option that would make

peace a private matter and also diminish or do away with public baptism. The spiritualist seeks to escape the world, while the theocrat would change it overnight, but the New Testament charts a different course. It summons us to participate in the new humanity God has created through Jesus Christ. The Christian believer is situated in the world but owes total allegiance to Jesus. Sometimes believers act like leaven to permeate society slowly, sometimes they will take a sudden conscientious stand that results in martyrdom, but always they are guided by the proclamation that Jesus is Lord (and no one or nothing else).[1]

Baptism is for believers. Baptism means we become members of Christ and members of his church. Baptism is not thereby just a social rite of passage, for the church is not like other social organizations. The church is "a new covenant people responding freely to God's call."[2] As a kind of divine "pilot project"[3] the church is called to be the harbinger and herald, the foretaste and model of God's kingdom.[4] Thus it does not impose its will upon the world or attempt to bring about peace through violence. Instead, the church "tells the world what is the world's own calling and destiny . . . by pioneering a paradigmatic demonstration of both the power and practices that define the shape of restored humanity."[5]

In his book *Body Politics: Five Practices of the Christian Community before the Watching World*, Yoder has entitled one chapter "Baptism and the New Humanity." He connects baptism with other biblical practices such as reconciliation and breaking bread together. He connects the new humanity with the new community that is the church and the new phase of history that commences with Jesus Christ. Everywhere baptism and "newness" go together. The newness that baptism proclaims is eternal and universal, but also personal and particular, for baptism typically (and prototypically) embodies the repentance and new start in life that God opens to each person, both the neighbor one knows and the enemy one learns, in Christ, to love.

Loving our enemies, as Jesus taught us, means we do not kill them, or even

1. "The central affirmation of New Testament faith is that 'Jesus is Lord'" (Yoder, "How H. Richard Niebuhr Reasoned: A Critique of *Christ and Culture*," *Authentic Transformation: A New Vision of Christ and Culture* [Nashville: Abingdon Press, 1996], 68). Cf. Yoder, *The Politics of Jesus* (Grand Rapids: Wm. B. Eerdmans, 2003), 156–57.

2. "A People in the World," in *The Royal Priesthood: Essays Ecclesiological and Ecumenical*, edited by Michael G. Cartwright (Scottdale, PA: Herald Press, 1998), 91.

3. John Howard Yoder, "Why Ecclesiology Is Social Ethics: Gospel Ethics versus the Wider Wisdom," in *Royal Priesthood*, 126.

4. "Why Ecclesiology Is Social Ethics," 106.

5. John Howard Yoder, "Sacrament as Social Process: Christ the Transformer of Culture," in *Royal Priesthood*, 373.

baptize them at swordpoint. Instead we allow baptism and other practices of our new humanity to change how we view and treat all people. While baptism does not change a whole society right away, still it is the right way to engender peaceful change. It is God's way of calling people into a new society that confesses Jesus is Lord, and "the people of God is called to be today what the world is called to be ultimately."[6] In fact, says Yoder, "the confessing people of God is the new world on its way."[7]

John Howard Yoder (1927–1997) was probably the most prominent Anabaptist theologian of the twentieth century. He stood firmly within a tradition that has been variously labeled "believers' church" (Max Weber), "free church" (Franklin Littell), and "Radical Reformation" (George Williams).[8] While Yoder's theological roots go back to sixteenth-century Germany, his contemporary influence branched out to Roman Catholics at Notre Dame, to evangelical Protestants at Fuller, and to any number of receptive readers everywhere. James McClendon, Stanley Hauerwas, Nancey Murphy, Marva Dawn, and U.S. senator Mark Hatfield are among those who report they learned a lot from John Howard Yoder.

His obituary in *The New York Times* on January 7, 1998, ends by relating how a friend once congratulated him because scholarly papers presented at a conference showed the deep imprint of his thought. "Your influence must really be spreading," the friend said. "Not mine," Yoder replied. "Jesus's."[9] Whether this reply evinces humility or confidence, or both, clearly it typifies how Yoder saw Jesus at the center of his writing, including his view of baptism.

THE PRIMARY MEANING OF BAPTISM

Centuries of what Yoder calls "fruitless debates" over sacramental theology have obscured the straightforward meaning of baptism, the Eucharist, and other Christian practices.[10] These debates were fueled by philosophical assumptions and superstitious notions foreign to the New Testament. The first

6. John Howard Yoder, *Body Politics: Five Practices of the Christian Community before the Watching World* (Scottdale, PA: Herald Press, 2001), ix.

7. "Sacrament as Social Process," 373.

8. John Howard Yoder, "A 'Free Church' Perspective on Baptism, Eucharist, and Ministry," in *Royal Priesthood*, 279.

9. Peter Steinfels, "John H. Yoder, Theologian at Notre Dame, Is Dead at 70," *New York Times*, January 7, 1998; quoted in Mark Thiessen Nation, *John Howard Yoder: Mennonite Patience, Evangelical Witness, Catholic Convictions* (Grand Rapids: Wm. B. Eerdmans, 2006), 143.

10. *Body Politics*, 14.

theologians, such as Paul, did not attempt to describe in detail what changes take place in which elements when certain words are spoken. Rather they were trying to comprehend the change taking place in people as a result of Christ, which they witnessed, even though it ran counter to their prior assumptions about religious and ethnic identity.

Jews and Gentiles were worshiping together. Jews and Gentiles were eating together and sharing other economic resources. Jews and Gentiles were now members of the same community, for they were alike baptized in Christ and clothed in Christ (Gal. 3:27–28). Further, they came to see how "the fundamental breakthrough at the point of the Jew-Gentile barrier demands and produces breakthroughs of the same type where the barrier is slavery, gender, or class."[11]

Baptism is how this new way of living starts. Baptism "introduces or initiates persons into a new people. The distinguishing mark of this people is that all prior given or chosen identity definitions are transcended." Thus, says Yoder, "the primary narrative meaning of baptism is the new society it creates, by inducting all kinds of people into the same people. The church is . . . that new society."[12]

Newfound unity is evident in the way Paul calls all the Christians of Galatia "children of God" (Gal. 3:26; 4:5–7), then goes on to remind them that "neither circumcision nor uncircumcision is anything; but a new creation is everything!" (6:15). We find substantially the same message in Ephesians 2:14–15, where the key words are *peace* and *new humanity*:

> He is himself our peace. Gentiles and Jews, he has made the two one; and in his own body of flesh and blood has broken down the enmity which stood like a dividing wall between them; for he annulled the law with its rules and regulations, so as to create out of the two a single new humanity in himself, thereby making peace.[13]

Or again, as Paul tells the Corinthians, "If anyone is united to Christ, there is a new world; see, everything has become new!" (2 Cor. 5:17).[14] The whole world is new, not just the individual, and with it comes a new way of seeing

---

11. *Body Politics*, 29.

12. *Body Politics*, 28–29. Cf. Yoder's essay "The Apostle's Apology Revisited," in *The New Way of Jesus: Essays Presented to Howard Charles*, ed. William Klassen (Newton, KS: Mennonite Press), 124–33.

13. This is Yoder's translation (*Body Politics*, 29).

14. Yoder mixes phrases from the New English Bible and New Revised Standard Version "in order to render the meaning most clearly" (*Body Politics*, 83). He notes that in the New Testament the noun *ktisis* (creation) most often refers more to categories or institutions than to individuals ("The Apostle's Apology Revisited," 130).

other people: "Worldly standards have ceased to count in our estimate of any-one" (2 Cor. 5:16).

The phrase "worldly standards" (*kata sarka*; literally, "according to the flesh") refers to ethnic identities. There is a clear contrast between being and knowing "in Christ" (*en cristo*) versus being and knowing "ethnically" (*kata sarka*). In the early church, Yoder surmises, the baptismal ritual may well have referred to this contrast and employed these phrases (new humanity, peace, new creation) to describe "the changed status of one who becomes publicly a confessing believer."[15]

Not only the confessing believer is changed through baptism—there are cosmic consequences. The mystery, kept hidden but now revealed, is that "from all eternity the purpose of God was going to be making one humanity out of Jew and Gentile. . . . The unity of two kinds of people, those born within the law and those without, is what God was about from all history." This reconciliation of peoples is not a by-product of the gospel; it *is* the gospel, and Yoder goes so far as to say that "where Christians are not united, the gospel is not true in that place."[16] For while in the Bible "justification" and "righteousness" refer to persons being reconciled to God, equally they refer to people being reconciled to one another. We cannot separate personal salvation from its social dimensions.[17]

The phrases *new humanity* and *new community* thus refer to the same reality, as depicted in Colossians 3:9–11:

> Do not lie to one another, since you have let yourselves be divested of the old humanity with its practices and have let yourselves be clothed with the new [humanity], which is being renewed in knowledge according to the image of its creator, where there is not Jew nor Greek.[18]

Yoder emphasizes, "Note that the 'new humanity' is defined directly as a state 'where there is no Jew and Greek.'"[19] Pastors and teachers might focus more on this communal dimension of salvation if they realized how many New Testament writings were written in a context of debate over the church's ethnic policy. When this context is overlooked, however, they may impose on these

---

15. *Body Politics*, 29–30.

16. John Howard Yoder, "The Imperative of Christian Unity," in *Royal Priesthood*, 291; cf. Yoder, "A People in the World," in *Royal Priesthood*, 91.

17. John Howard Yoder, *The Politics of Jesus* (Grand Rapids: Wm. B. Eerdmans, 2003), 215.

18. This is Yoder's translation ("The Apostle's Apology Revisited," 132).

19. "The Apostle's Apology Revisited," 132.

writings "the agenda of modern Western self-doubt," so that the Christian life becomes a matter of new mental ideas or psychic self-understandings.[20]

CHARACTERISTICS OF THE NEW COMMUNITY

At this point our basic definition that baptism creates the new community of Christ requires added clarification. First, *this new community does not erase the particularity of persons who enter it*. As a "multi-ethnic community," the church does not quash ethnicity but relativizes it to the central claim that Jesus is Lord; the same is true for other human attributes.[21] The unity that Christ creates in the church also honors the particularity of each person's history; in fact, unity and particularity become heightened simultaneously. This vision contrasts sharply with the individualism that dominates Western culture, an approach that celebrates the "individual," then enjoins individuals to leave behind their ethnic identity to join in the "melting pot." Says Yoder, "the melting pot metaphor does not include the separate identities of each community in the reconciliation as Paul does."[22]

Speaking of particularity, Yoder observes how Jesus himself "was a particular kind of politically committed poor palestinian preacher of a coming Kingdom."[23] In the global encounter of various religions, the "specificity of the Jewishness" of Jesus—his "particularity and provincialism"—may become embarrassing to some Christians. They may minimize such particulars in an attempt to glean universal truths found in all faiths. But there may be another reason behind this "drive to disavow particularity"; it may evince a desire to avoid the risk of any particular allegiance, especially one that entails being "bound to the crucified Jesus and the cost of following his way."[24] Union with Christ means honoring his particular claims, just as unity among Christians means honoring one another's particular cultures, which come "to flow into one new humanity, a new creation."[25]

Second, *in this new humanity the reality of the community precedes the individuals who enter it*. "It is not enough," Yoder explains, "to say that each of us is

---

20. "The Apostle's Apology Revisited," 133.
21. *Body Politics*, 29.
22. *Body Politics*, 30.
23. "How H. Richard Neibhur Reasoned," 83. Glen Harold Stassen, D. M. Yeager, and John Howard Yoder, *Authentic Transformation: A New Vision of Christ and Culture* (Nashville: Abingdon Press, 1996), 83.
24. "Why Ecclesiology Is Social Ethics," 111.
25. *Body Politics*, 30.

individually born again and baptized, with the result that all born-again individuals are collected in one place, commanded by God to plant churches." Rather, the church comes first: "The order is thus the reverse of our modern expectations. There is a new inter-ethnic social reality into which the individual is inducted rather than the social reality being the sum of the individuals."[26]

Yoder acknowledges that becoming a Christian has personal and inward dimensions, but it cannot be reduced to these.[27] He takes issue with a model that claims real change starts within the individual and expands out from that center.[28] In the New Testament, the new community comes first:

> The reconciliation of Jew and Gentile in the "new humanity" is first a community event. It cannot happen to a lone individual. The prerequisite for personal change is a new context into which to enter. A Gentile can only find Abraham by meeting a Jew. A Jew can only celebrate the messianic age by welcoming a Gentile.[29]

A biographical note may be in order. Growing up in a Mennonite church in Ohio,[30] Yoder no doubt experienced a strong sense of community, but as he recalled later, there was "never any coercion to stay within it. So that my choice to stay within it, although predisposed obviously by generations of ethnic continuity and by the church faithfulness of my parents, was by no means a matter of bowing to superior pressure but was rather a willing choice made in small stages in young adulthood."[31] Here his own life seems to exemplify aspects of the ecclesiology he gleans from Scripture: There is respect for particularity in the context of Christian community, and concern for ethnicity in the context of Christian unity.

Third, *the new community of Christ is at root a political reality*. The adjective "political" comes from the Greek word *polis*, which means a "structured social body."[32] As a set of relationships, which Paul calls Christ's body, the church is itself a *polis*—which "makes the Christian community a political entity in the simplest meaning of the term."[33] But the church is also political in the sense

---

26. *Body Politics*, 30.
27. "The Apostle's Apology Revisited," 132.
28. "The Apostle's Apology Revisited," 130.
29. "The Apostle's Apology Revisited," 133.
30. The church where he grew up was, until the 1920s, Amish Mennonite (not to be confused with Old Order Amish).
31. This is from an unpublished transcript of an autobiographical recording made by Yoder for James Wm. McClendon Jr. and Karen Lebacqz in 1980; quoted in Nation, *John Howard Yoder*, 9.
32. *Body Politics*, viii.
33. *Body Politics*, viii–ix.

that it is called to affect all spheres of surrounding society, including economics, law, the military, and government: "The will of God for human socialness as a whole is prefigured by the shape to which the Body of Christ is called. Church and world are not two compartments under separate legislation or two institutions with contradictory assignments, but two levels of the pertinence of the same Lordship."[34]

In modern times, however, people have wrongly supposed that "there is a vast qualitative distance between the realm we call 'politics' and the one we call 'church.'" This chasm, once inserted, becomes a problem to be solved by some sort of bridge. From one perspective, often called "liberal," the bridge becomes a set of *insights* into human nature and the world, including ideas about justice and freedom. Worship and church life are said to inculcate these insights so that people can act more responsibly in public affairs. From another perspective, often called "pietist," the bridge is a new set of *insides* (a new heart or will). Worship and church life are said to change a person "on such levels as guilt, self-esteem, and love" so that "the changed person will behave differently and thereby change the world."[35]

Neither of these perspectives is the biblical one. It is not that new insights or insides are wrong. What is wrong is the supposition that there are two realms, a spiritual nonpolitical realm and a political nonspiritual realm. What is wrong is the assumption of a bridge and the notion that crossing it must mean leaving behind dimensions of the church in order to reenter the world. It will be said, for example, that for baptized believers inside the realm of the church violence is never a way to address conflicts, but in the world one must be more "realistic." In response, Yoder says Christians must be more biblical. The same Lord, Jesus, is Lord of both the church and the entire world, even if the whole world does not know it yet. And the best way for the world to come to know it is by seeing believers who do know it and who act accordingly in all spheres of life, though the cost may be considerable, even of life itself.

Fourth, *the lordship of Christ does not depend on particular results*. "That Christ is Lord," says Yoder, is "a social, political, *structural* fact."[36] Again, this fact is true even if many people do not believe it, or even if many times believers do not see immediate results. Certainly we may anticipate results. The new humanity belongs to a new community that "will move history. It will create cultures and institutions. Yet its truth is not dependent upon those effects for its verification."[37]

34. *Body Politics*, ix.
35. *Body Politics*, vii.
36. *Politics of Jesus*, 156–57.
37. *Body Politics*, 30.

The temptation may be to look too much at outward circumstances and so succumb to external pressures. But Christian social action has Christ as its continual reference point. By his life and death Jesus triumphed over the fallen powers of the world, "concretely and historically."[38] Christians can keep in mind the strength of his victory when their position, say, of pacifism, appears weak in the world's eyes. Yoder quotes Johann Christoph Bumhardt, a nineteenth-century heir of the Radical Reformation: "'Dass Jesus siegt ist ewig ausgemacht. Sein ist die ganz Welt!' 'That Jesus is conqueror is eternally settled: the universe is his!'" This reality is the "eschatalogical foundation of Christian involvement in politics."[39]

A BRIEF HISTORY OF WHAT WENT WRONG

Both eschatology and ecclesiology were enduring concerns for Yoder. He reports how when discussing baptism in ecumenical settings, he was intent on "asking not about the theory of ordinances but about lived ecclesiology."[40] In the life of the church, baptism announces the lordship of Christ at the same time it embodies the union of particular and universal, of spiritual and political, and of worship and everyday life. These terms are meant to refer to concrete social reality.

But how did the church lose sight of the fact that the basic meaning of baptism is this new humanity, new society, and new reign of Christ? Yoder sketches a brief history of how the social meaning of the sacraments was lost:

> After the second century, the previously porous border between the church and the Jews was closed so that the lived meaning of the Pauline age was impossible. After the fifth century there were no more outsiders to convert because the whole world had been declared Christian by imperial edict. That made baptism a celebration of birth, reinforcing in-group identity rather than transcending it. Then it was natural that a new theology had to be developed to discuss what the ritual of baptism does to or for the infant who receives it without asking for it.[41]

In the development of sacramental theology, some aspects were consistent with the biblical witness. For example, Yoder readily accepts a common post-Reformation definition of "sacrament": it is a specific human activity whereby

---

38. *Politics of Jesus*, 144.
39. *Politics of Jesus*, 157.
40. John Howard Yoder, "The Believers' Church Conferences in Historical Perspective," *Mennonite Quarterly Review* 65 (January 1991): 8.
41. *Body Politics*, 32.

God at the same time acts "in, with, and under" that human activity.[42] But whereas the New Testament describes how God, in and with baptism, is acting to effect the in-breaking of a new era, along with the "breaking down of barriers between classes of people," in later centuries theologians came to construe baptism as God acting to wash away the guilt of an inherited, individual sinfulness.[43]

Then in the sixteenth century, Zwingli and his followers replaced this "sacramentalist" view with a "symbolic" one. Here the focus is on human action; the sacrament or ordinance is basically "an acted-out message." By baptism, it was said, the individual offers an outward and symbolic confession of an inward and spiritual birth. But this position loses as much ground as it gains. It corrects the error of infant baptism (infants cannot make public confession), but it does not reintroduce the original social meaning of baptism. It does not enact unity among people or imply equality between them. "It does not make the world new," says Yoder.[44]

Subsequently, Western society sought to establish unity and equality by other means, philosophical and theological, which were far less adequate. The Stoic tradition affirmed the dignity of all persons but also called for people to find their place in society and stay there. The modern Reformed vision said the equal worth of persons was intrinsic to the order of creation. Both Stoic and Reformed strands could be seen in the Declaration of Independence, the founding document of the United States: "We hold these truths to be self-evident, that all men are created equal, that they are endowed by their Creator with certain inalienable Rights."

This noble statement is empirically false, notes Yoder. These truths are not self-evident. "Self-evident" means that people do not need to be told or convinced, yet the current created order displays evident inequality and division, and even the founding fathers could not see, by looking at creation, how *all* people are equal: "they meant all land-owning white men—excluding all women, black men, Native American men, and poor men." To disentangle Americanism from racism a century later, it took a different message—"not a notion of equality through creation but the good news of redemption." Abolitionist preaching portrayed equal dignity as a gift of grace. To push emancipation a notch further another century later, it took the unmerited suffering and reconciling impact of people such as Martin Luther King Jr.[45]

---

42. *Body Politics*, 1.
43. *Body Politics*, 32.
44. *Body Politics*, 33.
45. *Body Politics*, 35.

In sum, much Renaissance and Enlightenment thinking tried to find an order in nature that could be transposed into the civil order and then into the church. Yoder avers the influence ought to run the other way: we find in the gospel an order for the church that is "the paradigm for what God intends for all humankind."[46]

SACRAMENTAL REALISM

Unity and equality matter to Christ, his church, and to the wider world.[47] Jesus makes unity imperative when in John 17 he prays for future believers, asking the Father that they may be one as the Father and the Son are one. The unity of future believers is meant to "make credible the fundamental Christian claim" that the Son was sent by the Father.[48] Their unity proclaims to principalities and powers the new reality God is making possible.

This unity is "the true internationalism," for what it offers is not an elusive plan to restructure governments but an "already achieved transformation of vision and community."[49] This path is better than "the lazy solution of pluralism."[50] Pluralism supposes that unity must be based on agreement, and where there is disagreement the result is division. The Spirit of Christ teaches that of course there will be disagreement, but disagreement calls for reconciliation. Baptism provides the reference point for this reconciliation, reminding us that the locus of unity is loyalty to Jesus.

Too often, however, churches have followed the world's way of hoping to find unity—through mergers, centralized church control, a melting-pot polity, and a common-denominator theology. Whether or not such an approach has merit on the level of business administration, it runs the risk of enervating the

46. John Howard Yoder, "Karl Barth: How His Mind Kept Changing," *How Karl Barth Changed My Mind*, ed. Donald K. McKim (Grand Rapids: Wm. B. Eerdmans, 1986), 170.

47. Does Yoder see the world beyond the church as being "wider"? He does, when speaking about the wide relevance of the gospel: "To include the jubilee message in our vision for the wider world is by no means unrealistic" (*Body Politics*, 25). He does not, when responding to people who say the gospel is too narrow to apply to the meaning system of the "wider world": "But that wider world . . . is still a small place. It still speaks only one language at a time, and that is still insider language" (*The Priestly Kingdom* [Notre Dame, IN: University of Notre Dame Press, 1984], 49). There is no "universal" location purged of all provincial particularity; all we can choose is our place of particularity.

48. "Imperative of Christian Unity," 291.

49. John Howard Yoder, "Let the Church Be the Church," in *Royal Priesthood*, 180.

50. "Imperative of Christian Unity," 292.

churches' main sources of vitality, for the Spirit of Christ moves in the local congregation and in the midst of believers who have strong, even widely divergent, convictions.[51] In Christ, as baptism shows, differences do not melt away or get left out for sake of "consensus"; rather they draw people into deeper conversation, undertaken in the faith that more clarity will come as Christians mutually submit to Jesus. If baptism is a gift, so too is the Christian unity it helps to enact. This unity is not a human thing we fabricate but a divine thing in which we participate. As Yoder puts it, "Christian unity is not to be created, but to be obeyed."[52]

In general the sacraments (the practices Jesus mandated) offer guidelines for ways the church can give direction to, instead of taking cues from, the wider society. What is true for unity is also true for equality and for economic justice. Says Yoder: "Baptism could again come to be, as it was in the New Testament, the basis of Christian egalitarianism." The Eucharist could again be what it once was: not only the expression of Christ's death for our sins but also "the sharing of bread between those who have and those who have not."[53]

Yoder calls this approach one of "sacramental realism." In each case it does not ask what the action symbolizes, or what external reality it mediates, but rather what it was in fact, in the immediate lived experience of the first Christians, and what it could be again for the present church community. For example, how did the first Christians hear Jesus' famous "words of institution"? While breaking bread for the disciples he said, "Whenever you do *this*, do it in my memory." *This* could refer to celebrating the Passover, but Passover was a once-a-year event, whereas bread breaking in Christ's memory was done much more often. Perhaps *this* referred simply to their ordinary eating together, something they did for months while living with Jesus and more than once after the Resurrection.

How would the disciples view this bread? For them, "bread *is* daily sustenance. Bread eaten together *is* economic sharing. Not merely symbolically, but also in fact."[54] In Acts, Luke describes how the disciples remain faithful to a way of life centered around the apostles' teaching, the fellowship, the breaking of bread, and the prayers (2:42). These practices set the pattern for the formation of economic community: "All who believed . . . had all things in

---

51. John Howard Yoder, "The Nature of the Unity We Seek," in *Royal Priesthood*, 229–30.

52. John Howard Yoder, *The Ecumenical Movement and the Faithful Church* (Scottdale, PA: Mennonite Publishing House, 1958), 21.

53. *Priestly Kingdom*, 93. Cf. Yoder, "Sacrament as Social Process: Christ the Transformer of Culture," in *Royal Priesthood*, 369.

54. *Body Politics*, 20.

common" (2:44); "no one claimed private ownership of any possessions" (4:32); "there was not a needy person among them" (4:34).

"In short," says Yoder, "the Eucharist is an economic act." To do it rightly "is a matter of economic ethics."[55] This same approach of sacramental realism lets us see that "baptism *is* the formation of a new people whose newness and togetherness explicitly relativize prior stratifications and classification."[56] The true church that one enters by baptism is not just invisible but is a visible believing community, an empirical social body, and a power for change in the present world.[57] Typically an institution or social body is less caring and less moral than its best individual members. But the body of Christ is called to be distinct in this regard—"it is not less moral than its individual members."[58]

THE NEW START WITHIN THE NEW COMMUNITY

Interethnic inclusiveness is one dimension of baptism, perhaps the central one, but there are others. They likewise involve issues of both ecclesiology (what the church is called to be now) and eschatology (how the world is meant to be ultimately).

At the same time baptism creates the new society, for example, it offers to each person who enters a new start in life. Yoder notes, "Before Paul and the new humanity, even before Jesus, baptism also meant repentance and cleansing. It meant 'You can leave your past behind.' John's annunciation of the kingdom enabled his hearers to begin a new life."[59] If that was the case in the days of John the Baptist, what does it mean for people today to hear the message of baptism: "You can change"? The *you* here must refer not just to each person but to the other person—the stranger, the outcast, even the enemy or oppressor that one is inclined to view in terms of their past actions. Baptism directs us to view them also in terms of Christ's plan for their future redemption.

Here is where Yoder connects baptism and peacemaking. Pacifism is the prophetic vocation of all baptized believers.[60] The true power of nonviolence

---

55. *Body Politics*, 21.
56. *Body Politics*, 33.
57. *Priestly Kingdom*, 91.
58. John Howard Yoder, "Reinhold Niebuhr and Christian Pacifism," *Mennonite Quarterly Review* 29 (April 1955): 115.
59. *Body Politics*, 41.
60. John Howard Yoder, "Peace without Eschatology?" in *Royal Priesthood*, 158.

does not lie in making aggressors more guilty or ashamed, but in moving them toward conversion. Baptism and nonviolence both proclaim that transformation is possible for all people. In the following section of *Body Politics*, Yoder discusses how the message of baptism is better than some models for human action based on the social sciences:

One of the standard challenges of social ethics is the temptation to borrow from the social "sciences" a model of what it means to be scientific, which in turn had been borrowed from the natural sciences. That model assumes the fixity of character and therefore promotes quasi-mechanical understandings of psychic and social causation. Within this context we are then predisposed toward models of social process that box the offender or the adversary into his or her past path.

The gospel says, however, and baptism celebrates that a new life is possible. At least in analogical ways, the category of repentance can be communicated beyond the church. For one example, the power of nonviolence is that it gives operational shape to our permanent readiness to see our adversary as able to change. Gandhi learned this by reading Tolstoy, although he had not encountered it among the Christians he knew well . . . . The goal of nonviolent action is not the destruction or even the repression of the adversary, but his or her conversion. Nonviolent techniques in the struggle for civil rights do much to celebrate the dignity of the downtrodden, without which such techniques would not "work." Yet their uniqueness is greatest at the point of their protecting the dignity of the adversary. They appeal to the conscience of the oppressor. They refuse to deal with the oppressor in terms of the oppressor's past and past or present guilt.

If nonviolence were only an appeal to the guilt of the beneficiaries of injustice then its appropriateness and probably some of its pragmatic effectiveness would be dependent on the presence of guilt feelings on the part of those whom one seeks to influence. Some racists feel less guilty than others. If the meaning of the civil rights struggle or of any nonviolent action was that it could exploit the guilt feelings of the white middle class, then we might have less to say to those who feel less guilt. There might be nothing at all to say to those who feel righteous about their oppressive role. If on the other hand, Christian baptism proclaims and celebrates that change in identity, understanding, and behavior (what the apostles call "repentance") is possible after all, then whether people feel guilt may not be so important. What is important is the clarity of the call to reconciliation, to which the nonviolent provocation calls the adversary. It is possible for all because it has already been celebrated in Christian baptism by some of us.

I have been describing nonviolent conflict here as an analog to the call to conversion. This is the way such activities have functioned, for example, at the edge of the constitutional order in the campaigns of Gandhi or King. The same witness must apply as well closer to the middle range of social process, in conflict management within institutions, and in exercising the skills of conflict resolution. Within the social sciences in the last generation, there has grown up a broad dissatisfaction with the "equilibrium" models that sociologists used to use for understanding a society in favor of patterns that observe conflict and change. To approach any conflict under the axiom that the adver-

> sary shares the same human dignity that God has ascribed to us without any merit on
> our part is to bring to the management of that conflict a powerful *a priori* ground,
> founded in baptism, for expecting redemptive change.[61]

Within the body of Christ, the repentance and redemptive change that baptism epitomizes are ongoing activities. "If I am a Christian at all," Yoder writes, "what I do is my brother's and my sister's business. We owe one another counsel and, sometimes, correction and pardon."[62]

THE NEW COMMUNITY WITHIN THE NEW REALITY

Baptism says that no one is beyond the possibility of repentance and redemption. All are invited to be united and equal with fellow believers. At the same time baptism draws people into the church, it also means the church is sent to the world in mission. Baptism entails not just a new start for a person, or that plus a new society that is the church, but overall it commences the entirely new regime and new reality of Jesus Christ. Jesus is "the bearer of a new possibility of human, social, and therefore political relationships. His baptism is the inauguration and his cross is the culmination of that new regime in which his disciples are called to share."[63]

To share in the new reign that began with Jesus's baptism is to participate simultaneously in the kingdom of Christ and in the life of the world. This participation is that of *theosis*. Like other authors in this book, Yoder speaks of "sharing in the divine nature as the definition of Christian existence"—but *theosis*, he makes clear, transpires in the arena of social ethics and political action.[64] Living between Pentecost and the Parousia, the disciple of Jesus lives simultaneously in "two aeons," which exist at the same time but point in different directions.[65] The one points back to history outside and before Christ, and the other points forward to the fullness of God's kingdom. The

---

61. *Body Politics*, 41–42.

62. John Howard Yoder, "Binding and Loosing," in *Royal Priesthood*, 158. These words, first published in 1967, became especially poignant twenty-five years later, when Yoder submitted himself to a four-year process of church discipline after allegations of sexual misconduct.

63. *Politics of Jesus*, 52.

64. *Politics of Jesus*, 115.

65. John Howard Yoder, "If Christ Is Truly Lord," in *The Original Revolution: Essays on Christian Pacifism* (Scottdale, PA: Herald Press, 1971), 58.

social manifestation of the one is the world and of the other is the church. The aim is for the church to exist in the world and embody the gospel, without caving in to the world's systems of "structured unbelief." ("Structured unbelief" is sometimes what the New Testament means by "world.")[66] Each baptized believer is automatically a missionary. The mission is not to conquer the world by strength and submission, but more simply to resist the world's seduction, while instead enticing people toward the way of Christ.[67]

The terms *church*, *world*, and *mission* are key here because they have bearing on current issues such as political action and interfaith dialogue. The "world" (*aion houtos* in Paul, *kosmos* in John) refers to creation or the universe not as God intended them, but in their fallen form. "Over against this 'world' the church is visible; identified by baptism, discipline, morality, and martyrdom," says Yoder.[68] The church is visible, also vocal and active in the world; it is the "foretaste/model/herald of the kingdom."[69] The completion of the kingdom will occur when all creation is restored and set right.

Between the church and the world there is this duality, even dichotomy, but behind or above it there is also a "believed unity," since Jesus is now Lord of both.[70] This unity ought to instill in Christians a quiet confidence. They ought never minimize the power of evil, yet they can and must affirm that Christ's love is stronger.[71] Sometimes Yoder uses a stark military image to state the position of believers in history: They are like the Allied forces of World War II between D-Day and VE Day; victory is assured, though not quite consummated and though the weapons of their warfare are not carnal but instead the gospel of peace.

We can picture the situation of the first Christians. They may appear weak, but because Jesus, their king, priest, and prophet, is also sovereign over the world, they know they too are "participating in God's rule over the cosmos."[72] They know the power of the state is not the ultimate force determining history, because Jesus is Lord over the principalities and powers.[73] This fact is secure, despite any evidence to the contrary, despite oppression and persecu-

66. John Howard Yoder, "The Otherness of the Church," in *Royal Priesthood*, 62.

67. *Politics of Jesus*, 150: "The church does not attack the powers; this Christ has done. The church concentrates upon not being seduced by them. By existing the church demonstrates that their rebellion has been vanquished."

68. "Otherness of the Church," 55–56.

69. "Why Ecclesiology Is Social Ethics," 106.

70. "Otherness of the Church," 56.

71. "How H. Richard Niebuhr Reasoned," in *Authentic Transformation*, 89.

72. John Howard Yoder, "To Serve Our God and to Rule the World," in *Royal Priesthood*, 130. For more on the roles of Jesus, see Yoder, *Preface to Theology: Christology and Theological Method* (Grand Rapids: Brazos Press, 2002), 240–376.

73. "Otherness of the Church," 56; cf. "How H. Richard Niebuhr Reasoned," in *Authentic Transformation*, 68.

tion, and as reason to hope they find signs within the church and beyond that Christ has begun a new phase of world history. The so-called delay of his second coming does not dim this hope, for the new community is ever vibrant, and baptism manifests this newness:

> Now within history there is a group of people whom it is not exaggerating to call a "new world" or a "new humanity." We know the new world has come because its formation breaches the previously followed boundaries that had been fixed by the orders of creation and providence.[74]

God is doing a new thing, and the emblem for this "new worldliness" is the way that "status differences—whether sexual, ritual, ethnic, or economic—are overarched in a new reality."[75] Baptism is a missionary action whereby people voluntarily enter this new reality; hence "Abraham has more sons and daughters than only his biological descendants: Even the language of family is broken open to adopt the outsider."[76]

But how changed was the situation, and how polluted the connection between baptism and mission, when church and state power became fused in the era of Christendom after Constantine.[77] Christ's triumph was replaced by a human triumphalism that co-opted his reign, and baptism became much less a voluntary entry into God's new reality and much more a vehicle for reinforcing the old regime. Whole societies were declared "Christian"; whole populations were "baptized" in response to subtle or blunt social pressure, for theocracy would baptize the world, along with the world's ways of distributing power and doing politics.

Today the world will no longer let itself be baptized that way.[78] The situation is now "post-Christendom" in two ways: We cannot assume the church presently has the same power in the world, and we cannot forget the church's abuse of power in the past. The present situation is also not bad: "Now that the church has become weak may we not recognize with joy that her calling is to be weak? Should we not, by definition and without reluctance, renounce all grasping for the levers of control by which other people think they can govern history?" Yoder is not against Christians holding political office; his

74. *Body Politics*, 37.
75. *Body Politics*, 37.
76. *Body Politics*, 39.
77. "[Christendom] speaks of a place and a time where the name of Christ was invoked over a global cultural/social/political phenomenon without regard for whether all the participants in that process were invoking that name as their own confessional identity" ("Why Ecclesiology Is Social Ethics," 106).
78. "People in the World," 93.

point is more that Christ's power is often manifest in human weakness. Among other things, this changed position of the church means we do not have to spend a lot of time fretting over the question challenging Christian pacifism: "What would happen if everybody did this?"[79] In fact, everybody will not. But radical disciples of Jesus will, not because they are intent on being radicals but because they desire to serve their Lord.[80]

Serving Christ means being in mission to the world, but given the past mistakes of missionaries and the general abuse of power in Christendom, how do we go forth? One corrective is to be less Christian, the other to be more. One corrective proposes that in the interfaith encounter with other religions, Christians ought to atone for triumphalism, along with Mediterranean and Germanic tribalism, by seeking a dialogue that "relativizes Jesus," stripping off distinctiveness to find common ground. The other "radicalizes the particular relevance of Jesus," focusing on the content of his message—love of the adversary, dignity of the lowly, repentance, servanthood, and the renunciation of coercion. Says Yoder, "One [path] corrects for the error of provincialism by embracing variety: the other corrects for the sin of pride by repenting. Only experience can tell when and where either one of these stances will enable a genuine interfaith meeting."[81] On balance, Yoder favors the second stance. The error of triumphalism, he says, was "not that it was too tied to Jesus but that it denied him, precisely in its power and its disrespect for the neighbor."[82]

THE CHURCH IN MISSION TO THE WORLD

However the difficulties of interfaith encounters are handled, baptism means that all believers are ordained to ministry and sent in mission to the world. Amid the various ways that mission takes place, we can limn some general principals. To summarize, mission begins with a large frame of reference, it proceeds often by small degrees, addressing particular issues, and it calls for human behavior that is impossible except by the Holy Spirit.

After disavowing the Constantinian vision of baptizing the whole world "from the top down," we might be inclined to construe Christian mission today in one of three ways:

79. "Let the Church Be the Church," 175.
80. Cf. *Priestly Kingdom*, 88.
81. John Howard Yoder, "The Disavowal of Constantine," in *Royal Priesthood*, 258.
82. "Disavowal of Constantine," 257.

1. Individuals join themselves to Christ. The new humanity has social dimensions, but social dimensions are secondary to what truly matters, namely, having an "individual inner transforming experience."[83]
2. People join the world. They align themselves with all the processes of liberation and empowerment that are happening anywhere and everywhere, since God works through them all.
3. People join the church. They come together to plant church communities, accepting that growth is easiest when a community is ethnically and culturally homogenous. The spanning of diversity that marked the first Christians was a good ideal, but church growth experts have taught us to think more realistically.[84]

None of these three visions of mission is the understanding Paul sets forth in the New Testament when he refers to baptism. Here mission is not centered "in the heart or in the total course of history," though it touches both.[85] According to this proclamation of mission:

- the messianic age has begun, there is a new reality;
- there is a real separation between the new community that embraces this reality and the world that does not;
- there is no separation between personal salvation and life in this community;
- this new life transforms all social relations, healing divisions, for the cause of Christ, and to the effect of transforming the world.

Given this frame of reference for mission, we can say that in baptism people voluntarily join the church that is joined to Christ and are thus joined together as God's chosen vessel for transforming creation. The church has visible and peculiar marks of holy living, baptism being one of them. There are many more. Says Yoder, "When people keep their promises, love their enemies, enjoy their neighbors, and tell the truth, as others do not, this may communicate to the world something of the reconciling, i.e., the community-creating, love of God. If, on the other hand, those who call Christ 'Lord, Lord' do whatever the situation calls for just as do their neighbors," this behavior also becomes a visible witness, a confirmation to the world that church people are really no different from them.[86]

However, when Christians really do engage in peculiar holy living, it does more than offer the world new information; it has a "leavening effect on

83. *Body Politics*, 36.
84. *Body Politics*, 37.
85. "People in the World," 101.
86. "People in the World," 81.

non-Christians and non-Christian society. It would even be possible to speak of a limited doctrine of progress within this context."[87] Thus holy living is not confined to behavior within the church community; it extends to working for social justice and peace in many venues. Such action is not optional for Christians; neither is Christianity an optional part of such action: "Christian ethics calls for behavior that is impossible except by the miracles of the Holy Spirit."[88]

THE VOLUNTARY NATURE OF BAPTISM

Put another way, "Christian ethics is for Christians," Yoder says simply. One needs the Holy Spirit and the whole church to respond to Jesus's call. Baptism makes this response clear and concrete; it is both "personal and public."[89] It is essential for a person to have the freedom to choose for or against baptism, and Yoder gives several reasons why.

God who is peaceful and not coercive has always given "the freedom of unbelief . . . to a rebellious humanity."[90] Freedom is also intrinsic to the new humanity; a chief error of Christendom was that it robbed people of the freedom not to believe, or to believe differently, and for Anabaptists the consequence was often harsh persecution. To kill an Anabaptist by drowning was seen as some kind of poetic justice—and this by Reformers who opposed the strictures of Rome.

By challenging infant baptism, the Anabaptists also questioned the parish pattern that assumed one pastor had responsibility for a given area "by virtue of the [infant] baptism of all members of that community."[91] Anabaptists said the church should be based upon common commitment and believers' baptism, not common geography and infant baptism. The parish pattern started to come unraveled during the industrial revolutions, when urban growth gave people a new kind of anonymity and freedom to form associations. This change could help churches rediscover their true basis for unity, yet city life also poses the question more acutely: Can a person find the loving community that makes this new urban freedom a good thing? If not, then as Jesus put it, the last state of that person will be worse than the first.[92]

87. "Peace without Eschatology?" 159.
88. "Let the Church Be the Church," 174.
89. "Why Ecclesiology Is Social Ethics," 116.
90. "Why Ecclesiology Is Social Ethics," 109.
91. "People in the World," 99.
92. "People in the World," 83.

Here we begin to see the social implications of voluntary baptism. God gives people liberty, Christendom denied liberty, but liberty is basic to baptism and the new humanity, just as interethnic unity and the new start in life are basic. With the unity that baptism enacts, there is peace between diverse peoples. With the new start that baptism offers, there is peace toward enemies (since repentance is possible for all). With the liberty that baptism demands, there is peace with those who choose not to believe. Nowadays the threat of being drowned or burned at the stake has receded, but a civil order can still be coercive in other ways. Notes Yoder, "It is not really assured that our society will defend the rights of real dissent."[93] Believers' baptism serves as a continual reminder that this defense of liberty is vital.

One place where Yoder himself expressed dissent was in the World Council of Churches. In 1982, after more than fifty years of ecumenical study and dialogue, the WCC issued its Faith and Order Paper No. 111, on *Baptism, Eucharist and Ministry* (often called the BEM, or "Lima document" because the final draft was approved in Peru). The document said that "mutual recognition of Baptism is acknowledged as an important sign and means of expressing the baptismal unity given in Christ."[94] It was seen as something of a milestone that members of the World Council of Churches, representing more than three hundred denominations, could agree to acknowledge the validity of one another's baptism.

While commending the ecumenical process and the desire for unity, Yoder notes how the document does not do justice to the believers' church perspective. For example, the Lima text flatly rejects "rebaptism," but it is not very clear about what that term means. Certainly Baptist, Mennonite, Brethren, and other believing communities would not say they are intent on practicing "rebaptism" when they question the validity of infant baptism, or when they state that baptism calls for an authentic confession of faith.[95] Yet historically their practice of baptizing believers was labeled "rebaptism" (as "Anabaptist" literally means), though from their perspective it was a true first baptism.

"The time is ripe," says Yoder, "for a restatement of the case against infant baptism."[96] Even within pedobaptist churches the practice is being challenged on various grounds: it is inconsistent with the biblical witness; it is detrimental to catechesis and mission; and in a world of fraying social cohesion, church

93. *Body Politics*, 43.

94. World Council of Churches, *Baptism, Eucharist and Ministry: Faith and Order Paper No. 111* (Geneva: World Council of Churches Publications, 1982), 6.

95. "'Free Church' Perspective on Baptism, Eucharist, and Ministry," 283.

96. John Howard Yoder, "Another 'Free Church' Perspective on Baptist Ecumenism," in *Royal Priesthood*, 270.

communities may need to reclaim "a 'sectarian' style of high-commitment membership."[97] The practice of believers' baptism demonstrates this level of high commitment—though not always. Yoder points out some reasons why believers' churches have been reticent to press their critique of infant baptism:

> We are honestly aware of the limits of our own practice; we know how often baptisms in our churches do not represent adult commitment or moral covenant—how incomplete is our theology of the child, how manipulative our evangelism. We are aware that some of the simple biblicism and the simple views of religious experience used before to refute pedobaptism are not conclusive.[98]

Thus believers' churches also need to strive toward deeper thinking and purer practice. In particular, as Yoder noted in 1980, "the time will soon be ripe for a restatement of what is and is not meant by the individuality of personal saving faith."[99]

The rudiments of this restatement can be given in the following contrast. On the one hand, we have what personal saving faith meant to the first Baptists and Anabaptists. It meant that God's offer of renewing grace was to be personally appropriated "in the local fellowship where every member is uniquely cherished and every gift needed."[100] This personal appropriation entailed counting well the cost of discipleship. Even recently one finds evidence of this understanding among the Doopegezinde of the Netherlands, where there is a concern for "personal, moral, and religious maturity."[101]

On the other hand we have seen what can happen to this vision when it collides with thinking prevalent in the world after the Enlightenment. There is a temptation to lower the age of baptism to eight or even five (ironically, in churches that oppose infant baptism). There is a tendency to base baptism upon a "particular modern understanding of the subjective conversion experience and being born again," and so neglect baptism's inherently social and communal character.[102] There is the danger of losing the meaning of believers' baptism in "the thicket of false kinds of individualism: narcissism in the search for experience and fulfillment at the cost of commitment and community, selfishness as economically legitimate, the celebrity as role model." Thus

---

97. "Another 'Free Church' Perspective," 270. Yoder attributes this last analysis to the influence of Ernst Troeltsch.

98. "Another 'Free Church' Perspective," 270.

99. "Another 'Free Church' Perspective," 275.

100. "Another 'Free Church' Perspective," 275.

101. "Another 'Free Church' Perspective," 272.

102. "Another 'Free Church' Perspective," 272.

believers' churches also need correction, to draw out the "corporate dimension" of baptism and to "clear the way for a new focusing of genuinely person-
alized conviction."[103]

With such correction baptism can indeed be what God intends—not a rein-
forcement of the old humanity, but an induction into the new:

> Baptism for Jesus at the hands of John, and for the first believers at the
> hands of the first disciples, for Bunyan and Carey, meant a radically
> new life in the light of the inbreaking of God's reign. Social defensive
> child raising, cheaply persuasive evangelizing, a focus on guilt or fear
> and its relief rather than on God's sovereignty and glory, and negli-
> gence of moral catechesis before or after baptism have brought many
> of our churches to the point where the social impact of a person's bap-
> tism is that of a rite of passage deepening his or her rootage in the
> known world rather than launching him or her into a new life possi-
> ble only by grace.[104]

103. "Another 'Free Church' Perspective," 275.
104. "Another 'Free Church' Perspective," 276.

3

Thomas Aquinas

Baptism Is the Act of Washing

Christ loved the church and gave himself up for her, in order to make her holy by cleansing her with the washing of water by the word.

Eph. 5:25–26

THE DESIRE FOR PRECISION

Precision is a recognized virtue in certain spheres. When going in for surgery or dentistry, we hope and pray for precision. Makers of many products, from silicon chips to turbine engines, pride themselves on precision, as do figure skaters, basketball players, and other athletes. And in the world of words, there are people such as lawyers, journalists, and poets whose livelihood depends on an ability to speak and write precisely.

Yet in religious matters, is it so important to be precise? For many people religion seems to be relegated to the sphere of imponderable opinions and never-ending question marks. Everyone is entitled to an opinion, even a strong personal conviction, but to argue one position against another is not only impolite but also rather pointless—for how can you ever really know about such things? Those who purport to have precise knowledge of God's ways may be met with suspicion.

Thomas Aquinas (1224–74) held a different view. He labored to think and speak about God and topics such as Baptism with great precision. However, the question remains whether precision, though prized in most spheres of a high-tech culture, is necessary or even desirable when speaking about Christian faith. We can probe this question using Thomas's dialectical style of reasoning.

It seems that in matters of Christian faith precision is not so desirable.

1. Something is not desirable if it leads to disharmony or violence. Historically, when people have claimed precise knowledge in religious matters it has caused division and bloodshed within the Church and among people of different faiths. With Baptism, for example, there have been fierce disputes over issues such as infants versus adults, immersion versus sprinkling, and so on. Striving for precision has led to division; therefore precise knowledge in such matters is not desirable.

2. Further, a thing is not desirable if it is impossible to attain. Precise knowledge of faith is impossible to attain, for precision applies to what can be seen and measured, whereas faith pertains to what is "unseen" (Heb. 11:1) and immeasurable. As the Apostle writes, quoting Isaiah: "No eye has seen, no hear ear has heard, no mind has conceived what God has prepared . . . " (1 Cor. 2:9, NIV). What is unseen, unheard, and inconceivable cannot be measured; therefore precise knowledge of it is not possible or desirable.

3. Further, something is not desirable if observation shows that most people do not in fact desire it. It is commonly accepted that faith is good if it gives someone confidence in the trials of life, or comfort in the face of death. But people care far less about the precise content of faith; therefore precision is not desired or desirable.

4. Further, something is not desirable if striving for it even in basic steps leads to futility. Baptism is a basic step. Yet this book you are reading exemplifies how even in Baptism there is no precise knowledge or agreement of opinion. We find as many views of Baptism as there are theologians. Trying to keep them straight or decide which is best leads to futility. Therefore precise knowledge about Baptism or other matters of faith is not desirable.

On the contrary, Jesus says, "teach ye all nations, baptizing them in the name of the Father, and of the Son, and of the Holy Ghost: teaching them to observe all things whatsoever I have commanded you" (Matt. 28:19–20, RNT).

I answer that, in order to teach about baptizing and all things Jesus commanded, it is needful to distinguish one thing from another, saying what it is and is not, and helping people to know its purpose and its power for daily living. The more precisely we can think and speak of these things, the better we fulfill our Lord's commission. Therefore precision in these matters of faith *is* desirable.

Reply to 1: Divisions and factions are not caused by the desire for precision, but by wrongful motives and lack of self-examination, wherefore the Apostle says, "There are divisions among you" (1 Cor. 11:18), then instructs, "Examine yourselves, and only then eat of the bread and drink of the cup" (1 Cor. 11:28). At the Council of Jerusalem (Acts 15), prayerful discussion and precise reasoning enabled the apostles and elders to avert division in the Church, leading to greater harmony.

Reply to 2: It is possible to know what "no eye has seen" when, as Paul goes on to say, "God has revealed it to us by the Spirit" (1 Cor. 2:10, NIV). Likewise the Spirit can reveal what is naturally "inconceivable." As the Angelic Doctor (Thomas Aquinas) notes, "It was necessary for human salvation that certain truths which exceed human reason should be made known by divine revelation."[1] Revelation oftentimes provides the premises for precise reasoning. Given Christ's revealed command to baptize, for example, we strive to know precisely why and how.

Now this desire for precision is quite different from supposing we can know everything. We cannot know God in his essence, as only God knows himself. (Some people suspect Thomas did catch a glimpse of God's essence in a mystical vision shortly before he died, which is why he could not go on writing his monumental *Summa theologiae*, his comprehensive summary of theology.)[2] But early on in the *Summa*, Thomas puts himself in the "apophatic" tradition of theologians such as Pseudo-Dionysius, whose quest for knowledge entails saying precisely what we do not know. As Thomas notes: "we cannot know what God is, but rather what he is not."[3] For example, we know God is not finite but infinite, not created but uncreated, and so forth. Yet even if we do not know the quiddity, or essence, of God's existence, we *can* know that God does exist, that we exist in relation to God, and that God chooses to act toward us in certain ways. Moreover we can respond by bringing our own faith and actions into alignment. Toward that end, precise reasoning based both on divine revelation and human observation can guide us.

Reply to 3: While some people may not care about precision in matters of faith, many in fact do. Thus in bookstores we find volumes spelling out precise steps for Christian living, while in seminaries we see movements— neo-Aristotelian, Radical Orthodox, and so on—that seek to develop more

---

1. Thomas Aquinas, *Summa theologiae*, trans. Fathers of the English Dominican Province (Westminster, MD: Christian Classics, 1981), First Part, Question 1, Article 1. Unless otherwise noted, all citations of the *Summa* are to this edition.

2. While saying mass one day in December 1273, he had an experience that he described to a friend as a special revelation. Afterward he stopped writing, for he said that everything he had written seemed like straw in comparison with what had been revealed. He said he now wanted to die, and he did shortly thereafter, in March 1274. (See Eleonore Stump, *Aquinas* [London: Routledge, 2003], 12; cf. Aidan Nichols, *Discovering Aquinas* [Grand Rapids: Wm. B. Eerdmans, 2002], 17–18).

3. *Summa theologiae*, First Part, Question 1, Article 3, prologue (vol. 1, p. 14). To read more about Thomas's apophaticism, see Nicholas Healy, *Thomas Aquinas: Theologian of the Christian Life* (Burlington, VT: Ashgate Publishing Co., 2003), 58; and Jean-Pierre Torrell, *Saint Thomas d'Aquin: Maître Spirituel: Initiation 2* (Paris: Cerf, 1996), 61–62.

precisely those habits and modes of reason that are intrinsic to a tradition. Further, people in parishes and congregations are asking for specific answers to practical questions. Like many pastors, I have been asked: is Baptism necessary for salvation?; can I be rebaptized?; and other such questions, which Aquinas precisely answers.

Reply to 4: Feelings of futility do not come from grasping many points precisely but rather from sensing an enterprise is pointless. Moreover, the goal of this book is not to arrive at a single correct view but rather to see how several views can shed more light and reflect more radiance. To reason by analogy, as Aquinas often does: Lawyers write different legal briefs on the same matter, each precise, to arrive at a better judgment. Poets may compose several, equally precise poems on the same topic, yet all of them can excite the imagination. Journalists convey different accounts of the same matter, each precise, to tell a more complete story. By the same token, Thomas gives us precise questions and answers about Baptism—to hone our ministerial judgment, to spark our pastoral imagination, and to help us grasp the story of Baptism in the Church.

DIVISION AND UNION

Thomas divides—and he also unites. He divides the entire *Summa*, which contains his best exposition of Baptism, into three parts. Each part contains many questions, each question contains many articles (a total of 1473), and each article contains a mini-debate such as I imitated above. In each case Thomas puts forth a statement ("It seems that . . . ") and offers specific arguments in its favor (usually, if oddly, called "objections"). Next he launches a counterargument, in which he first cites an authority on the subject ("*On the contrary*, it is written . . ."), then states his own position, then replies to each of the initial arguments. One question builds on another, and the back-and-forth, crisscross structure of his writing is often compared to the architecture of the Gothic cathedrals that were being erected in Europe at the time he was writing.

Thomas explains sacraments in general before turning to Baptism in particular. In his six questions on Baptism, divided into thirty articles, he addresses specific issues: for example, whether a person can be baptized more than once (the answer is no); whether an unbaptized person can baptize someone else (the answer is yes); whether several people can baptize one and the same person—say, in the case of "a child in danger of death, and two persons present, one of whom is dumb, and the other without hands or arms" (the answer is no).[4]

---

4. *Summa theologiae*, Third Part, Question 67, Article 6, objection 3.

Before seeing why such specifics matter, it is worth noting how Thomas was not only picking things apart but also working to bring everything into a grand unity; his mind could synthesize ideas like no other. Within Baptism he presses us to see how the visible act of washing is united to removal of sin and spiritual rebirth, and how both are united with the Passion of Christ.

The desire to unify extends to his method of reasoning. Some scholars have claimed the world is divided into Platonists and Aristotelians, but Thomas unites these two ways of thinking. Plato is the father of the philosophy of idealism, of all those who say the invisible realm is more real than the visible. Aristotle is the father of realism, of those who say the real world is the one we see. But to Thomas's mind both ways of thinking make sense, and there is a dynamic movement between the two. God is revealed by what we can hear, see, taste, and touch. Even knowledge that comes by revelation is mediated through sensible things—"all our knowledge springs from the senses"—which is one reason why God gives us visible, sensible sacraments such as Baptism.[5] The invisible comes to us through the sensible, and in turn the study of sensible things draws us to the realm of the invisible, and to questions that only revelation and faith can answer. Thus Thomas integrates observation and revelation; more precisely, he finds these two come together in Baptism as a gift.

SACRAMENTS SIGNIFY OUR SANCTIFICATION

The Eucharist is the most glorious sacrament since it "contains Christ substantially,"[6] but Baptism is the most necessary for it is the "door" or "gateway" (*janua*) to all the others.[7] But what exactly is a sacrament?

Here Thomas quotes Augustine, who says that a sacrament is a "sacred sign."[8] Sacraments signify our sanctification, that is, our transformation from sinfulness to holiness. Sacraments are visible signs of what is invisible, enabling us to "discover the unknown by means of the known."[9]

More specifically, a sacrament signifies Christ's Passion—the cause of our sanctification. Second, it signifies grace and virtues—the form sanctification

---

5. *Summa theologiae*, Third Part, Question 60, Article 4, reply to objection 1.

6. *Summa theologiae*, Third Part, Question 65, Article 3, *responsio* ("I answer that . . .").

7. *Summa theologiae*, Third Part, Question 62, Article 6, objection 3; also, Question 63, Article 6, *responsio*.

8. *Summa theologiae*, Third Part, Question 62, Article 6, objection 3.

9. *Summa theologiae*, Third Part, Question 60, Article 2, *responsio*.

takes within us. Third, it signifies eternal life—the ultimate destiny of sanctification. Put another way, sacraments point to the *past*, Christ's Passion, to the *present* effect of his Passion in us, and to the *future* glory of that effect being made complete.[10]

Sacraments are Christ centered and have a strong vertical dimension. They are how we worship God, and how God in turn (and in time) sanctifies us. As one writer expresses Thomas's view: they are both the worship we give to God and the holiness we receive.[11] Sacraments are not anything and everything, but specifically those sensible elements God has prescribed for our use; and since God is the One we worship and who sanctifies us, it is God who decides what shall be a sacrament. When, for example, Jesus says, "No one can enter the kingdom of God without being born again of water and the Spirit," we are in no position to argue that physical water should not be necessary for spiritual regeneration.[12] We are, however, usually in a position to obtain water for baptizing people to that end; likewise all "the things which need to be used in the sacraments are either in everyone's possession or can be had with little trouble." Sacraments thus do not narrow the path of salvation.[13]

Sacraments utilize specific materials—and precise words. To explain why a sacrament must have words as well as visible elements, Aquinas quotes Ephesians 5:25–26: "Christ loved the Church, and gave himself up for her that he might sanctify her, cleansing her by the washing of water in the word of life."[14]

It is fitting to join the washing and the word in Baptism, and to join word and element in every sacrament. For the cause of our sanctification is Christ, the Word incarnate. In the Incarnation, the Word of God is united with sensible flesh; the sacrament likewise joins word with sensible sign. Then too, a person is composed of both body and soul, and so the "sacramental remedy" to our sin-sickness is a fitting combination that "touches the body through the sensible element, and the soul through faith in the words."[15]

Words also lend greater precision to a sacrament. In itself water may "signify cleansing by reason of its humidity" or "refreshment by reason of its being

10. *Summa theologiae* (London: Blackfriars, 1975), Third Part, Question 60, Article 3, *responsio*.

11. Aidan Nichols, *Discovering Aquinas: An Introduction to His Life, Work, and Influence* (Grand Rapids: Wm. B. Eerdmans, 2002), 124.

12. John 3:5, as quoted in *Summa theologiae*, Third Part, Question 60, Article 5, *sed contra* ("on the contrary"), Blackfriars.

13. *Summa theologiae*, Third Part, Question 60, Article 5, reply to objection 3.

14. *Summa theologiae*, Third Part, Question 60, Article 6, *sed contra*, Blackfriars.

15. *Summa theologiae*, Third Part, Question 60, Article 6, *responsio*.

cool," yet the words of Baptism make clear that we use water to signify spiritual cleansing. Hence the words we use should not be haphazard, but precise and predetermined, just as Jesus in consecrating the sacrament of the Eucharist "did utter predetermined words when he said, 'This is my body.'"[16] At the same time it is permissible to insert words for explanation or emphasis, and the sacrament is still valid so long as the addition does not "destroy the essential sense."[17] Likewise certain variations are valid. For example, in the West the minister says, "I baptize you in the name of the Father, and of the Son, and of the Holy Spirit," whereas in the East the minister says, "The servant of God, N., is baptized in the name of the Father, . . ." The Western way makes perfect sense, because it points to both the principle cause from which Baptism receives its power, the Holy Trinity, and the instrumental cause that confers this power outwardly, the minister. But the Eastern way also makes sense, because it guards against the error of those who in the past thought the power of Baptism came from people, and thus they said, "I belong to Paul," or "I belong to Cephas" (1 Cor. 1:12), because these people had baptized them.[18]

Sacraments are not just nice to have, but vitally necessary. We need them for our entire sanctification, starting with salvation. Certainly the all-sufficient cause of our salvation and sanctification is Christ's suffering, death, and resurrection; but faith and the sacraments are how the power of his Passion is applied to us.[19] Certainly within us God's grace is the sufficient cause of our salvation; but God imparts grace in a way that is suitable to humanity.[20] Why are sacraments so suitable? Thomas can think of three reasons. First, it suits the condition of our human nature: we need to be led from corporeal and sensible things to spiritual and intelligible things. Second, humanity in sinning became emotionally attached to material things, and subject to them. To reverse the situation, God uses physical signs as "spiritual medicine" to free people from this bondage.[21] Third, it is simply a fact that people are drawn toward physical objects and actions. God gave the sacraments to direct this energy in salutary ways, lest people fall into superstition, demon worship, and other harmful practices involving physical elements.

---

16. *Summa theologiae*, Third Part, Question 60, Article 7, *sed contra* (Blackfriars).

17. *Summa theologiae*, Third Part, Question 60, Article 8, *responsio*.

18. *Summa theologiae*, Third Part, Question 66, Article 5, *responsio* and reply to objection 1; also, Question 60, Article 8, *sed contra*.

19. *Summa theologiae*, Third Part, Question 64, Article 3, *responsio*; Question 61, Article 1, reply to objection 3; and Question 62, Article 6, *responsio* ("the power of Christ's Passion is united to us by faith and the sacraments").

20. *Summa theologiae*, Third Part, Question 61, Article 1, reply to objection 2.

21. *Summa theologiae*, Third Part, Question 61, Article 1, *responsio* (Blackfriars).

CAUSALITY, CHARACTER, AND CORRESPONDENCE

Causality, character, and *correspondence* are good terms to remember in studying Thomas's view of sacraments. Like Aristotle, Thomas is concerned with the causes or factors (*aitia*) that make a thing what it is; and like Augustine, he focuses on the causal connection between sacraments and grace. Do sacraments *cause* grace?

It would seem they do not, for three reasons. A sacrament is a sign, not a cause, of grace. Second, a sacrament is physical while grace is spiritual, and "no physical thing can act upon a spiritual reality." Third, as Psalm 83 says: "The Lord will give grace and glory." God is the One who bestows grace, not "certain created words and things."[22]

On the other hand, notes Thomas, we have Augustine's statement that the baptismal water "touches the body and cleanses the heart." Since only grace can cleanse the heart, we may infer that Baptism does indeed cause grace, and so do other sacraments. If we do not believe Augustine, we have another authority, St. Paul, who writes: "As many of you as have been baptized into Christ have put on Christ" (Gal. 3:27, RNT). Here Paul says we become members of Christ by Baptism; only grace makes us members of Christ, so Baptism must cause grace.

Thomas acknowledges that some people think the sacraments are not the cause of grace by their own operation. In this view humans perform the sacraments while God simultaneously but independently causes grace in the soul. Thomas himself once held this view, then realized its error. For this interpretation turns the sacraments into "mere signs of grace"—whereas "we have it on the authority of many saints that the sacraments of the New Law not only signify, but also cause grace."[23] He repeats a phrase from Peter Lombard's *Sentences*: "they effect what they signify."[24]

To put the matter more precisely, if we are referring to the force or "efficient cause" that brings about grace in a person, we must recognize that "there are two kinds of efficient causes, principal and instrumental." Yes, the principal cause of grace is God alone. It must be God alone, because "grace is nothing else than a certain shared similitude to the divine nature," says Thomas, quoting 2 Peter 1:4.[25] But the sacrament is the instrumental cause, and it too

---

22. *Summa theologiae*, Third Part, Question 62, Article 1, objections 1–3 (Blackfriars).
23. *Summa theologiae*, Third Part, Question 62, Article 1, *responsio*.
24. Peter Lombard, Sentences, IV: 4, 1; quoted in *Summa theologiae*, Third Part, Question 62, Article 1, reply to objection 1.
25. *Summa theologiae*, Third Part, Question 62, Article 1, *responsio* (Blackfriars).

has power when connected to the principal cause. An axe has power to cut, and in the hands of a skilled carpenter it becomes a cause of furniture. Likewise by the hand of God the sacraments are instruments that cause grace, enabling people to become "partakers of the divine nature."

Thus to reply to the initial arguments: (1) as an *instrumental cause*, a sacrament is both sign and cause; (2) by the power of the *principal cause*, a sacrament can act upon both the body and the mind; and (3) God alone is this principal cause who can "give grace and glory," as the psalm says.

If this depiction makes grace seem like an impersonal operation, we can refer to an earlier section of the *Summa* (part 2a, question 110). Here Thomas says not how sacraments act upon the soul as an *efficient cause* but how within the human soul grace is already an essential quality (or *formal cause*).[26] The soul has a God-given destiny to participate in the divine life, which the sacraments enable it to fulfill. For while grace is present in all creation, God gives more grace through the "certain special effects" of the sacraments: "thus Baptism is ordained unto a certain spiritual regeneration" by which a person "dies to vice and becomes a member of Christ."[27]

The sacraments are not isolated, detached events, as Thomas makes clear in his subsequent discussion in part 3. Rather they are intimately connected to Christ and the Church. While Baptism really does contain grace, it "derives its spiritual power from Christ's blessing and from the action of the minister";[28] and beyond that all the sacraments ultimately "derive their power from the Passion of Christ."[29]

Through his Passion "Christ delivered us from our sins," and "he also inaugurated the Rites of the Christian Religion by *offering himself as an oblation and sacrifice to God* (Eph. 5:2)."[30] These two acts of the Passion are precisely the two primary effects of sacramental grace—namely, removing defects resulting from sin and perfecting the soul for divine worship. God even gave a sign that power was passing through Christ's Passion into the sacraments: "From the side of Christ hanging on the Cross there flowed water and blood, the former of which belongs to Baptism, the latter to the Eucharist, which are the principal sacraments."[31]

Paul calls the sacraments of the old law "weak and needy elements" (Gal.

26. *Summa theologiae*, First Part of the Second Part, Question 110, Article 2, reply to objection 1.
27. *Summa theologiae*, Third Part, Question 62, Article 2, *responsio*.
28. *Summa theologiae*, Third Part, Question 62, Article 4, reply to objection 3.
29. *Summa theologiae*, Third Part, Question 62, Article 5.
30. *Summa theologiae*, Third Part, Question 62, Article 5, *responsio* (Blackfriars).
31. *Summa theologiae*, Third Part, Question 62, Article 5, *responsio*.

4:9), but sacraments of the new law are different. The former sacraments, such as circumcision, were good in that they signified faith, but sacraments of the new covenant not only signify faith, they also cause grace.[32]

A little later in the *Summa*, Thomas revisits this issue to be more precise. There is a sense in which circumcision also brings about grace, for in both the old and new covenants people are set right with God by faith. Since grace comes through faith, and since "circumcision was a profession of faith and through it the Fathers of old were joined to the body of believers," therefore we must say that circumcision did indeed resemble Baptism "in regard to its spiritual effect."[33] Because of its connection to faith, we must go so far as to say that circumcision "bestowed sanctifying grace."[34] But we must be careful not to go too far, for if circumcision or any other rite of the old law could fully justify sinners, then Christ suffered and died in vain.[35]

There must be a difference between circumcision and Baptism, and the difference is this: one was given before the Passion, the other after. Before the Passion, the sacrament derived its sanctifying grace solely from the faith that looked forward to the Passion, whereas after the Passion the sacrament derives its power from this faith but also contains within itself, its very operation, the grace *of* Christ's Passion. Furthermore it imprints upon the human soul an indelible character, which is in fact the very character of Christ.[36]

We move now from causality to the theme of sacramental character. In this context, character means not just an indelible mark, but a "spiritual power."[37] All the sacraments confer grace.[38] They all work to unite people with Christ in such a way that people have a share in Christ's priesthood.[39] But three of the sacraments—namely, Baptism, confirmation, and holy orders—do something more. They imprint on people the character of Christ in such a way that people can worship God as Christ worships God.[40] Christ's priesthood is everlasting; so too is the character given through these sacraments.[41] Because it is permanent, these sacraments need not be, indeed cannot be, repeated.[42] To summarize and clarify: both effects of the sacraments—grace and character—

---

32. *Summa theologiae*, Third Part, Question 62, Article 6.
33. *Summa theologiae*, Third Part, Question 70, Article 1, *responsio* (Blackfriars).
34. *Summa theologiae*, Third Part, Question 70, Article 4.
35. *Summa theologiae*, Third Part, Question 70, Article 4, objection 1.
36. *Summa theologiae*, Third Part, Question 63, Articles 1–3.
37. *Summa theologiae*, Third Part, Question 63, Article 2, *sed contra* and *responsio*.
38. *Summa theologiae*, Third Part, Question 63, Article 6, *responsio*.
39. *Summa theologiae*, Third Part, Question 63, Article 6, reply to objection 1.
40. *Summa theologiae*, Third Part, Question 63, Article 3, *responsio*.
41. *Summa theologiae*, Third Part, Question 63, Article 5, *responsio*.
42. *Summa theologiae*, Third Part, Question 63, Article 5, *sed contra*.

are the power of God, but grace resides in the soul in a changeable manner, character in an indelible manner.[43]

All believers participate in Christ's priesthood, but priests who receive the sacrament of holy orders have a special role when it comes to the sacraments. The power of the priest is connected to the power of Christ. Christ as God produced the inward effects of grace and character by his authority; as human he produced these effects by his operation.[44] The power of *authority* still rests with God alone, but the operational power of *excellence* he passed on to other ministers.[45] Thus Christ works in the sacraments, and he works through people—both through bad people as "lifeless instruments" and through good people as "living instruments."[46]

Therefore a sacrament has a distinct human dimension: it cannot happen by chance and it cannot be performed by angels.[47] It requires human intention, which is not the same thing as human perfection. The recipients of sacraments need never doubt that God is able to work through ministers, even faithless or wicked ones, to bestow grace and character.[48] God will judge the ministers, but the sacraments themselves are valid provided ministers "observe the form prescribed by the Church."[49] To insist on the correct form is not being too picky or precise, for it ensures the identity and integrity of what is done, so the recipients of sacraments can rest assured that God has acted. In this way there is a balance between human action and divine action, yet with clear priority given to the latter.

In speaking of this action, we come to the theme of *correspondence*. Thomas remarks that there is also a wonderful correspondence between how God acts in the Church and how God acts in nature, and thus between the life of the spirit and the life of the body.[50] This correspondence figures into his argument for why there should be seven sacraments, in the following way.

If we think of the goal as human perfection (wholeness or completeness), then we can see that it is a process involving both the person and the community. In regard to myself, I attain perfection both directly (through being born, eating, and growing) and indirectly (through removing hindrances, such as sickness, and by restoring vigor). In relation to the community, I attain perfection

43. *Summa theologiae*, Third Part, Question 63, Article 5, reply to objection 1.
44. *Summa theologiae*, Third Part, Question 64, Article 3.
45. *Summa theologiae*, Third Part, Question 64, Article 4.
46. *Summa theologiae*, Third Part, Question 64, Article 5, reply to objection 2.
47. *Summa theologiae*, Third Part, Question 64, Articles 7–8.
48. *Summa theologiae*, Third Part, Question 64, Articles 9–10.
49. *Summa theologiae*, Third Part, Question 64, Article 9, reply to objection 2.
50. *Summa theologiae*, Third Part, Question 65, Article 1, *responsio*.

by exercising power well in some sphere of activity, and by propagating the species. All these things are true of everyday physical life, they are how we attain physical perfection or wholeness, but they also correspond to sacramental life and how we attain spiritual wholeness. Baptism corresponds to generation. Confirmation corresponds to growth. The Eucharist corresponds to nourishment. Penance corresponds to healing. Extreme Unction corresponds to restoring vigor. Ordination corresponds to ruling. And Marriage, in both spheres, corresponds to propagation.

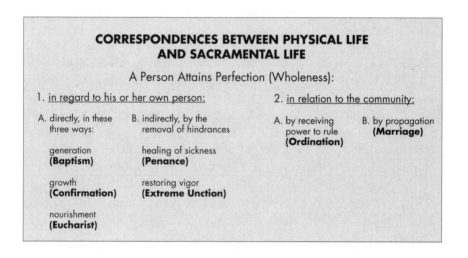

WHAT IS BAPTISM?

In moving from the sacraments to Baptism in particular, Thomas starts with the event we can see and the fact upon which we can all agree: "Baptism is the act of washing."[51]

This seems to be a mild definition for such a momentous event, as Aquinas is the first to point out. It seems that Baptism could not be the mere act of washing, for bodily washing is transitory, whereas Baptism is permanent. Should we not, like St. John Damascene, say that Baptism is rebirth, enlightenment, safeguarding, and seal?[52] Or, as a quite different consideration, Hugh of St. Victor and other authorities have equated Baptism with the element of water, not this particular use of water—*washing*.[53] Augustine likewise says,

51. *Summa theologiae*, Third Part, Question 66, Article 1, *responsio* (Blackfriars).
52. *Summa theologiae*, Third Part, Question 66, Article 1, objection 1.
53. *Summa theologiae*, Third Part, Question 66, Article 1, objection 2.

"The word is added to the element, and this becomes the sacrament."[54] The basic element is water itself, not washing.

On the other hand, the Latin (Vulgate) translation of the book of Sirach uses the word *baptize* in a context where it clearly does mean washing. But really this whole discussion requires us to make a distinction between three things when talking about Baptism or any sacrament:

First, there is the *sacramentum tantum* or "sacrament only."

Second, there is the *res et sacramentum*, or "reality (thing) and sacrament together."

And third, there is the *res tantum*, or "reality only."

If we are speaking of (1) the *sacrament only*, then we must, scientifically as it were, say first what we observe; "and this outward something that can be perceived by the sense is both the water itself and its use, which is washing."[55] It is important to say not just the water but the act of washing—for this more precise language will help us when we consider the *reality and sacrament together*. As just noted, God uses the sacrament as an instrument to convey grace and imprint character, and the participation of people is vitally important; it requires not just water but a minister who washes and a person who is washed. Baptism is this washing activity. Peter Lombard is right when he says that the perfection (completion) of Baptism consists in "the external washing of the body with the prescribed form of words."[56]

Now the *reality only* is an inward justification that comes about by God's grace. The baptismal sign and this justifying grace are not totally locked together; one can exist without the other, for God is free to give grace when the sign is absent, and people are free to resist grace when it is present. But when sign and reality do come together in Baptism, an event takes place that can never be erased, and something is given that will never be retracted— namely, the baptismal *character*. Even if people resist grace and run from God, the baptismal character is permanent. It remains as an identity to which a person can always return.

Thus to reply to the initial objections: *rebirth* and *enlightenment* refer to the "ultimate reality of the sacrament,"[57] while *seal* and *safeguarding* aptly describe the baptismal character (the reality and sacrament together). Meanwhile, *water* imprecisely describes the sacrament only.[58]

---

54. *Summa theologiae*, Third Part, Question 66, Article 1, objection 3.

55. *Summa theologiae*, Third Part, Question 66, Article 1, *responsio*.

56. Lombard, *Sentences*, IV: 3, I; quoted in *Summa theologiae*, Third Part, Question 66, Article 1, *responsio* (Blackfriars).

57. *Summa theologiae*, Third Part, Question 66, Article 1, reply to objection 1.

58. *Summa theologiae*, Third Part, Question 66, Article 1, reply to objections 1–3.

We can understand Baptism not only by such analysis but also by its history. There are two critical turning points. First, when Christ was plunged into the waters of the Jordan, he connected Baptism to himself and imbued it with power to confer grace. Second, when he was crucified and risen, he commanded Baptism to be the means by which people of faith die to sin and begin a new life of righteousness. Baptism first prefigures the Passion and Resurrection, then configures people to it.[59]

The new life in Christ is both death-and-resurrection and a new birth, and Baptism is fitting for both. Jesus says a person must be born of water and the Holy Spirit to enter the kingdom of God (John 3:5). Since water is the first principle of physical life, it is fitting to use it for regeneration unto spiritual life.[60] Water is also an excellent way to signify death and resurrection; as John Chrysostom noted, when we dip our heads under it, water becomes a kind of tomb. Further, water can be found the world over, which is fitting since the command to baptize is universal.

If water is the fitting matter of Baptism, then without doubt the fitting form is: "I baptize you in the name of the Father, and of the Son, and of the Holy Spirit." Jesus himself uses these words in commanding Baptism, as Matthew records. These words are not to be taken lightly, since "Baptism receives its consecration from its form, according to Ephesians 5:26: 'Cleansing it by the laver of water in the word of life.'"[61] Christ commanded people to baptize in the name of the Trinity. Only for a limited time and by special revelation were people in the early Church permitted to baptize in the name of Christ alone, "in order that the name of Christ, which was hateful to Jews and Gentiles, might become an object of veneration."[62]

We ought to be precise about what is essential for Baptism and what is not. Besides a suitable candidate, really the essentials are washing and speaking the correct form of words. Again Aquinas quotes Ephesians 5:26 to make the point that there must be both washing and the word. The washing signifies the "inward washing away of sins."[63] How should it be done? Immersion is "safer," since Christ's death and resurrection are the cause of sins being washed away, and "Christ's burial is more clearly represented by immersion: wherefore this manner of baptizing is more frequently in use and more commendable."[64] But

59. *Summa theologiae*, Third Part, Question 66, Article 2, *responsio*, reply to objection 3.

60. *Summa theologiae*, Third Part, Question 66, Article 3, *responsio*; reply to objection 3.

61. *Summa theologiae*, Third Part, Question 66, Article 5, *responsio*.

62. *Summa theologiae*, Third Part, Question 66, Article 6, reply to objection 1.

63. *Summa theologiae*, Third Part, Question 66, Article 7, *responsio*.

64. *Summa theologiae*, Third Part, Question 66, Article 7, reply to objection 1.

immersion is not essential, for Hebrews 10:22 implies sprinkling ("having our hearts sprinkled from an evil conscience"),[65] while Ezekiel 36:25 indicates pouring ("I will pour upon you clean water").[66]

Similarly, if Baptism is indeed done by immersion, then trine and single immersion are both acceptable. To immerse three times signifies the Trinity and three days of Christ's burial. To immerse once signifies the unity of the Godhead and oneness of Christ's death.[67] One mode or another may be favored at different times and places; in his day, Aquinas writes, "trine immersion is universally observed in Baptism: and consequently anyone baptizing otherwise would sin gravely, through not following the ritual of the Church. It would, however, be valid Baptism."[68]

Once Baptism is done validly it must not be repeated, and this point is essential to grasp. In fact, if in baptizing someone you are unsure whether this person has been baptized before, or unsure whether a prior Baptism was valid, then you ought to use this formula: "If thou art baptized, I do not rebaptize thee; but if thou art not baptized, I baptize thee in the name of the Father, . . ."[69] Why is it so wrong to repeat Baptism? After all, sins are repeated, and Baptism is meant to wash away sin. Thomas gives four reasons why Baptism cannot be reiterated. It is spiritual regeneration (John 3:5), and as Augustine puts it, just "as there is no return to the womb, so neither is there to Baptism."[70] Second, we are baptized into Christ's death (Rom. 6:10), and Christ died once and for all. Third, Baptism imprints a character that is indelible the first time. Fourth, and in response to the initial objection, "Baptism is conferred principally as a remedy against *original* sin. Wherefore, just as original sin is not renewed, so neither is Baptism reiterated."[71]

To the washing and the word, the Church has added prayers, blessings, anointing with oil, the giving of a white garment, and other ceremonies. These rites are not essential, but neither are they superfluous. They serve three valuable purposes. They arouse the devotion of the faithful by adding solemnity to the event of Baptism, lest anyone think it is just an ordinary washing. Second, they instruct, for "simple and unlettered folk need to be taught by some sensible signs." And third, they restrain the power of the devil "from hindering the sacramental effect."[72]

---

65. *Summa theologiae*, Third Part, Question 66, Article 7, *sed contra*.
66. *Summa theologiae*, Third Part, Question 66, Article 7, *responsio*.
67. *Summa theologiae*, Third Part, Question 66, Article 8, *responsio* and *sed contra*.
68. *Summa theologiae*, Third Part, Question 66, Article 8, *sed contra*.
69. *Summa theologiae*, Third Part, Question 66, Article 8, *sed contra*.
70. *Summa theologiae*, Third Part, Question 66, Article 9, *responsio*.
71. *Summa theologiae*, Third Part, Question 66, Article 9, *responsio*.
72. *Summa theologiae*, Third Part, Question 66, Article 10, *responsio*.

If we are speaking of "sacramental effect," then we ought to note that there are three kinds of Baptism—namely Baptism of Water, of Blood, and of the Spirit. (That is why Heb. 6:2 speaks of Baptisms in the plural.)[73] Through water Baptism a person is conformed to the Passion of Christ, and here the Holy Spirit is the prime cause. But the Holy Spirit can also cause a person to be conformed to Christ's Passion without water. For example, if a person suffers for Christ in a way similar to how Christ suffered for our salvation, this is the martyr's Baptism of blood; or if the Holy Spirit brings a person to deep repentance, this is the Baptism of the Spirit, also called the Baptism of repentance (here Aquinas quotes Isa. 4:4).[74] The unity of Baptism is not destroyed by speaking of three Baptisms, for all three can be included in water Baptism,[75] and at any rate only water Baptism is the *sacrament* because it has the sign.[76] At the same time, however, the most excellent of these three is the Baptism of blood, for Christ's Passion acts in the water in a figurative way, and in the Baptism of repentance by way of desire, but the Baptism of blood is closer to the work of the Passion in that it imitates it.[77]

Having said what baptizing is (the act of washing), Thomas goes on to answer these questions:

- Who should baptize and how?
- Who should be baptized and when?
- Why are we baptized?

Let us look at each question in turn.

THE MINISTERS OF BAPTISM

The "principal purpose of the priesthood" is to celebrate the Eucharist, but priests are also consecrated to baptize people.[78] "To baptize," says Thomas, "belongs to the priestly order by reason of a certain appropriateness and solemnity; but this is not essential to the sacrament."[79]

Baptism itself *is* essential; it is a person's "regeneration unto spiritual life,"

73. *Summa theologiae*, Third Part, Question 66, Article 11, *sed contra*.
74. *Summa theologiae*, Third Part, Question 66, Article 11, *responsio*.
75. *Summa theologiae*, Third Part, Question 66, Article 11, reply to objection 1.
76. *Summa theologiae*, Third Part, Question 66, Article 11, reply to objection 2.
77. *Summa theologiae*, Third Part, Question 66, Article 12, *responsio*.
78. *Summa theologiae*, Third Part, Question 65, Article 3, and Question 67, Article 2, *responsio*.
79. *Summa theologiae*, Third Part, Question 67, Article 3, reply to objection 1.

and God would have all people be saved (1 Tim. 2:4).[80] Therefore God causes Baptism to happen through any kind of water and any kind of person.[81] A deacon can baptize,[82] laypeople, both men and women, can baptize,[83] and even an unbaptized person can baptize another unbaptized person[84]—all provided the situation is urgent, a priest is not available, and the name of the Trinity is invoked.[85] If the Baptism is not done in the name of the Trinity, it is not valid. If the situation is not urgent, then the person who baptizes is sinning, but the Baptism itself is still valid.[86]

Though anyone can baptize in a dire situation, it is essential that Baptism be done by one person only. For Christ himself "is the chief Baptizer, according to John 1:33," and so Baptism occurs when a person speaks "the word of life" (Eph. 5:26) as Christ's representative.[87] There must one person speaking, because Christ is one person, even if other people assist in the physical act. Regarding assistance, it is quite needful, though not absolutely essential to the sacrament's validity, for the baptized person to have a sponsor.[88] The sponsor's duty is to "take charge of the instruction and guidance of the baptized."[89]

THE RECIPIENTS OF BAPTISM

"All are bound to receive Baptism," says Thomas.[90] But is it possible for an unbaptized person to be saved? This is not an easy question to answer, and Thomas weighs evidence and reasoning on both sides.

Here is why Baptism is necessary. John 3:5 says a person must be born of water and the Spirit, and church teaching makes clear that "the way of salvation is open only to those who are baptized."[91] Christ is the only way to salvation (Acts 4:12), and Baptism is the way to become a member of Christ, as Galatians 3:27 says: "As many of you as have been baptized into Christ, have

---

80. *Summa theologiae*, Third Part, Question 67, Article 3, *responsio*.
81. *Summa theologiae*, Third Part, Question 67, Article 3, *responsio*; Article 5, *responsio*.
82. *Summa theologiae*, Third Part, Question 67, Article 1, reply to objection 3.
83. *Summa theologiae*, Third Part, Question 67, Articles 3 and 4.
84. *Summa theologiae*, Third Part, Question 67, Article 5.
85. *Summa theologiae*, Third Part, Question 67, Article 4, *sed contra*; Article 5, *responsio*.
86. *Summa theologiae*, Third Part, Question 67, Article 4, reply to objection 3.
87. *Summa theologiae*, Third Part, Question 67, Article 4, *responsio*; Article 6, *responsio*.
88. *Summa theologiae*, Third Part, Question 67, Article 7, *responsio*; reply to objection 2.
89. *Summa theologiae*, Third Part, Question 67, Article 7, *responsio* (Blackfriars).
90. *Summa theologiae*, Third Part, Question 68, Article 1.
91. *Summa theologiae*, Third Part, Question 68, Article 1, *sed contra*.

put on Christ."[92] Thomas concludes, "Consequently it is manifest that all are bound to be baptized: and that without Baptism there is no salvation."[93]

Yet in the very next article Thomas states that a person *can* be saved without Baptism.[94] From the human side, the sine qua non for salvation, the absolutely essential thing, is faith. Before Christ came to earth, people were incorporated into Christ *by faith* in his future coming, and circumcision was the seal of this faith (Rom. 4:11). Since Christ has come, people are incorporated into him *by faith* (Eph. 3:17), and Baptism is the "sacrament of faith."[95] If people have faith in Christ, certainly they will want to be baptized, for Christ commands the faithful to receive Baptism. But what happens if a person desires Baptism yet dies before receiving it? The person is still saved. Indeed, Ambrose wrote of his pupil Valentinian: "I lost him whom I was to regenerate: but he did not lose the grace he prayed for."[96]

Was Valentinian baptized or not? Technically, of course, he was not; the water never touched his body. Yet if we recognize that a human action begins with volition or desire, then we can say that a person who desires to be "born again of water and the Holy Spirit" is indeed "regenerated in the heart though not in the body."[97] This regeneration is like the nonphysical "circumcision of the heart" to which Paul refers in Romans 2:29.[98] Valentinian was saved because he had faith in Christ and the desire to be baptized, and this desire was the first step to completed Baptism. Thomas refers to Augustine, who says a person can have "invisible sanctification without visible sacraments," a condition that is far better than the reverse—having visible sacraments without the invisible sanctification that comes by grace through faith.[99]

Thus we arrive at an interesting conclusion: Baptism is necessary for all, even though it is possible for someone to be saved without completing it. In the end the essential thing is faith in Christ—but let no one think little of Baptism. Anyone who has free-will and refuses the sacrament is doomed; even Valentinian or other catechumens who die before being baptized must suffer punishment for past sins before entering eternal life. They "will be saved, but only as through fire" (1 Cor. 3:15).[100]

---

92. *Summa theologiae*, Third Part, Question 68, Article 1, *responsio*; reply to objection 1.

93. *Summa theologiae*, Third Part, Question 68, Article 1, *responsio*.

94. *Summa theologiae*, Third Part, Question 68, Article 2.

95. *Summa theologiae*, Third Part, Question 68, Article 1, reply to objection 1.

96. *Summa theologiae*, Third Part, Question 68, Article 2, *responsio*.

97. *Summa theologiae*, Third Part, Question 68, Article 2, reply to objection 1.

98. *Summa theologiae*, Third Part, Question 68, Article 2, reply to objection 1.

99. *Summa theologiae*, Third Part, Question 68, Article 2, *sed contra*.

100. *Summa theologiae*, Third Part, Question 68, Article 2, reply to objection 2 (Blackfriars).

Given the vital necessity of Baptism, it is worth asking whether it should ever be delayed. Here Aquinas makes a distinction between children and adults. An adult convert should not be baptized immediately, but instead the Baptism should be deferred until a fixed time. The intervening period is a time for the Church to "test the spirits" (1 John 4:1), ensuring the conversion is genuine, and also a time for the convert to approach the sacrament with greater devotion. For children, however, there should be no delay, "because in them we do not look for better instruction or fuller conversion," and also because we are aware of the danger of death. For infants the only remedy for original sin is Baptism; they cannot come to God by their own repentance and desire, so they must be baptized before they die.[101] Indeed, if sickness or death threatens adults, then they too should be baptized without delay. Another valid reason not to delay would be when adults appear perfectly instructed in the faith at the time of their conversion, as Philip judged the eunuch to be in Acts 8.[102]

While clearly both adults and infants should be baptized, their situations differ somewhat when it comes to central issues of sin and faith. For both, Baptism has the primary effect of washing away original sin, the inherited corruption and disharmony that infects all Adam's descendants. Baptism also removes all past personally committed sins, and it even "hinders the commission of future sins."[103] Yet adults must express a desire to be baptized, and this desire must include a desire to turn from sin. Should adult "sinners" be baptized? Yes, if by that we mean they have incurred a "stain and debt of punishment" for past sins; indeed, God instituted Baptism to wash away the stain of sin: "*having cleansed her*, namely the Church, *by the washing of water with the word of life.*"[104] However, an adult who obstinately wills to sin and wishes to remain in sin should not be baptized, because Baptism unites a person with Christ (Gal. 3:27), and attempting to unite "righteousness and iniquity" (1 Cor. 6:14) would be wrong.[105] This is not to say a person must be perfect in every way, but there needs to be repentance before Baptism.

Hence Baptism is not an event that overpowers an adult apart from his or her free will and participation. In speaking of how a person cooperates with God, Aquinas quotes Augustine: "He Who created thee without thee, will not justify thee without thee."[106] The adult does not need to confess sins outwardly to a priest before Baptism, but there should be an inward confession to God.[107]

101. *Summa theologiae*, Third Part, Question 68, Article 3, *responsio*.
102. *Summa theologiae*, Third Part, Question 68, Article 3, *responsio*.
103. *Summa theologiae*, Third Part, Question 68, Article 3, reply to objection 3.
104. *Summa theologiae*, Third Part, Question 68, Article 4, *responsio*.
105. *Summa theologiae*, Third Part, Question 68, Article 4, *responsio*.
106. *Summa theologiae*, Third Part, Question 68, Article 4, *sed contra*.
107. *Summa theologiae*, Third Part, Question 68, Article 6.

Also, the priest should not impose "works of satisfaction" along with Baptism, for, to quote Ambrose, "faith alone is required and freely remits everything."[108]

This last statement raises the question of faith: How much and what kind is needed for Baptism? Basically an adult must have enough faith freely to say *yes* to being baptized. The intention to receive the sacrament expresses the necessary and sufficient faith. It is necessary, because the human passiveness in Baptism "is not violent but voluntary."[109] And it is sufficient because the person who truly and freely says *yes* to Baptism is also saying *no* to a former way of life and intending "to lead a new life, the beginning of which is precisely the receiving of the sacrament."[110] Human faith may be defective in many ways; a person may lack moral stamina or even hold some heretical ideas. But if the Baptism is voluntary and done with the right form, then by the power of God it bestows its indelible character; and hopefully in time the person will grow in faith, while God's grace, which is the sacrament's "ultimate effect," will more and more be manifest.[111]

INFANT BAPTISM

From what has been said thus far, "it seems that infants should not be baptized."[112] To make the argument more explicit, Thomas names three reasons. First, infants cannot have the necessary intention to receive the sacrament "since they have not the use of free-will."[113] Second, infants do not have faith, and "Baptism is the sacrament of faith."[114] Third, as 1 Peter 3:21 says, Baptism saves people "*not as a removal of dirt from the body, but as the examination of a good conscience towards God.* But infants have neither good nor bad conscience since they do not have the use of reason."[115]

On the other hand, there are compelling reasons why infants can and should be baptized. "*Our heavenly guides*, the apostles, *approved of infants receiving Baptism*," writes Aquinas, here quoting Pseudo-Dionysius, a theologian once thought to have been Paul's contemporary.[116] Children contract original sin

---

108. *Summa theologiae*, Third Part, Question 68, Article 5, *sed contra* (Blackfriars).
109. *Summa theologiae*, Third Part, Question 68, Article 7, reply to objection 1.
110. *Summa theologiae*, Third Part, Question 68, Article 7, *responsio*.
111. *Summa theologiae*, Third Part, Question 68, Article 8, reply to objection 3.
112. *Summa theologiae*, Third Part, Question 68, Article 8, reply to objection 3.
113. *Summa theologiae*, Third Part, Question 68, Article 9, objection 1.
114. *Summa theologiae*, Third Part, Question 68, Article 9, objection 2.
115. *Summa theologiae*, Third Part, Question 68, Article 9, objection 3 (Blackfriars).
116. *Summa theologiae*, Third Part, Question 68, Article 9, *responsio*.

through Adam; that they have the disease of original sin is clear from the fact that "they are under the ban of death," for death passed to all descendants of Adam because of his sin, as Romans 5:12 says. If children can receive original sin through Adam, then "much more, therefore, can children receive grace through Christ, so as to reign in eternal life."[117] Indeed they must receive this grace, for again as John 3:5 says, a person must be born of water and the Spirit to enter God's kingdom.

It is both "necessary" and "fitting" to baptize infants. Thomas replies to the original objections. First, spiritual regeneration is like physical birth; in both cases we receive something (spiritual salvation or physical nourishment) not by our own act, but by our connection to another (to the Church, as to the mother). For the same reason we can even say that children have the intention to be baptized, "not by their own act of intention, since at times they struggle and cry; but by the act of those who bring them to be baptized."[118] Second and similarly, we can say that "little children believe through others," and these others are the whole Church. Aquinas cites Augustine, who reasons that since children contract sin through other people, they can also obtain through others the faith and Baptism that remit sin.[119] Third, and again likewise, the infant is questioned and responds through others. Thus the "good conscience" of Baptism is not an act the infant does but a capacity the infant receives by baptismal grace. Baptism is called the "sacrament of faith," which here means that adults profess the faith of the Church and in this way bring a child into the faith.[120]

At the same time, Baptism should not be done without regard to natural law or common sense. For example, one should not try to force Baptism on Jewish children or other children whose parents are not of the Christian faith, since a child is naturally under parental care and responsibility.[121] Adults with severe mental deficits may be brought to Baptism as if they were children, but if they have moments of lucidity, then naturally at that time they should be asked and not brought against their will.[122] Meanwhile the case of baptizing unborn children is more complex, and Aquinas addresses several aspects. Clearly one should not try to baptize babies while they are still in the womb, for a person must be born physically before being reborn spiritually.[123] If there is danger of death, however, and "the head, which is the seat of consciousness,

117. *Summa theologiae*, Third Part, Question 68, Article 9, *responsio*.
118. *Summa theologiae*, Third Part, Question 68, Article 9, reply to objection 1.
119. *Summa theologiae*, Third Part, Question 68, Article 9, reply to objection 2.
120. *Summa theologiae*, Third Part, Question 68, Article 9, reply to objection 3.
121. *Summa theologiae*, Third Part, Question 68, Article 10.
122. *Summa theologiae*, Third Part, Question 68, Article 12.
123. *Summa theologiae*, Third Part, Question 68, Article 11, *sed contra*.

should come forth first," then the child ought to be baptized.[124] But the general principle is that a child living in the mother is not subject to human action so as to receive the sacrament; however, in the womb he or she can still be "subject to the operation of God in whose presence they live so that by a privilege of grace they attain sanctification."[125]

THE EFFECTS OF BAPTISM

In explaining why people are baptized, Thomas stresses that Baptism takes away original sin and also the actual sins that a person has committed. Here Ezekiel 36:25 is scriptural evidence: "I will pour upon you clean water, and you shall be cleansed from all your filthiness." Even more conclusive evidence is in Romans 6, where Paul says, "All of us who have been baptized into Christ Jesus were baptized into his death," and further on says, "So you also must consider yourselves dead to sin and alive to God in Christ Jesus our Lord" (6:3, 11).[126] Hence, says Thomas, it is clear that by Baptism a person "dies unto oldness of sin, and begins to live unto the newness of grace. But every sin belongs to the primitive oldness. Consequently every sin is taken away by Baptism."[127]

In cleansing a person from sin, Baptism also frees a person from divine punishment. For the Passion of Christ becomes "communicated" to the baptized, providing payment for sins and healing for sinners. It is worth quoting this section of the *Summa*. It typifies Thomas's manner of reasoning and also shows how he uses multiple images to depict baptismal atonement, such as cleansing, refreshing, freeing from debt, healing from sin, and sufficient satisfaction.

Is a person freed from all punishment due to sin through Baptism?

THE FIRST POINT: 1. It seems not, for St. Paul says, *The things that are of God are well ordered* (Romans 13:1). But sin is not put in order except through punishment, as Augustine says. Therefore Baptism does not take away the punishment due to past sins.

2. Moreover, the effect of a sacrament has a resemblance to the sacrament itself because the sacraments of the New Law *effect* what they *signify*, as was said above (Question 62, Article 2). But the washing of Baptism has a certain likeness to the wash-

---

124. *Summa theologiae*, Third Part, Question 68, Article 11, reply to objection 4.
125. *Summa theologiae*, Third Part, Question 68, Article 11, reply to objection 1.
126. *Summa theologiae*, Third Part, Question 69, Article 1, *sed contra* and *responsio* (Blackfriars).
127. *Summa theologiae*, Third Part, Question 69, Article 1, *responsio*.

ing away of stain, but it seems to have none with the taking away of the debt of punishment. Therefore the debt of punishment is not taken away by Baptism.

3. Moreover, when the debt of punishment is removed, a person no longer is deserving of punishment and it would be thereby unjust to punish him. If, therefore, the debt of punishment is taken away by Baptism, it would be unjust after Baptism to hang a brigand who had previously committed murder. Thus through Baptism the rigour of human discipline would be weakened, which is not fitting. Therefore the debt of punishment is not taken away by Baptism.

ON THE OTHER HAND, Ambrose, commenting on the words of St. Paul, *The gifts and call of God are without repentance* (Romans 6:8), says, *The grace of God in Baptism freely remits everything.*

REPLY: As was said above [Question 49, Article 3; Question 68, Articles 1, 4, 5], a person is incorporated into the passion and death of Christ through Baptism: *If we have died with Christ, we believe that we shall also live with him* (Romans 6:8). It is clear from this that to every one baptized the passion of Christ is communicated for his healing just as if he himself had suffered and died. But the passion of Christ, as was said above [Question 68, Article 5], is sufficient satisfaction for all the sins of all men. Therefore the one who is baptized is freed from the debt of all punishment due to him for his sins, just as if he himself had sufficiently made satisfaction for all his sins.

HENCE: 1. Since the one baptized, inasmuch as he becomes a member of Christ, participates in the pain of the passion of Christ just as if he himself suffered that pain, his sins are thus set in order by the pain of Christ's passion.

2. Water not only washes but it also refreshes. So its refreshing quality signifies the removal of the debt of punishment just as the cleansing aspect signifies the washing away of sin.

3. In punishments meted out by a human tribunal, consideration must be given not only to the punishment that a man deserves before God, but also to the extent to which he is indebted to his fellow men who are injured and scandalized by another's sin. Therefore, although a murderer is freed by Baptism from the debt of punishment due with respect to God, he still remains in debt to men who are justly edified at his submission to punishment as they were scandalized at his sin. However, a ruler can mercifully remit the due punishment.[128]

In saying that Baptism frees a person from divine punishment, Aquinas refers to the punishment of hell, which "Christ entirely abolished." In this life and even in relation to God there are still "temporal punishments"[129] such as "death, hunger, thirst, and the like."[130] Baptism actually has power to remove these penalties too, since they are ultimately a consequence of the world's sin, but it exercises this power in the resurrection. This world is a place of "spiritual

128. *Summa theologiae*, Third Part, Question 69, Article 2.
129. *Summa theologiae*, Third Part, Question 69, Article 3, reply to objection 2.
130. *Summa theologiae*, Third Part, Question 69, Article 3, reply to objection 3.

training," and it is fitting for the faithful to participate in suffering as Christ did, and also to emerge victorious.[131]

Baptism aids immensely in this victory. It removes sin and divine punishment, and simultaneously instills a positive benefit. Like other sacraments, it confers grace and virtues, since it causes people to become members of Christ's body, and from Christ the head flows "the fulness of grace and virtues," just as John 1:16 says: "Of his fulness we all have received."[132] The water cleanses to signify removal of guilt, water refreshes to signify remission of punishment, and water is translucent to signify the splendor of baptismal grace and virtues.[133]

Grace empowers without overpowering us. Just as there are still penalties from sin in this world, so there remains a proneness to sin in each person. But baptismal grace can make a crucial difference. Concupiscence, or disordered desire, loses its gripping power in the face of baptismal grace, so a person does not need to be enslaved by it; other human defects are likewise diminished.[134] Baptized infants likewise receive "an influx of grace and virtues."[135] In dying with Christ "they die to that sin which they contracted in birth."[136] Like adults, they are made members of Christ.

But is it really proper, Thomas asks, to speak of Baptism in these exalted ways, calling it "incorporation in Christ, enlightenment, and fruitfulness"? It would seem that union with Christ is caused by faith, enlightenment by teaching, and fruitfulness by active generation.[137] How can we properly attribute all this to Baptism? We can do so by recognizing that each of these acts has more than one aspect. Yes, faith causes a person to be united *spiritually* with Christ, but Baptism unites the person *physically*. Yes, teaching enlightens a person *outwardly*, but Baptism enlightens the person *inwardly* so the heart can receive truth. Yes, fruitfulness can refer to generating *spiritual children* (as Paul writes to the Corinthians, "I begot you in Christ Jesus through the gospel"), but fruitfulness is also an effect of Baptism in the sense that Baptism engenders *good works*.[138]

Thomas goes even further, declaring that "the effect of Baptism is to open the gates of the heavenly kingdom."[139] After Jesus was baptized, "heaven was opened" (Luke 3:21), which points to the power that Baptism has for others:

---

131. *Summa theologiae*, Third Part, Question 69, Article 3, *responsio*.
132. *Summa theologiae*, Third Part, Question 69, Article 4, *responsio*.
133. *Summa theologiae*, Third Part, Question 69, Article 3, reply to objection 1.
134. *Summa theologiae*, Third Part, Question 69, Article 4, reply to objection 3.
135. *Summa theologiae*, Third Part, Question 69, Article 6, *responsio*.
136. *Summa theologiae*, Third Part, Question 69, Article 6, *sed contra*.
137. *Summa theologiae*, Third Part, Question 69, Article 5, objections 1–3.
138. *Summa theologiae*, Third Part, Question 69, Article 6, replies to objections 1–3.
139. *Summa theologiae*, Third Part, Question 69, Article 7.

It opens heaven by removing the obstacle that prevents people from entering, namely, "sin and the debt of punishment."[140] Baptism does not accomplish this (or any other) effect as some independent operation, but rather by incorporating people into Christ's Passion and "applying its power" to them.[141]

Thus we catch the sweep of Thomas's perspective: While Baptism is first washing, it is ultimately union with Christ in his Passion, and it is the power of his Passion applied to human lives. Thomas uses this word "applied" (*applicatur*) more than once. We can observe how water is applied to the body, but how is the Passion applied to the baptized?[142] Even if we cannot say in terms of operation, we can see and stress that the pattern is definitely one of union. Humans are a union of spirit and body, and likewise "Christ's humanity is simultaneously spirit and body," as Thomas says in one treatise (*Disputed Questions on Truth*).[143] There is another union, the union of Christ and a person, that sanctifies a person in both spirit and body—"*spiritually* through faith and *bodily* through the sacraments."[144] In this way, as Catholic scholar Jean-Pierre Torrell puts it, "everything the Savior did and suffered in the flesh reaches us even today."[145] It reaches us due to the union of Christ and us, and the union of spirit and body, and the union of faith and sacraments.

The effect of Baptism is the same for all, but also different. It is the same in that Baptism gives all people the grace to be born into spiritual life. For all Baptism is both new birth and dying with Christ, in view of both John 3:5 and Romans 6:3. However, the effect is different in that not everyone receives the

140. *Summa theologiae*, Third Part, Question 69, Article 7, *responsio* (Blackfriars).

141. *Summa theologiae*, Third Part, Question 69, Article 7, reply to objection 1.

142. *Summa theologiae*, Third Part, Question 61, Article 1, reply to objection 3; Article 3, objection 1. Thomas employs a similar idea in speaking of how the faith of the Church is applied to or shared with (*communicatur*) the infant (see Question 69, Article 6, reply to objection 3).

143. *Quaestiones disputatae de veritate*, Question 27, Article 4, quoted in Jean-Pierre Torrell, OP, *Saint Thomas Aquinas*, vol. 2, *Spiritual Master*, trans. Robert Royal (Washington, DC: Catholic University Press, 2003), 139.

144. *Quaestiones disputatae de veritate*, Question 27, Article 4. See also *Summa theologiae*, Third Part, Question 62, Article 6, *responsio*: "The power of Christ's Passion is united to us by faith and the sacraments."

145. Torrell, *Saint Thomas Aquinas*, 2:139. Torrell poses the "vast and delicate question" of whether Christ's saving acts "can touch the just pagans who did not have access to the sacraments." Yes, he answers "without hesitation," for while faith and the sacraments are normally united, they could in cases be separated and the functions of each fulfilled in other ways. Spiritually, just pagans can participate in the grace of Christ's Passion through a faith that is not explicitly Christian, and bodily they can participate "through certain mediations that are proper to them and that God alone knows" (140). This language, combining notions of function and participation, is Thomistic, though the argument is not one Thomas himself makes.

exact same power to overcome sin and live the new life. Some receive more because God simply chooses to give more.[146] Others receive more because they approach Baptism with more devotion. And even when two people receive the same grace, one may utilize it better than the other.[147] Thus while the effect of Baptism is reliable, it does not overrule God's freedom or the freedom of people in responding. For example, if a person comes to Baptism with a deficient faith or devotion, this insincerity or deceit (*fictio*) will certainly hinder the effect of baptismal grace; but if and when this obstacle is removed (through the sacrament of Penance) the grace will just as certainly flow forth.[148]

Human participation is important in other ways. Catechism should precede Baptism, since Baptism "is a profession of the Christian faith" and people must be instructed in the faith they are to profess. As Romans 10:4 says, "How are they to believe in him of whom they have never heard? And how are they to hear without a preacher?"[149] Infants also hear because sponsors listen in their stead, and infants respond to the questions of Baptism because sponsors respond in their stead. The sponsor does not respond by saying the infant "will believe," for who can predict what will happen down the road? Rather, the sponsor says, "I do believe," to answer in the infant's stead at that moment and to show that the faith of the Church is at that moment being communicated to the infant.[150] Thus Mother Church lends to infants the feet of others so they may come to Baptism, the heart of others so they may believe, and even the ears and mind of others so they may hear and understand the instruction that precedes Baptism.[151] In other matters it might not be right for one person to be bound thus to others, but it is fitting in the case of infants and the "things necessary for [their] salvation."[152]

Exorcism should also precede Baptism. Jeremiah 4:3 tells us to break up unplowed ground and not to sow among thorns—in other words, to remove obstacles to our work. The devil opposes the salvation people receive at Baptism, "consequently it is fitting that before Baptism the demons should be cast out by exorcisms."[153] The act of breathing forth signifies this expulsion, while the blessing and imposition of hands bars the way against a demon's return.

---

146. *Summa theologiae*, Third Part, Question 69, Article 8, *responsio*.
147. *Summa theologiae*, Third Part, Question 69, Article 8, reply to objection 2.
148. *Summa theologiae*, Third Part, Question 69, Article 9, *sed contra*; Article 10, *responsio*.
149. *Summa theologiae*, Third Part, Question 71, Article 1, *responsio*.
150. *Summa theologiae*, Third Part, Question 71, Article 1, reply to objection 3.
151. *Summa theologiae*, Third Part, Question 71, Article 1, reply to objection 2.
152. *Summa theologiae*, Third Part, Question 71, Article 1, reply to objection 3.
153. *Summa theologiae*, Third Part, Question 71, Article 2, *responsio*.

Then salt is placed in the mouth, and spittle is used to anoint ears and nostrils, to "signify that the ears receive the teaching of faith, the nostrils approve its fragrance, and the mouth confesses it."[154] Anointing with oil signifies a person's "ability to fight against the demons."[155] Along with these signs, the priest speaks words, for example, "accursed devil, go out from him or her," and so forth. Together the words and signs accomplish the very things said and done, thus removing both outward and inward impediments to baptismal salvation.[156]

After Baptism the priest anoints the top of the head, which signifies, and also effects, the preservation of baptismal grace. The baptized is given a white garment, which signifies, but does not effect, the newness of life. Thus not every ritual is the same. Some, like the anointing, enact what they represent, while others, like the white garment, are simply representations.

Here as elsewhere, Thomas strives to be precise, in order to do justice to the magnitude of the gift God has given in Baptism—the washing with water that becomes union with Christ in his Passion.

154. *Summa theologiae*, Third Part, Question 71, Article 2, *responsio* (Blackfriars).
155. *Summa theologiae*, Third Part, Question 71, Article 2, *responsio*.
156. *Summa theologiae*, Third Part, Question 71, Article 3, *responsio*.

4

Martin Luther

Baptism Is God's Word with Water

The one who believes and is baptized will be saved; but the one who does not believe will be condemned.

Mark 16:16

FACING DOUBT AND ANXIETY

Some people say we live in an age of anxiety; others that we live in an age of doubt. If doubt and anxiety are prevalent problems today, they were also problems Luther faced—and addressed in his teaching on Baptism.

As a starting point, we might ask what these terms mean. *Doubt* can be a general posture of skepticism about religious statements. But doubt can also be a specific parasite or demon that attacks people who want to have faith and live faithfully. Some people, probably Luther among them, would say that doubt and ensuing despair can even be trials that God uses to break us or make us more open, and ultimately more faithful. For just as there are differing doubts, so too with faith. *Faith* can be a human ability to understand the divine, or an ability to construct ultimate meaning in life. But faith can also be a human being clinging completely, even desperately, to God. Amid doubt about the former kinds of faith, one may come more to the latter—then as a gift find the former restored, in a deeper understanding of God, and a greater clarity of meaning.

Martin Luther (1483–1546) knew deeply about such doubt. He wrote of the *Anfechtungen* he faced. This word has no direct English equivalent, but the experience of it does. An *Anfechtung* may be the devil's attack or God's trial. It is, as one writer puts it, "all the doubt, turmoil, pang, tremor, panic, despair, desolation, and desperation" that invade the human spirit.[1]

For Luther, Baptism is "the Word with the water."[2] Baptism speaks directly to the condition of *Anfechtung*. In turn, Luther's view of Baptism may speak to people today because it addresses this *Anfechtung*, this doubt and anxiety.

Just as there are different kinds of doubt, there are various sorts of anxiety. *Anxiety* can be a psychological condition, a free-floating fear in which the fear has become separated from its proper object. Here the therapy may consist in connecting the feelings back to the object, so the fear can be examined realistically, and reduced. I realize, for example, that my anxiety about spider webs is really a fear of entangling relationships. But other sorts of anxiety may be more spiritual than psychological, and require a different sort of therapy. These anxieties arise not from specific fears but from a general apprehension of the human condition.

It is said that people living in different times have experienced different anxieties about the human condition.[3] In Luther's day, anxiety was connected to feelings of moral condemnation. People experienced life not simply as a gift, but also as a responsibility for which there would be a day of reckoning. The threat of purgatory and hell was very real. Everyone must stand before a righteous Judge who punishes unrighteous sinners.

Today and in Western societies, anxiety about the human condition may be connected to feelings of emptiness or purposelessness. You work your whole life and then you die—period? What if it all adds up to nothing? The notable success in recent years of approaches to life that advocate being "purpose driven" may have a shadow side: many people may be anxiety driven at the prospect that life has no ultimate purpose. They may suspect, even if they do not articulate it, that the meaning and purpose they attach to things is simply a fiction, a story rehearsed each Sunday to keep anxiety at bay throughout the week. The bedrock reality of their science speaks of a universe that is terrifying in magnitude but empty of eternal meaning. Everything, including the human person, can be reduced to random matter or motion, atoms or vibrating loops of energy. Recent years have brought countercurrents. There has been a slight return of the metaphysical, with some physicists speaking about

---

1. Roland Bainton, *Here I Stand: A Life of Martin Luther* (New York: Abingdon-Cokesbury Press, 1950), 42.

2. Martin Luther, *Luther's Works*, vol. 51 (Philadelphia: Muhlenberg Press, 1959), 321. Hereafter, references to vols. 1–30 (ed. Jaroslav Pelikan; St. Louis: Concordia Publishing House, 1958) and to vols. 31–55 (ed. Helmut T. Lehman) will use the abbreviation LW.

3. See Paul Tillich, *The Courage to Be* (New Haven, CT: Yale University Press, 1980).

"meaning" and "soul," or some mathematicians postulating "intelligent design." Nevertheless anxiety about the human condition is a real option for people in churches today.

While the *moral* anxiety of Luther's day differs from the *meaning* anxiety of today, there is common ground between the two historical eras. People in the sixteenth century could be anxious about the vanity of life, just as people today can feel condemnation. Postmoderns may not have well-developed ideas about hell or purgatory, yet there is still the sense that life is not only a gift but also a responsibility. People feel responsible for their families, or even for helping to create a more just society—for doing something and not nothing about the starvation, disease, and violence in the world. People today may feel moral anxiety when they consider the magnitude of these problems and how little their efforts have helped, or how sometimes they have done harm; just as people today may feel meaning anxiety when they consider how all the large problems in the world may be quite inconsequential in the final analysis, because we inhabit a pale blue dot in the midst of infinite space that ultimately leads nowhere and means nothing.

EMBRACING GOD'S COVENANT, COMMAND, AND COMFORT

In response to anxiety and doubt, Luther declared, "But I am baptized!"[4] He calls Baptism "divine water" and "priceless medicine."[5] To see how Baptism becomes medicine that enables people to face anxiety and doubt, let us look at Luther's teaching on Baptism in context.

In writing about Baptism, Luther was facing *Anfechtungen*, but he was also facing human adversaries and addressing different audiences. Against Rome, he argued that Baptism requires faith, while against the Radical Reformers he argues that one should not make an idol out of faith. Against the devil, he pointed to the external water of Baptism as a visible sign of God's promise.

His writing is polemical, sometimes pastoral, and often personal. His life brought historic sea change, but there is constancy in his depiction of Baptism as God's Word with water. He returns to that basic description, whatever his adversary or audience. In the Small Catechism of 1528, Baptism is "the Word

---

4. Martin Luther, *The Book of Concord: The Confessions of the Evangelical Lutheran Church*, trans. and ed. Theodore G. Tappert (Philadelphia: Mulhenberg Press, 1959), 442. Hereafter, this work will be referred to as BC.

5. BC 438, 442.

of God connected with the water"; in a sermon on the catechism it is "water connected with the Word of God."[6] He goes on to say, "Therefore Baptism is water with the Word of God, and this is the essence and whole substance of Baptism."[7] He holds to this understanding in a later sermon (1540), calling Baptism "the Word with the water."[8]

The reality of Baptism resides in both God's Word and the water, but the Word has conceptual priority: "Baptism is a living, saving water on account of the Word of God which is in it."[9] But what is this Word?

Contra Rome, it is a Word of "divine covenant."[10] Luther opposes an *ex opere operato* view of Baptism; the power of Baptism does not come "by the work worked," by its proper administration. Rather God promises forgiveness to those who enter into the covenant by faith: "Therefore, let this irrefutable truth stand fast: Where there is a divine promise, there everyone must stand on his own feet; his own personal faith is demanded."[11] Luther quotes Mark: "The one who believes and is baptized will be saved; but the one who does not believe will be condemned" (Mark 16:16). The *one who believes* and is baptized—this verse says that one must believe in order for Baptism to be salvific. The stress is on faith.

Contra the Radicals, God's Word is a command. Mark 16:16 once more comes into play, against those who say that since faith is everything, water avails nothing: "The one who believes *and is baptized* will be saved"—the same verse says one must be baptized in order for faith to be salvific. Now the stress falls on Baptism. "It is solemnly and strictly commanded that we must be baptized or we shall not be saved."[12] Because Baptism is a command, Luther opposes an insistence on adult Baptism. The surest course, following church practice down through the centuries, is to baptize infants in obedience to this command. Faith is still necessary, but faith is ultimately a gift from God, as Romans 12:3 suggests. Whether God imparts faith as a gift to infants or whether faith arises later in life, it is best to obey the clear command to baptize.

6. BC 349; LW 51:185.

7. LW 51:185.

8. LW 51:321.

9. LW 51:183.

10. LW 1:228 (written in 1535). Luther describes Baptism as *covenant* even more often in earlier writings, particularly "The Holy and Blessed Sacrament of Baptism" (1519) (LW 35:29–43), but see also "Concerning Rebaptism" (1528) (LW 51:252). However, if the word *covenant* connotes the term *covenant theology*, then it needs to be clarified that Luther was not a covenant theologian in the manner of some earlier medieval or later Reformation thinkers, such as Occam or Bullinger.

11. LW 36:49.

12. BC 437.

Against Rome Baptism is covenant, against the Radicals it is command, but against the devil it is God's Word that speaks comfort and even confidence:

> Certainly when the devil sees Baptism and hears the Word sounding, to him it is like a bright sun and he will not stay there, and when a person is baptized for the sake of the Word of God, which is in it, there is a veritable oven glow. . . . Say, therefore, that Baptism is water and God's Word comprehended in one.[13]

Preaching at the funeral of a prince, Luther says Baptism makes a person bold to face demonic doubt and anxiety because it makes God's Word visible. At root, comfort and confidence come from being joined to Jesus Christ. The prince has died, but *death* is not really the right word to use; since the prince is joined to Jesus Christ, God has promised to carry him "through death and hell." Thus "without doubt our beloved lord and prince lies in a sweet sleep. . . , not because he was a mild, merciful, kindly master, but because he confessed Christ's death and clung to it and stuck to it."[14]

There is supreme comfort in clinging to Christ, but "the devil's real strategy . . . [is] to tear us away from this comfort and meanwhile lead us into an argument about how good we are."[15] The devil already possesses those who care nothing for Christ and "live their lives away in reveling," so he focuses his attacks on those who try to live for Christ, yet who in times of self-reflection have doubts about their faith or anxiety over their sins. The devil, says Luther,

> also wants these others, the discouraged, the timid, and terrified consciences. . . . These he tries to get through despondence and despair. But you must learn to say: Devil, you're coming at the wrong time. No devil is going to argue with me now, but rather I shall talk with my Lord Jesus Christ, that I may learn that he suffered and died and rose again for my sins, and that God will bring me with him on the last day. And for a sign of all this I have his dear Baptism, his gospel, his Word and sacraments. . . . These seals and letters cannot fail me, any more than God himself can fail me.[16]

Here Baptism is not the sole source of confidence; Luther lists it with other "seals and letters." Christ's dear Baptism comes first in this list, perhaps because it comes first to Luther's mind, or took place first in his life, or else because it is his first line of defense against the devil. Penance and the Lord's Supper are also God-given, but centuries of wrongful teaching have polluted

13. LW 51:184.
14. LW 51:242.
15. LW 51:242.
16. LW 51:242.

the experience of these sacraments. Baptism remains more pure. Certainly hearing the Gospel preached can inspire comfort and confidence, but there is something visible and palpable about Baptism. It is an external event to which a person can point when doubts or anxieties rage inside the mind.

More can be said about these audiences or adversaries that Luther faced— Rome, the Radicals, and the devil—and how in facing them Luther formed a view of Baptism that puts his theology in microcosm. What needs to be said first is an acknowledgment that these shorthand terms (Rome, Radicals, and the devil) are imprecise. Luther himself began as a Roman Catholic monk. The Roman Church of his day was not monolithic, any more than it is today. Likewise the term *Radicals* refers to any number of groups whom Luther opposed for any number of reasons, though in this essay the sole reason in view is their Baptismal theology. Like Luther they challenged Rome, but unlike Luther they said people who were baptized as infants ought to be rebaptized as believers, and some said people need not be baptized in water at all, since what truly matters is being baptized by the Spirit. As for the "devil" (*Teufel*), that is the name Luther uses most often for his invisible foe, the Satan, though it may be said to stand for all the demons that arouse anxiety and doubt.

DEFEATING THE DEVIL BY ENDURING DOUBT AND ANXIETY

If the devil's sole strategy is to tear Christians away from the comfort of clinging to Jesus Christ, then the strategy of Baptism, we may surmise, is twofold. It is God's Word, and it is water. The strength of having both is clearer if we see first how Luther hears the Word, and second, how he views the water.

Baptism is God's Word. If we want to hear God's Word, why not go directly to the Scriptures? Luther did so continually but was not immune to attack when reading them. For example, it says "the righteous shall live by faith" (Rom. 1:17). At first Luther heard this text to mean he must become actively righteous and live faithfully, or else die and suffer God's wrath. The Romans passage speaks in detail of God's wrath, and so the devil made Luther anxious about his sin. Even if he confessed his sins incessantly, how could he be certain his heart was pure enough? He writes, "For whatever work might be accomplished, there would always remain an anxious doubt whether it pleased God or whether he required something more."[17]

---

17. LW 33:289.

Then came a remarkable insight, often said to have sparked the Reformation. Luther heard this same text to mean that God, being completely righteous, even makes sinners righteous by uniting them with Christ. He had only to believe, to receive passively the righteousness that comes from having faith in Christ. The justice of God makes us just. The power of God makes us powerful. The wisdom of God makes us wise.[18] All these gifts are received by faith.

But now the devil could attack in another way. If Luther staked everything on faith, how could he be sure his faith was firm enough? He knew enough of such doubts to warn against requiring personal faith before Baptism. To be sure, "personal faith is demanded," but this faith may grow gradually, even as a consequence of Baptism.[19] The problem with making faith a prerequisite for Baptism can be put this way. Let us say a person is baptized as an infant, then later in life confesses faith in Christ and becomes rebaptized. But then, even the following day, Satan will come and say: Yes, you were baptized upon your faith, but your faith was not the right kind. It was not complete or mature enough. You need to be baptized a third time. Luther did not poll Anabaptists to find out what happened to them. Rather he intuited what could happen to himself or others, based on his knowledge of the devil. "You think," he writes, "the devil can't do such things? You had better get to know him better. He can do worse than that, dear friend. He can go on and cast doubt on the third [Baptism], and the fourth and so on . . . just as he has done with me and many in the matter of confession. . . . Baptizing without end would result." Further, the result would be "constant peril and anxiety."[20]

Human faith is an inadequate basis for Baptism; not only is it imperfect, it is also hard to gauge. External observation does not always tell us whether a person truly has faith, and there is great potential for internal self-deception. It may be that someone who claims confidently to have faith really does not believe, while the person who "is in despair, has the greatest faith."[21] The

---

18. LW 34:337. Lutheran scholars Cynthia Moe-Lobeda and Robert Jenson see in this "glorious exchange" (LW 51:316) an implicit doctrine of *theosis*. In Luther's words: "The soul of the one who clings to the word in true faith is so entirely united with it that all the virtues of the word become virtues of the soul also" (*Weimar Ausgabe*, 7, 24. Hereafter, this work will be referred to as WA). See Moe-Lobeda, *Healing a Broken World: Globalization and God* (Minneapolis: Fortress Press, 2002), 74–82; and Jenson's essay, "Luther's Contemporary Theological Significance," in Donald K. McKim, ed., *The Cambridge Companion to Martin Luther* (New York: Cambridge University Press, 2003), 281–84.

19. LW 36:49.
20. LW 40:240–41.
21. LW 40:241.

question of reBaptism, therefore, raises questions about the nature of faith and what it means to hear God's Word.

Let us review the matter. First Luther hears God's Word telling him to do good works in order to be saved. The devil attacks his conscience and brings anxiety, which is good in that it brings him to the end of his efforts and into the good news that he is saved by faith. Thus "even the devil is God's devil," whom God uses for that good purpose. But the devil does not stop there. The point of contact between God's Word and the human mind or soul is the point of vulnerability. If faith involves human participation, a focusing on and trusting in Christ, then how can I be sure I have trusted sufficiently?

Presumably if one hears God speaking through Scripture the message of salvation by faith, then one can also hear God speaking assurance that one *has* faith and *is* saved. This latter speaking and hearing implies ongoing revelation. It claims that God not only inspired people to write the Scriptures but continually speaks to people. Luther does not deny that possibility, but he is suspicious of people in his day who claimed to hear things from God. If someone challenged the unique supremacy of biblical revelation by claiming new revelations in the Spirit, Luther said he would not trust them, though they "had swallowed the Holy Ghost, feathers and all."[22] Rather he returned to Scripture and found, starting with Genesis, that everything reinforced for him the importance of Baptism. Here the devil was God's devil who drove him to Baptism.

Baptism was removed from the internal machinations of Luther's mind. Baptism was not something he did, but God's action: "There is a great comfort and mighty aid to faith in the knowledge that one has been baptized, not by man, but by the Triune God himself, through a man acting among us in His name."[23] Having no recollection of this event, he could in theory doubt his parents' report of it, but that fleeting doubt at least could be quenched—he may as well doubt he was alive, having no recollection of his physical birth. In sum, if God's Word of salvation is hard to hear, not because one's mind does not comprehend, but because one has doubts and anxieties, then there is a cleansing simplicity in looking to Baptism, God's Word in water.

But now, turning to the second issue, how are we to view this water? The water could look insufficient. It is quite possible to doubt its efficacy, as Luther well acknowledged. Indeed, he says Baptismal water is "in no wise better in quality than that which the cow drinks." This description was not just a charge leveled by some Radicals opposed to water Baptism. It was how

---

22. Quoted in Bainton, *Here I Stand*, 261.
23. LW 36:63.

Luther himself countered Roman theologians when they claimed "the Baptismal water brings about justification by its own power."[24] No, the power of the water is the power of God's Word that is in it. God's Word makes all the difference in the world. "Take the Word away and it is the same water with which the maid waters the cow; but with the Word it is a living, holy, divine water. He who considers the words: 'will be saved' (Mark 16:16) will find it [salvation]; for with his words 'will be saved,' Christ puts salvation into Baptism."[25] Again Luther is quoting Mark 16:16, but now the emphasis of this key verse falls neither on the faith nor the command, but on Christ who speaks the promise.

This promise is powerful, though hidden in weakness. In Jesus, God comes to us, disguised in human weakness. In Baptism, God comes to us, hidden in weak water. So you can call it the water of "pigs and cows," but it becomes "a divine, heavenly, holy, blessed water—praise it in any other terms you can—all by virtue of the Word."[26] As with the water of Baptism, so with other "external things" ordained by God: They "should not be regarded according to the gross, external mask (as we see the shell of a nut) but as that in which God's Word is enclosed."[27] To put it boldly, "God wraps himself up in Baptism."[28] Faith believes this reality about the water, but the water also calls forth faith. God may even use this water to instill the gift of faith in an infant.

In sum, this is how Luther hears the Word and views the water. Against the devil, it provides a twofold strength and strategy. If the water looks weak, listen to God's Word. If the Word is hard to hear, simply look to the water.

This approach may not remove all doubt and anxiety, and perhaps God intends it that way—not that life should be free from such struggles, but that the struggles should draw us closer to Christ. After all, where is the place where people first doubted God's Word? The tree of forbidden fruit—but this tree was also the first "church," the first place God appointed for "divine worship," since here the man and woman were to show through their obedience that they knew, honored, and feared God. The tree itself was not poisonous, for all things God created were good. The tree became fatal because God's Word "had been attached to it" and because of human disobedience.[29] But God attaches a better promise to Baptism, and its benefits come from the second Adam, who in a different garden chooses obedience through a different tree.

24. LW 1:228.
25. LW 51:184.
26. LW 51:376; BC 438.
27. BC 439.
28. LW 1:11.
29. LW 1:227.

FAITH OVER WORKS (CONTRA ROME), BUT WORD
OVER FAITH (CONTRA RADICALS)

While Luther is keenly aware of the human struggle against doubt and anxiety, he does not want the battle to become too human-centered. Thus he stresses the two points we have just examined—that Baptism is divine covenant and divine command. Against Rome, as we have seen, Luther emphasizes the former. This covenant is not an agreement between equals but rather a promise given by God and grasped by faith. "Now if this covenant did not exist . . . there could be no sin so small but it would condemn us."[30] By the same token, there are no human works so great that they could save us. We are not saved by our works, but by God through faith: "This faith is of all things the most necessary, for it is the ground of all comfort." Faith lets us "hold fast to our Baptism and set it high against all sins and terrors of conscience." We sin repeatedly but return continually to the fact of our Baptism, saying, "But I am baptized, and through my Baptism God, who cannot lie, has bound himself in covenant with me. He will not count my sin against me, but will slay it and blot it out."[31]

Baptism is primarily God's action, by which God chooses to accomplish the Christian covenant. Since Jesus in Mark 16 says Baptism is needed for salvation (though there may be extraordinary cases, such as the thief on the cross, where God sovereignly saves a person without it), therefore Baptism *must be* God's work, since salvation cannot be dependent on human works.[32]

Likewise, Baptism and salvation cannot be dependent upon human faith. Against Rome, Luther emphasized the priority of faith over works, but against the Radicals, the priority of Word over faith. "Note well," he says, "that Baptism is water with the Word of God, not water and my faith. My faith does not make the Baptism but rather receives the Baptism."[33]

This important distinction between divine initiating and human receiving, between divine accomplishing and human accepting, has at least two implications. First, it means that God is pleased with infant Baptism. For just as God is the One acting to save people in this covenant, so too God can impart faith as a gift to the infant. Faith always comes as a gift anyhow. Even if faith were to come subsequent to Baptism, there is no harm and much good in baptizing infants. It is good simply because God has commanded us to baptize (Matt.

30. LW 35:34.
31. LW 35:36.
32. BC 437.
33. LW 51:186.

28:19). By analogy, God has commanded that the Word be preached, and we do not wait for people to express faith before preaching. We preach to all and leave the fruit of it to God. Likewise God has commanded Baptism, so we baptize all and leave the fruit to God. And we can tell the fruit has been good, for God has given the Holy Spirit to mighty people who were baptized as infants, people such as John Hus, whom even the Radicals revere. If infant Baptism were somehow wrong, God would have included at least one word of Scripture to forbid it, but there is none. If it were wrong, God would not have let the Church, in both the East and West, continue for so long in such an error. But it is not wrong. God is pleased with infant Baptism, for primarily it is something God does.

Second, the distinction between divine initiating and human receiving means that the human response is a real response. There is real work to do—both in the Baptismal service and throughout one's entire lifetime—since Baptism is an event that takes a lifetime to complete and becomes completed only in death.

LUTHER'S BAPTISMAL SERVICE

In the Baptismal service that Luther translated into German he included a letter exhorting participants to "serious prayer," for in this service the church is confronting the devil, and "it is no joke to take sides against the devil." The church confesses "in plain undoubting words" that the child to be baptized "is possessed by the devil and is a child of sin and wrath, and prays very diligently for aid and grace through Baptism that he or she may become a child of God." Luther instructs priests to pray "very clearly and slowly" so others can join in the prayers.

In addition to prayer, the service has a number of "external things" about which Luther felt some ambivalence. The signs that God ordains in the Scriptures are not the same as these "human additions." The devil fears the former, not the latter. Yet Luther lets the additions remain "in order to spare weak consciences" and so he will not be accused of creating a "new Baptism."

Thus we find some continuity between this Baptismal service and ones dating to the fourth and fifth centuries. At the start, the officiant blows three times under the child's eyes, telling any unclean spirit to depart, then makes the sign of the cross on the child's forehead and breast. A prayer is said, then some salt is given to the child with the words, "Receive the salt of wisdom." There follows a "flood prayer," recounting Noah and other times in Scripture when God's actions involved water. Then come the exorcisms, including: "So hearken now, thou miserable devil, adjured by the name of the eternal God and of our Savior Jesus Christ, and depart trembling and groaning, conquered together with thy hatred so that thou shalt have nothing to do with the servant of God who now seeks that which is heavenly." Luther says more than once that such a prayer of exorcism is "no joke," for to drive the devil away from the child is also to "burden the child with a strong and lifelong enemy."[34]

There is a reading from the Gospel of Mark (10:13–16), which speaks of adults bringing children to Jesus. Then the priest places a hand on the child's head and prays the Lord's Prayer while the sponsors kneel. The priest takes spittle and touches the right ear of the infant, saying, "*Ephphatha*," that is, "be opened" (Mark 7:34), then touches the nose and left ear and says, "But thou, devil, flee, for God's judgment cometh speedily."

Afterward the child is led into the church, and the priest asks the child, through sponsors, to renounce the devil and to affirm the Creed. The child is anointed on the breast and between the shoulders with holy oil. Then comes the Baptism itself. The priest takes and dips the child in the font and says, "I baptize thee in the name of the Father and of the Son and of the Holy Ghost." The child is given a white garment to wear and a lit candle to hold.[35]

The Baptism does not end when the service is over but remains an ever present reality. In an early writing, Luther distinguishes the "sign" from the "significance" of Baptism. The sign is a person being thrust into the water and drawn out. Here he advocates immersion of "the infant, or whoever is to be baptized," since *baptismos* in Greek and *mersio* in Latin mean "to plunge something completely into the water"; also the German word *Taufe* "comes undoubtedly from the word *tief*" (meaning "deep").[36] The significance of Baptism is "a blessed dying unto sin and a resurrection in the grace of God." The sign is done quickly, but the significance "lasts as long as we live and is completed only in death."[37] Only physical death deals the ultimate blow to sin, for a sinful nature abides in human flesh: "For sin never ceases entirely while the body lives, which is so wholly conceived in sin that sin is its very nature."[38]

But Baptism makes the crucial difference, because it unites us with Christ. "Christ is given us,"[39] which means sin is "not imputed" to us, and we can commence a lifetime of dying to sin and rising to righteousness. The gradual "drowning of sin" is what Luther means by "spiritual Baptism."[40]

---

34. WA 12, 42–48.
35. Ibid.
36. LW 35:29.
37. LW 35:30.
38. LW 35:31.
39. LW 35:34.
40. LW 35:30.

REMEMBERING YOUR BAPTISM

Baptism, therefore, is divine action that summons human response. Throughout his writings Luther urges people to remember their Baptism. Some scholars suggest that the weight of Luther's own remembrance shifted during the course of his life—and that he came to focus increasingly on "the Word and act of God" more than any human action.[41] A brief comparison explains this shift.

The words just quoted regarding *sign* and *significance* are from an early writing, "The Holy and Blessed Sacrament of Baptism." It contains many references to human effort. Luther says God "will not count sin against us if only we keep striving against it with many trials, tasks, and sufferings, and at last slay it to death. To them who do this not, God will not forgive their sins. For they do not live according to their Baptism and covenant."[42]

Paradoxically, the trials, struggles, and suffering in life are to be welcomed, because they suppress our evil nature: "When we do not suffer and are not tested, then the evil nature gains the upper hand, so that a person invalidates his Baptism."[43] Luther walks a fine line between reassurance and warning. Nothing exhausts Baptismal grace, he makes clear. The baptized person can always return to God. But he cautions against a "false security" that says, in effect: I can forget about God for now and go about my own business—then, sometime down the road, "I will remember my Baptism and remind God of his covenant."[44] Yes, it is true, if you turn from sin and appeal to the covenant of Baptism, your sins are forgiven. But if you "wickedly and wantonly sin" you may well find that down the road you have too little faith to turn back: "Beware lest, even if you then desired to believe or trust in your Baptism, your trial [*Anfechtung*] be, by God's decree, so great that your faith is not able to stand."[45]

We can compare these statements with later ones Luther makes, where the emphasis shifts. Perhaps because he experienced trials that suppressed his "evil nature," Luther finds his own faith is able to stand, bringing over time an increased trust in his Baptism. Preaching at the Baptism of Bernhard von Anhalt in 1540, he focuses on God's activity. Baptism means more than simply that sin is "not imputed" (his earlier understanding, following Augustine's). In Baptism, a "blessed exchange"—indeed, "a beautiful, glorious exchange"—

---

41. LW 51:323.
42. LW 35:37, cf. 32: "They become remiss and negligent in the killing of their sinful nature."
43. LW 35:34.
44. LW 35:42–43.
45. LW 35:43.

transpires: "Christ changes places with us." We are "freed from sin and death and given his righteousness and life as our own."[46]

Luther anticipates an objection: "I do not see such great and glorious things in Baptism as you have been talking about." Here he replies that if "God were to reveal visibly how the Holy Spirit and the whole Trinity works in Baptism . . . and how all the angels are present, you would not be able to stand it, you could not endure such majesty for an instant. Therefore he must so cover and veil himself that you may be able to endure it."[47]

Here we see the contrast. The earlier writing warns that persons may not be able to stand if they are lax in doing their part to live out the Baptismal covenant. The later sermon suggests that a person could not stand if they glimpsed the glory of what God has done for them. The former focuses more on human response, the latter more on divine initiative. But we should not overdraw this contrast. Even at the later date, Luther states that Baptism summons a human response. Those who know what Baptism is, "and who the Founder and real Baptizer is, will also experience the power of it in [their] heart and be bettered by it." Luther names the fruits that must surely follow in life, including a love of neighbor that extends to economic life.[48]

In the past several years, Lutheran scholar Cynthia Moe-Lobeda has written on the ramifications of Baptism, not only for the whole lifespan, but the whole earth. Her proposal for Lutherans to play a role in public life and to care for the earth is grounded in present-day Baptismal vows. The ELCA (Evangelical Lutheran Church in America) service begins, "You have made a profession of your faith. Do you intend to continue in the covenant God made with you in Holy Baptism?" Specifically it asks: Do you intend "to serve all people, following the example of our Lord Jesus, to strive for justice and peace in all the earth?"[49] Moe-Lobeda makes it clear that following the example of Jesus is not done by human energy alone. She says that for Luther the center of Christian moral life is "Christ who dwells in us, in whom we dwell, with whom we are united, and who transforms us."[50]

The indwelling of Christ, given in Baptism, means that "Christ is not only object of faith but also active agent of faith."[51] In other words, says Moe-Lobeda, "faith is both 'faith in Christ' and 'faith of Christ.'"[52] Thus, in both

46. LW 51:316.
47. LW 51:328.
48. LW 51:329.
49. Cynthia D. Moe-Lobeda, *Public Church for the Life of the World* (Minneapolis: Augsburg Fortress, 2004), xii–xiii.
50. Moe-Lobeda, *Healing a Broken World*, 75.
51. Ibid.
52. Ibid., 74.

the Baptismal covenant and the lifetime of living it out, Christ can supply what is lacking in human resources. This indwelling does not minimize human responsibilities but rather elevates them; it inspires a heightened concern for the earth and for "earthly, earthy, bodily life" wherein "the faithful become agents of Christ's love, lovers of neighbors and doers of good."[53] From this perspective, the movement of Baptism is ultimately one of *theosis*; through union with Christ, people become "partakers in the divine."[54]

In the past, Lutherans have not always thought of Luther's theology in this light, and even today the exact nature of Baptismal union with Christ is debated. While most scholars might say that Luther's conviction of sin curbs any notion of *theosis*, Robert Jenson is another Lutheran scholar who thinks *theosis* is important in Luther's writings, and as evidence he quotes Luther: "Everything [Christ] is and does is present in us and there works with power, so that we are utterly deified, so that we do not have some part or aspect of God, but his entire fullness."[55]

We began this chapter on Luther by noting how the human condition can evoke swirling doubt and anxiety. We are born into a world in which the devil is against us, and when a person is plunged into Baptism this struggle intensifies. But Baptism also bestows union with Christ and the indwelling of Christ, and so by the end of this chapter we have come to see how some Lutherans today focus less on the devil and more on divinization, the process of humanity becoming like God. No doubt in Luther's mind the struggle against Satan is not separated from total salvation in Christ. Baptism involves both. So too it involves both death and resurrection. It involves both body and soul. It involves both the Word and the water: "I therefore admonish you again that these two, the Word and the water, must by no means be separated from each other."[56]

Most of the themes covered in this chapter can be found in the following excerpt from Luther's *Large Catechism* (1528). The catechism has three parts: "the nature, benefits, and use of Baptism."[57] Luther asks three basic questions: What is Baptism (its nature)? What are its benefits? And how do people come to "use" these benefits?

What is Baptism? It is, as we have seen, "not simply common water, but water comprehended in God's Word and commandment and sanctified by

---

53. Ibid., 84.
54. Ibid., 74.
55. WA 17/1, 438; quoted in Jenson, "Luther's Contemporary Theological Significance," 281.
56. BC 439.
57. BC 442.

them. It is nothing else than divine water."[58] Luther extols the water and Word, then turns to his second and third questions. Here is a portion of his answers:

In the second place, since we now know what Baptism is and how it is to be regarded, we must also learn for what purpose it was instituted, that is, what benefits, gifts, and effects it brings. Nor can we understand this better than from the words of Christ quoted above, "He who believes and is baptized shall be saved." To put it most simply, the power, effect, benefit, fruit, and purpose of Baptism is to save. No one is baptized in order to become a prince, but as the words say, to "be saved." To be saved, we know, is nothing else than to be delivered from sin, death, and the devil and to enter into the kingdom of Christ and live with him forever.

Here you see again how precious and important a thing Baptism should be regarded as being, for in it we obtain such an inexpressible treasure. This shows that it is not simple, ordinary water, for ordinary water could not have such an effect. But the Word has. It shows also (as we said above) that God's name is in it. And where God's name is, there must also be life and salvation. Hence it is well described as a divine, blessed, fruitful, and gracious water, for through the Word Baptism receives the power to become the "washing of regeneration," as St. Paul calls it in Titus 3:5.

Our know-it-alls, the new spirits, assert that faith alone saves and that works and external things contribute nothing to this end. We answer: It is true, nothing that is in us does it but faith, as we shall hear later on. But these leaders of the blind are unwilling to see that faith must have something to believe—something to which it may cling and upon which it may stand. Thus faith clings to the water and believes it to be Baptism in which there is sheer salvation and life, not through the water, as we have sufficiently stated, but through its incorporation with God's Word and ordinance and the joining of his name to it. When I believe this, what else is it but believing in God as the one who has implanted his Word in this external ordinance and offered it to us so that we may grasp the treasure it contains?

Now, these people are so foolish, as to separate faith from the object to which faith is attached and bound on the ground that the object is something external. Yes, it must be external so that it can be perceived and grasped by the senses and thus brought into the heart, just as the entire Gospel is an external, oral proclamation. In short, whatever God effects in us he does through such external ordinances. No matter where he speaks—indeed, no matter for what purpose or by what means he speaks—there faith must look and to it faith must hold. We have here the words, "He who believes and is baptized will be saved." To what do they refer but to Baptism, that is, the water comprehended in God's ordinance? Hence it follows that whoever rejects Baptism rejects God's Word, faith, and Christ, who directs us and binds us to Baptism.

In the third place, having learned the great benefit and power of Baptism, let us observe further who receives these gifts and benefits of Baptism. This again is most beautifully and clearly expressed in these same words, "He who believes and is baptized will

---

58. BC 438.

be saved," that is, faith alone makes the person worthy to receive the salutary, divine water profitably. Since these blessings are offered and promised in the words which accompany the water, they cannot be received unless we believe them whole-heartedly. Without faith Baptism is of no use, although in itself it is an infinite, divine treasure. So this single expression, "He who believes," is so potent that it excludes and rejects all works that we may do with the intention of meriting salvation through them. For it is certain that whatever is not faith contributes nothing toward salvation, and receives nothing. . . .

In Baptism, therefore, every Christian has enough to study and practice all his life. He always has enough to do to believe firmly what Baptism promises and brings—victory over death and the devil, forgiveness of sin, God's grace, the entire Christ, and the Holy Spirit with his gifts. In short, the blessings of Baptism are so boundless that if timid nature considers them, it may well doubt whether they could all be true. Suppose there were a physician who had such skill that people would not die, or even though they died would afterward live forever. Just think how the world would snow and rain money upon him! Because of the pressing crowd of rich men no one else could get near him. Now, here in Baptism there is brought free to every man's door just such a priceless medicine which swallows up death and saves the lives of all men.

To appreciate and use Baptism aright, we must draw strength and comfort from it when our sins or conscience oppress us, and we must retort, "But I am baptized! And if I am baptized, I have the promise that I shall be saved and have eternal life, both in soul and body." This is the reason why these two things are done in Baptism: The body has water poured over it, though it cannot receive anything but water, and meanwhile the Word is spoken so that the soul may grasp it.

Since the water and the Word together constitute one Baptism, body and soul shall be saved and live forever: the soul through the Word in which it believes, the body because it is united with the soul and apprehends Baptism in the only way it can. No greater jewel, therefore, can adorn our body and soul than Baptism, for through it we obtain perfect holiness and salvation, which no other kind of life and no work on earth can acquire.[59]

59. BC 439–42.

5

John Calvin

Baptism Is Sign and Seal

He received the sign of circumcision as a seal of the righteousness
that he had by faith while he was still uncircumcised.

Rom. 4:11

FOCUSING ON GOD'S FAMILY

Families have always been basic to human life, but recent years have brought
an intense focus upon the family. We are used to hearing slogans such as, "It
takes a village to raise a child," and we read statistics, such as "35% of Amer-
icans have divorced (and 34% of born-again Christian adults)."[1] How our families have shaped us is a perennial concern of psychology and counseling. How
to define *family* has become a political concern. And how best to raise our children, how to help them find themselves and find God—these are clamant concerns of many parents as well as teachers and pastors.

By baptism "we are received into the family of God."[2] These words come
from the Genevan Catechism of John Calvin (1509–1564), which was written
to teach families. This teaching embraces both the biological family and the

---

1. "Born Again Christians Just as Likely to Divorce As Are Non-Christians," The
Barna Group, September 8, 2004, http://www.barna.org, last accessed October 23,
2006.

2. John Calvin, *Treatises on the Sacraments, Catechism of the Church of Geneva, Forms
of Prayer and Confessions of Faith*, trans. Henry Beveridge (Grand Rapids: Reformation
Heritage Books, 2002), 86.

ecclesial family. In the church, which is God's family, even adults are like children when it comes to needing visible signs of God's love. Baptism and the Lord's Supper are such signs. Importantly, they are the sort of signs by which God can elect to enact the very things being signified—forgiveness, regeneration, and union with Christ.

Baptism is both a sign from God to us and a sign by us before others that we belong to God's household. Baptism signifies and seals. Like the seal on a letter or government document, it confirms and gives assurance of God's promises.[3] Truly the Holy Spirit seals these promises upon our hearts. But God uses the sacraments as well, because "we are surrounded with this body of clay" and need physical things to show us "spiritual and heavenly things." The sacraments "nourish, strengthen, and advance" our faith. This aid to faith is what "Paul indicates, when he says that they have the effect of sealing the promises of God (Rom. 4:11)."[4]

Calvin is referring here to a section of Romans where Paul is writing about circumcision, not sacraments, but Calvin draws a clear line from circumcision to infant baptism. God called the children of Israel his family; all their biological children were included in the covenant by the sign and seal of circumcision. Children of Christians are not in an inferior position. They too are included in God's covenant and receive the sign and seal of baptism. In being baptized, they receive what is most essential in life: a seed of faith that God remarkably and secretly implants by the Holy Spirit. Even the seed of repentance is given through baptism.[5]

Parents want the best for their children starting out in life, and Calvin's view of baptism prompts us to think that it takes the Holy Trinity to raise a child.[6] Calvin forged this view while writing in a household with nine children, none of whom were biologically his own. Four were offspring of his brother Antoine, who lived with him; one was the daughter of Calvin's wife by her first husband. After Antoine's wife was convicted of adultery with Calvin's manservant, she was banished from Geneva. Antoine remarried and had four more children. Theirs was a blended household, with children belonging to several parents. Theologically speaking, however, children do not belong to their parents, but to God. This Calvin knew from sad experience. His only child, born prematurely, died. He wrote to his friend William Farel: "The Lord has cer-

---

3. John Calvin, *Institutes of the Christian Religion* (vol. 2) 4.14.5; ed. John T. McNeill, trans. Ford Lewis Battles (Philadelphia: Westminster Press, 1960), 1280; 4.15.1, 1304. Hereafter *Institutes*.

4. *Treatises on the Sacraments*, 84, 85.

5. *Institutes* 4.16.20, 1343.

6. This phrase was used by James Loder, in personal conversation.

tainly inflicted a severe and bitter wound in the death of our baby son. But He is Himself a Father and knows best what is good for His children."[7] In years when the bubonic plague swept through Geneva, many parents would have the occasion, if not the conviction, to write such letters.

Calvin did not write nearly as much as Luther about his personal life. What he did write reveals that he too experienced anxiety of conscience.[8] (The specific concerns highlighted in each chapter of this book are plainly not exclusive to any one theologian.) In his commentary on 1 Corinthians, he writes about the troubles and anxieties, great and small, that attend daily family life: "Trouble has its source in sad matters such as the death of children, parents, or a spouse; quarrels and petty differences that come of faultfinding; the delinquencies of children; the difficulty of bringing up a family; and similar things."[9] No doubt Calvin's view of baptism owes more to his steady attention to the Scriptures than his observations of family life. Still, concern for family—both biological and ecclesial—is one theme in his view of baptism and one reason among many that his view remains relevant today.

We can read Calvin to remind us that the pressing problems of children and families today are not isolated issues of human activity. Baptism places family failure and success into the framework of a covenant that clearly originates with God's activity—a covenant whose center is Christ and whose circumference covers the sweep of biblical history. If the future of a family is ever in doubt, baptism points us back to the assurance of God's promises. These promises are signed, sealed, and delivered by Jesus Christ. Baptism makes them visible for all to see.

TWO SACRAMENTS, ONE CLEAR DISTINCTION

There are only two sacraments, baptism and the Lord's Supper, "whose use is common among all believers."[10] God gave these sacraments to believers because believers need considerable help in believing. "For so scanty and weak

---

7. Quoted in Thomas H. L. Parker, *Portrait of Calvin* (Philadelphia: Westminster Press, 1954), 71.

8. See *Institutes* 3.14.6: "The thought repeatedly returns to my mind that I am in danger of being unjust to God's mercy by laboring with so much anxiety to assert it, as if it were doubtful or obscure." See also William Bouwsma, *John Calvin* (New York: Oxford University Press, 1988), 32–48.

9. Calvin, Commentary on 1 Corinthians 7:32; quoted in William J. Bouwsma, *John Calvin: A Sixteenth-Century Portrait* (New York, Oxford University Press, 1988), 39.

10. *Treatises on the Sacraments*, 86.

is our faith that, unless it is propped up on all sides and sustained by every means, it trembles, wavers, totters," writes Calvin in his first catechism (1538).[11]

Is the need for sacramental signs actually an "indication of unbelief"? No, Calvin replies, "the children of God" do not "cease to be believers," even though their faith is "small and imperfect." But as long as we live in this world, we must always advance and grow in faith. Toward that end, baptism is a kind of entrance into God's family, and the Supper "attests that God exhibits himself to us by nourishing our souls."[12] Some faith is required to receive the sacraments, or else they accomplish nothing and actually incur judgment.[13] But once received, even with feeble faith, the sacraments in turn build faith.

Calvin likes to define his terms, and in both the *Institutes of the Christian Religion* (1559) and the Genevan Catechism (1560) he starts by defining *sacrament*. "What is a Sacrament?" the catechism asks. Reply: "An outward attestation of the grace of God which, by a visible sign, represents spiritual things to imprint the promises of God more firmly in our hearts, and to make us more sure of them."[14] (This catechism, supposedly written to teach youth, presses us to imagine teenagers and parents engaged in substantive dialogue.)

As a "visible sign," baptism entails a kind of vertical movement from God to humanity. God "communicates himself to us," aiding our faith in his promises.[15] But secondarily and in response, we communicate our piety in a way that is plain for all to see: "A sacrament . . . is an outward sign by which the Lord seals on our consciences the promises of his good will toward us in order to sustain the weakness of our faith; and we in turn attest our piety toward him in the presence of the Lord and of his angels and before men."[16] Thus the sacrament entails both divine action and human action, as well as both vertical and horizontal dimensions.

Calvin says he basically agrees with Augustine, who taught that a sacrament is a visible sign of invisible grace.[17] If, like Calvin, we mean to define our terms, it may be hard to affix an exact definition to the word *sign*. Calvin wrote sev-

---

11. I. John Hesselink, *Calvin's First Catechism: A Commentary* (Louisville, KY: Westminster John Knox Press, 1997), 33. Cf. *Institutes*, 4.14.3, 1278, where the same language is used.

12. *Treatises on the Sacraments*, 85, 86.

13. Calvin writes, "If we lack faith, this will be evidence of our ungratefulness, which renders us chargeable before God, because we have not believed the promises given there" (*Institutes* [vol. 2] 4.15.15, 1315).

14. Calvin, *Catechism* (1560), part 4, question 310 (available at: http://www.apuritans mind.com, last accessed October 21, 2006).

15. *Catechism*, 309.

16. *Institutes* 4.14.1, 1277.

17. Ibid.

eral versions of the *Institutes* in both Latin and French, using various words such as *signum* (sign), *sceau* (seal), *enseigne* (badge), and *marque* (mark). Exactly what he meant by these words has been debated. Sometimes he describes the sacraments as *tessera* and *méreau*, which English versions often translate as "symbols."[18] But what exactly does this word mean? A symbol can be the most real instance of something, or it can mean a lesser reality—a token or visual aid. Clearly Calvin does think baptism is a visual aid, but it is also more than that. To provide some clarity, consider the following three guidelines into what Calvin means when he calls baptism a sign and seal.

First, there is the sense of proof or evidence. Calvin's background as a lawyer may come into play here, but more important is his belief that the natural world as a whole, and sacraments in particular, offer proof or evidence of God's benevolence toward humanity: "Sacraments are truly named the testimonies [or 'proofs'] of God's grace and are like seals of the good will that he feels toward us."[19]

Second, *sign* and *seal* include the sense of performance. By these signs God does what he says and performs what he promises. God "does not feed our eyes with a mere appearance only, but leads us to the present reality and effectively performs what it [baptism] symbolizes."[20] Note here that *God* performs what *it* symbolizes. It, the sacrament, does not by itself perform anything.

This observation brings us to a third guideline. It is somewhat subtle, but important. There is the need to distinguish clearly the sign from the reality, or as Calvin (following Augustine) puts it, the *signum* (sign) from the *res* (thing). The sign does not accomplish the thing. Baptism does not, of itself, bring about salvation. Thus Calvin opposes an *ex opere operato* view that says it "works through its working" (by its proper administration). On the contrary, "we are not to be taken up with the earthly sign so as to seek our salvation in it, nor are we to imagine that it has a peculiar power enclosed within it."[21] At the same time—and this is the important subtlety—baptism does in fact impart the reality it represents, so long as we are clear that God is the One acting here, through baptism. The reality of salvation is given through baptism, but the reality of salvation is not bound up in this particular sign, as if God could not use other means. Certainly God does use other means of salvation, especially the preaching of the Word.

Thus the firm distinction between sign and reality is not meant to denigrate

---

18. For example, see Hesselink, *Calvin's First Catechism*, 141.
19. *Institutes* 4.14.7, 1282.
20. *Institutes* 4.15.14, 1314.
21. *Catechism*, 318.

baptism. Rather the separation between the two serves a better union. We need to know that salvation is united to God's Word and Spirit on the one side, and to human faith on the other. We also need to know that baptism is united to God's Word and Spirit on the one side, and to human faith on the other. But there is no independent transaction going on between baptism and salvation. There is a rather a clear distinction between baptism and salvation—between sign and reality. Yet, paradoxically, once this distinction is grasped, so there is no confusion, then the God-given union between the two can be embraced: "Yet it is not my intention to weaken the force of baptism by not joining reality and truth to the sign," Calvin affirms. God does in fact join the reality to the sign, "in so far as God works through outward means. But from this sacrament, as from all others, we obtain only as much as we receive in faith."[22] Baptism is thus a meeting place of grace and faith, as well as a union of sign and reality.

Having clarified this distinction-yet-union between sign and reality, we can turn to what baptism becomes in the life of the church.

THREE THINGS GOD
PROMISES—AND PERFORMS—IN BAPTISM

We enter God's family through baptism. Calvin writes, "Baptism is the initiatory sign by which we are admitted to the fellowship of the Church, that being ingrafted into Christ we may be accounted children of God." Due emphasis upon the words "ingrafted into Christ" will keep us from viewing baptism as simply a ritual of socialization by which persons are initiated into a human community. As a sign of initiation, baptism is also a means by which God promises and performs things that are utterly transforming—matters of death and life. Specifically, says Calvin, baptism "brings three things to our faith which we must deal with individually."[23]

The first thing baptism brings to our faith is a sign and seal of forgiveness. It is "a token or proof of our cleansing; or (better to explain what I mean) it is like a sealed document to confirm to us that all our sins are so abolished, remitted, and effaced that they can never be charged against us. For God wills that all who believe be baptized for the remission of sins [Matt. 28:19; Acts 2:38]." This forgiveness of sins is not a one-time event, but rather baptism is a "token

---

22. *Institutes* 4.15.15, 1315. Probably "all others" refers to all other outward means, since Calvin believes there is only one other sacrament (the Lord's Supper).

23. *Institutes* 4.15.1, 1303, 1304.

of cleansing for the whole of life," Calvin emphasizes. There is no need for a sacrament of penance, since baptism never loses its cleansing power: "But we must realize that at whatever time we are baptized, we are once for all washed and purged for our whole life. Therefore, as often as we fall away, we ought to recall the memory of our baptism and fortify our mind with it, that we may be confident of the forgiveness of sins."[24]

But does baptism bring about forgiveness of sins? Calvin does not want us to attribute too much power to the water, or too little to the event of baptism. Thus the focus of baptism must be God. In keeping this focus, we can draw out from Calvin's various descriptions the following Trinitarian pattern.

- We receive forgiveness of sins because God the Father has promised forgiveness by his Word.[25] God's Word, contained in the Holy Scriptures, offers the promise that precedes baptism.[26] Indeed, "a sacrament is never without a preceding promise but is joined to it as a sort of appendix, with the purpose of confirming and sealing [it]."[27] Baptism brings about forgiveness because it is attached to the Word that promises forgiveness.
- We receive forgiveness of sins because God the Son has obtained it by his blood: "Christ's blood is our true and only laver." Thus, "baptism promises us no other purification than through the sprinkling of Christ's blood, which is represented by means of water from the resemblance to cleansing and washing."[28] Baptism brings about forgiveness because it is related to Christ and his blood.
- We receive forgiveness of sins because God the Holy Spirit enters into us, making effective the promise of God and blood of Christ: "It is the proper office of the Holy Spirit to seal the promises of God in our hearts. . . . The Spirit of God in very truth is the only One who can touch and move our hearts, enlighten our minds, and assure our consciences; so that all this ought to be judged as his own work, that praise may be ascribed to him alone."[29] Baptism brings about forgiveness because it is an event of the Holy Spirit.

In sum, baptism expresses forgiveness of sins and helps to enact it, but its action is completely dependent upon the promise of God, the blood of Christ, and the convicting power of the Holy Spirit.

24. *Institutes* 4.15.1, 1304, 1305.
25. *Institutes* 4.15.2, 1304. Calvin's reasoning resembles Luther's when he says that baptism's "virtue [is] not in water without the Word: . . . For Paul joins together the Word of life and the baptism of water."
26. *Treatises on the Sacraments*, 82.
27. *Institutes* 4.14.3, 1278.
28. *Institutes* 4.14.2, 1305.
29. *Catechism*, 312.

Along with forgiveness, the second thing baptism brings to our faith is "a sign of . . . our participation in Christ's death and resurrection."[30] Here Calvin draws our attention to the baptismal rite: "A figure of death is set before us when the water is poured upon the head, and the figure of new life when instead of remaining immersed under water, we only enter it for a moment as a kind of grave, out which we instantly emerge."[31]

Death gives rise to new birth, which is another way to describe this benefit. Again a Trinitarian pattern unfolds. God promises regeneration, the death and resurrection of Christ makes it possible, and the Holy Spirit makes it ours. Baptism is the figure of this regeneration, but not just a figure: "The reality is annexed to it; for God does not disappoint us when he promises us his gifts. Accordingly, it is certain that both pardon of sins and newness of life are offered to us in baptism, and received by us."[32] To reiterate the same principle as before, baptism expresses regeneration and works to enact it, but its action is completely dependent upon the promise of God, the death and resurrection of Christ, and the power of the Holy Spirit.

As a figure of Christ's death and resurrection, baptism enacts a change that is greater than an outward imitation or even an ethical injunction to lead a new life. Baptism makes us share in Christ's death—we are grafted into it (Rom. 6:5). A twig draws life from the root to which it is attached; so too those who receive baptism with right faith can truly feel Christ's death working to mortify their flesh, and they can feel Christ's resurrection giving them life in the Spirit.[33] Thus baptism both imputes righteousness and imparts power.

Along with forgiveness and regeneration, the third thing baptism brings to our faith is a sign of our union with Christ. Baptism provides "sure testimony to us that we are not only engrafted into the death and life of Christ, but so united to Christ himself that we become sharers in all his blessings."[34] Again, these blessings are not bestowed magically, but they come from God who promises them, Christ who is their substance, and the Holy Spirit who is "the bond that unites us with Christ."[35]

In describing how people receive Christ's righteousness, Calvin uses two different but complementary ideas: *imputed* and *united*. By saying "righteousness is by imputation only," he means that God forgives our sin only because we are united to Jesus and credited with his righteousness. We are not "exempt

30. *Institutes* 4.15.1, 1303.
31. *Treatises on the Sacraments*, 86.
32. *Treatises on the Sacraments*, 87.
33. *Institutes* 4.15.5, 1307.
34. *Institutes* 4.15.5, 1307.
35. *Institutes* 4.14.6, 1291; 3.1.1, 537.

from original sin," and never do we cease to struggle against sin in this life.[36] However, this righteousness is not imputed at a distance; our union with Christ is real and close:

> the indwelling of Christ in our hearts—in short, that mystical union— is accorded by us the highest degree of importance, so that Christ, having been made ours, makes us sharers with him in the gifts with which he has been endowed. We do not, therefore, contemplate him outside ourselves from afar in order that his righteousness may be imputed to us but because we put on Christ and are engrafted into his body—in short, because he deigns to make us one with him.[37]

Baptism is the sign and seal of this intimate union with Christ. It fortifies us in the struggle against lust and other sin, because it "promises to us the drowning of our Pharaoh." We have God's constant assurance that sin will "not overcome us."[38]

TWO SEQUENCES, ONE SALVATION

Thus God uses baptism to bring about forgiveness, regeneration, and union with Christ. If we are to ask again and more pointedly how so, it appears the answer must be twofold: because baptism is attached to God's Word, which does what it says, and because baptism has the potential to touch people outwardly and inwardly, in the body but also the mind and heart. Here we need to consider two sequences: how baptism affects believers and how it affects infants.

In the previous section we were concerned with ontology, the study of *being* or what baptism *is*. Now we turn to epistemology, the study of *knowing* and how baptism connects to human knowledge and faith. Faith, Calvin makes clear, is not contrary to knowledge but is actually a kind of knowledge. Calvin's oft-cited definition of faith says: "Now we shall possess a right definition of faith if we call it a firm and certain knowledge of God's benevolence toward us, founded upon the truth of the freely given promise in Christ, both revealed to our minds and sealed upon our hearts through the Holy Spirit."[39] This definition hints at the pattern just depicted. God's Word makes a promise, Christ becomes the substance or "matter" of this promise, and the Holy Spirit seals the promise upon our hearts, making it effectual.[40] If, as just quoted, the Holy

---

36. *Institutes* 4.15.10, 1311.
37. *Institutes* 3.11.10, 737.
38. *Institutes* 4.15.11, 1312.
39. *Institutes* 3.2.7, 551.
40. *Institutes* 4.15.6, 1308.

Spirit *seals* the promise of God's benevolence, why do we need the "sign and seal" of baptism? Not to make God's Word more sure, but our faith more secure. There is no doubt "God's truth is of itself firm and sure enough," but not so our faith.[41] It is feeble and frail. It needs help to become the "firm and certain knowledge" that aptly corresponds to the firm and certain reality of God's promises.

In leading us to faith and knowledge, God knows well the human mind. Psychologists say an entrenched mental pattern is "overdetermined" when it has more than one cause. They also say people have "multiple intelligences," meaning we learn in different ways. There is something both "overdetermined" and "multiple" in how God teaches and imparts salvation to people. Through preaching we hear, through the sacraments we see, and through the Holy Spirit giving us a "teachable disposition," we become convicted and convinced.[42] The process can be depicted this way: "First, the Lord teaches and instructs by his Word. Secondly, he confirms it by the sacraments. Finally, he illumines our minds by the light of the Holy Spirit and opens our hearts for the Word and sacraments to enter in."[43] This process can be understood not only as teaching but in terms of God's parental care. By baptism the heavenly Father "receives us into the family of God, so as to be counted of his household."[44] Meanwhile "the church is the common mother of all the godly, which bears, nourishes, and brings up children to God, kings and peasants alike; and this is done by the ministry."[45]

In this two-parent home, as it were, God does many things by twos. There is a twofold ministry; the ministry of sacraments is never divorced from the ministry of the Word. (For example, baptism and teaching belong together.) Of the sacraments, there are two, baptism and the Lord's Supper, the one to receive us, the other to sustain us in God's family. In baptism there are at least two parts, forgiveness of sins and new birth.[46] In the Lord's Supper there are two elements, "the symbol of bread" and "the symbol of wine."[47] Presumably God could work with one or none of these things, but in each case provides two, so that the weak faith of God's children may grow strong.

---

41. *Institutes* 4.14.3, 1278.

42. *Institutes* 4.14.10, 1285.

43. *Institutes* 4.14.8, 1284.

44. *Treatises on the Sacraments*, 86.

45. Calvin, *Commentaries on the Epistles of Paul to the Galatians and Ephesians*, trans. William Pringle (Grand Rapids: Wm. B. Eerdmans, 1957), 282.

46. These two are named in all Calvin's catechisms. The third benefit, union with Christ, is added in the *Institutes*, but it is already implicit in the second benefit (regeneration).

47. *Treatises on the Sacraments*, 90.

Faith is central to life in general and baptism in particular. Since "Baptism is a kind of entrance" into God's family, it must be available to both infants and adults.[48] But since baptism is also never effective without faith, God provides two temporal sequences of salvation, one for adults, the other for infants. For adults, or those "old enough to be taught," the sequence is precisely what Paul implies in Romans 10:17: "Faith comes from what is heard, and what is heard comes through the word of Christ."[49] A person hears the word preached, comes to repentance and faith, then becomes baptized—that is the normative sequence for adults. "We indeed admit that to such persons the Word of the Lord is the only seed of spiritual regeneration," notes Calvin.[50]

But this "ordinary arrangement" is not an "unvarying rule."[51] With infants, "God keeps his own timetable of regeneration."[52] This timetable cannot violate the principle that faith is needed for baptism, since "what is a sacrament received apart from faith but the most certain ruin of the church?"[53] Nor does this timetable violate the principle that repentance and faith are needed for regeneration. However, it does recognize that God works not only by his Word being heard, but also directly by the Holy Spirit. Thus, "infants are baptized into *future* repentance and faith, and even though these have not yet been formed in them, the seed of both lies hidden within them by the secret working of the Spirit."[54] Therefore, the sequence of salvation for the children of believers begins with infant baptism. Later in life, when they hear the Word, the seed that God implanted can blossom and flower into fuller faith.

The aim here is not to pinpoint a precise moment of regeneration, but to recognize that babies as well as adults can be "regenerated by God's power."[55] Clearly they are not "endowed with the same faith as we experience in ourselves," and yet (to switch metaphors) they can still have "a tiny spark" of faith. That spark of faith or seed of faith is a gift from God. For some children, "whom death snatches away in their very first infancy," that spark will be what they carry with them to heaven, to be illumined by the full splendor of God's light.[56] Calvin first penned these ideas in 1539, three years before his only child died at the age of two weeks.

48. *Treatises on the Sacraments*, 86.
49. *Institutes* 4.16.31, 1357.
50. *Institutes* 4.16.18, 1341.
51. *Institutes* 4.16.19, 1342.
52. *Institutes* 4.16.31, 1357.
53. *Institutes* 4.14.14, 1289.
54. *Institutes* 4.16.20: 1343; italics added.
55. *Institutes* 4.16.18, 1341.
56. *Institutes* 4.16.18, 1342.

Calvin does not advocate "emergency" baptism. An infant's eternal destiny is entrusted to God's sovereign will and electing grace. Hence infant baptism is not a desperate measure to save a child from hellfire, but rather a deliberate measure by which parents offer a child up for adoption. "God declares that he adopts our babies as his own, before they are born, when he promises that he will be our God and the God of our descendants after us. Their salvation is embraced in this word."[57] Baptism is the "solemn symbol of adoption," given to children even before they are old enough to recognize God as their Parent.[58]

Baptism also gives an assurance to the child's earthly parents: "For God's sign, communicated to the child as by an impressed seal, confirms the promise given to the pious parent." This promise states that God will manifest goodness and grace not only to us but to "descendants even to the thousandth generation." This promise "floods godly hearts with uncommon happiness." It quickens a "deeper love of their kind Father, as they see his concern . . . for their posterity."[59]

As scriptural evidence for this sequence of salvation pertaining to infants, Calvin points to John the Baptist, who was sanctified from his mother's womb, and also Christ himself, who was "sanctified from earliest infancy."[60] In Scripture, the baptism of infants is implied when the apostles are said to baptize whole families. No infant is named explicitly, but, notes Calvin, no woman is named as receiving the Lord's Supper, yet we can be certain they did so.

To pray for infants in a service of dedication is not enough. When children and infants are brought to Jesus, it is true he does not baptize them, for he did not baptize adults either. But Jesus does say that the kingdom of heaven belongs to people such as these children (Matt. 19:14). So then Calvin asks, "if the Kingdom of Heaven belongs to them, why is the sign denied which, so to speak, opens the door into the church, that, adopted into it, they may be enrolled among the heirs of the Kingdom of Heaven?"[61]

By baptizing infants, the church can "attest that infants are contained within God's covenant."[62] God "gives them a place among those of his family and household." In this household, teaching is vital, and infant baptism ought to inspire parents to instruct children "in an earnest fear of God and observance of the law."[63]

57. *Institutes* 4.15.20, 1321.
58. *Institutes* 4.16.9, 1332.
59. *Institutes* 4.16.9, 1332.
60. *Institutes* 4.16.17–18: 1340–41.
61. *Institutes* 4.16.7, 1330.
62. *Institutes* 4.16.7, 1330.
63. *Institutes* 4.16.32, 1359.

TWO SIGNS, ONE REALITY

Calvin devotes as many words to defending infant baptism as discussing baptism's benefits. A large portion of this defense concerns the parallels between baptism and circumcision. To grasp their importance, one needs to see how circumcision fits into a larger pattern of covenant and sign—and a larger framework of God's creative, redemptive activity.

Down through history, God makes promises and gives signs that he intends to keep them. The promises are called *covenants*, and the signs are called *sacraments*.[64] Thus, "a sacrament is a seal by which God's covenant, or promise, is sealed," Calvin says.[65] "The term 'sacrament' . . . embraces generally all those signs which God has ever enjoined upon men to render them more certain and confident of the truth of his promises. He sometimes willed to present these in natural things, at other times set them forth in miracles."[66] Examples of "natural" signs, other than baptism and the Lord's Supper, include the tree of life in the garden and the rainbow after the flood. Examples of supernatural signs include the smoking fire pot that Abraham saw, the wet fleece of Gideon, and the sundial of Hezekiah going back ten degrees. However, the natural signs and supernatural signs are more alike than different, since both kinds give assurance of God's promises.

Likewise, there is continuity between Old and New Testament signs. Baptism "is today what circumcision was for the ancients."[67] What was circumcision for them, for Abraham and Sarah and their descendants? It was a sign to remind them that the whole nature of humankind "is corrupt and needs pruning"; thus it was a continual call to repentance. Then too it was the sign to remind them of God's promise, that one day all nations would be blessed through "the blessed seed" of Abraham (Gen. 22:18; Gal. 3:16). The descendants of Abraham were to put their faith in God's promise, the sign and seal of which was circumcision. "Accordingly, circumcision was . . . a sign of the righteousness of faith [Rom. 4:11]; that is, a seal by which they are more certainly assured that their faith . . . is accounted to them as righteousness by God."[68]

---

64. "The Lord calls his promises 'covenants' [Gen. 6:18; 9:9; 17:2]" (*Institutes* 4.14.6, 1280).

65. *Institutes* 4.19.2, 1450. The word "sacrament" comes from the Latin (*sacramentum*) rendering of the New Testament Greek word for "mystery" (*musterion*), and in the church age this word came to refer to "those signs which reverently represented sublime and spiritual things" (*Institutes* 4.14.2, 1278).

66. *Institutes* 4.14.18, 1294.

67. *Institutes* 4.14.24, 1300.

68. *Institutes* 4.14.21, 1297.

Thus circumcision and baptism are two signs that promise the same real-ity—the righteousness that comes through faith. Like baptism, circumcision involved repentance and faith. Circumcision was "a sacrament of repentance, as Moses and the prophets declare (Deut. 10:16; 30:6; Jer. 4:4); and it was a sacrament of faith, as St. Paul says (Rom. 4:11, 12). And yet God has not excluded little children from it."[69] Neither should the church exclude little children from baptism.

Calvin probes the connection between the physical and spiritual in circum-cision, in order to shed more light on baptism. Some opponents of infant bap-tism might say that a clear distinction needs to be made between the physical and spiritual, and between the old and new covenants; they might say that cir-cumcision was a physical act pointing forward to spiritual blessings bestowed by Christ. To an extent they are right. Gentile Christians are called Abraham's children, even though they have "no blood relationship with him by nature [Gen. 2:28; cf. Rom. 4:12]."[70] But we need to consider what circumcision is for male Jewish infants, following Abraham. They receive the physical act of circumcision due to a biological family connection, but this physical act car-ries a spiritual blessing. There is correspondence between the physical and the spiritual, and continuity between the biological family and the household of God. This same continuity applies to Gentile Christians, because of infant baptism.[71] "Otherwise," reasons Calvin, "if the testimony by which the Jews were assured of the salvation of their posterity is taken away from us, Christ's coming would have the effect of making God's grace more obscure and less attested for us than it had previously been for the Jews."[72]

Importantly, with both circumcision and baptism, the spiritual blessing is received by faith. That is why Paul says in Romans 4:11 that the sign of cir-cumcision was a seal of the righteousness that Abraham had already received because of his faith.[73] Along these lines, Paul often argued against those who stressed physical circumcision. One ought to be "spiritually circumcised in both soul and body." But Paul does not denigrate physical signs. True, when referring to the "circumcision" that Christ accomplishes by his death (Col. 2:11–12), Paul clearly distinguishes the sign from the reality; "far better than the shadow" is the reality of having sins forgiven and hearts made pure. How-ever, "outward circumcision was not superfluous," for Paul immediately tells

69. *Catechism*, 334.
70. *Institutes* 4.16.12, 1335.
71. *Institutes* 4.16.12–13, 1335; cf. 4.14.24, 1300.
72. *Institutes* 4.16.6, 1329. Cf. *Catechism*, 337: "If we denied Baptism to little infants, the grace of God would then be diminished by the coming of Christ."
73. *Institutes* 4.16.13, 1335.

the Colossians that they have its parallel or replacement in baptism—they have "been buried with Christ through baptism [Col. 2:12]."[74]

Because we humans are physical as well as spiritual beings, God gives us physical signs that correspond to spiritual realities. God knows that we are "bound up with our bodies" and kindly teaches us accordingly; "it is expedient for us to have all our senses exercised in his holy promises, in order to confirm them to us."[75] Calvin recalls how Augustine called a sacrament a "visible word," meaning it gives a picture of God's promises.[76] God is leading us by the hand as a tutor leads children.

While God is the consummate Teacher, it is vital to have human teachers as well. Indeed, "the sacrament requires preaching to beget faith."[77] The importance of teaching is an implicit theme throughout Calvin's view of baptism. For example, only people who are "publicly charged to teach in the Church" should administer baptism, because "the preaching of the Word and the distribution of the Sacraments are things conjoined."[78] Daily Bible studies were available for the entire populace of Geneva to learn about baptism and other subjects.

Speaking of continuity, family life in Geneva entailed a kind of cooperation between family, church, and state. The General Council was composed of all the heads of households in the city.[79] The infants of each household were to be baptized into the church, the family of God. Within the family of God, there is, as we have seen, continuity between old and new covenants, between covenant and sign, between supernatural and natural signs, and between circumcision and baptism. There is also, Calvin notes, complete continuity between John's baptism and that of the apostles, since they agreed on the same teaching: "Both baptized to repentance, both to forgiveness of sins, both into the name of Christ, from whom repentance and forgiveness of sins came."[80]

However, not everything is the same. There is a clear difference between the sign and the reality in baptism, and this difference rules out magical understandings, while at the same time we can affirm that God performs what baptism promises.

---

74. *Institutes* 4.14.24, 1300.
75. *Catechism*, 314.
76. *Institutes* 4.14.6, 1281.
77. *Institutes* 4.14.3, 1279.
78. *Catechism*, 366. Calvin's opposition to women baptizing was based on his belief that those ordained to teach should also baptize, since Christ "ordained the same [people] as heralds of the gospel and ministers of baptism" (Matt. 28:19) (*Institutes* 4.15.21, 1322).
79. Parker, *Portrait of Calvin*, 27.
80. *Institutes* 4.15.7, 1308.

Also, not everything is static. There are clear differences in how God acts in different eras of history. When Peter summons people to be baptized on Pentecost, he tells them how God promises them the Holy Spirit. This gift of the Holy Spirit, he declares, "is for you, for your children, and for all who are far away, everyone whom the Lord our God calls to him" (Acts 2:39). However, God's children manifest the Holy Spirit differently in Calvin's day than in apostolic times. After Pentecost, Christ commenced his kingdom with miracles that "lasted but for a time."[81] In his day, notes Calvin, people do not receive the Spirit to speak in tongues, be prophets, cure the sick, or work miracles. Instead the Spirit "is given us for a better use, that we may believe with the heart unto righteousness, that our tongues may be framed unto true confession (Rom. 10:10), that we may pass from death to life (John 5:24), that we . . . may withstand Satan and the world stoutly." For these enduring purposes, "the grace of the Spirit shall be always annexed unto baptism."[82]

ONE BAPTISM, NO ADDITIONS

God annexes his Spirit to baptism, but people should not annex any of their own "theatrical pomp" to it.[83] The service of baptism ought to be simple, clear in meaning, and easy to observe.[84] The person to be baptized should be offered to God. The church should be present to witness and pray.[85] The promises of God should be recounted and the confession of faith recited, since baptism signifies these promises and strengthens faith. The baptism should be done in the name of the Father and of the Son and of the Holy Spirit; and after the person is baptized, he or she should be dismissed with prayers and thanksgiving. "If this were done, nothing essential would be omitted; and that one ceremony, which came from God, . . . would shine in its full brightness."[86]

Candles, oil, and spittle are all examples of additions to the ceremony that pollute rather than augment it.[87] Calvin says that Christ and the apostles did not institute these actions, but they were added by leaders in the Roman

81. John Calvin, *Commentary Upon the Acts of the Apostles*, vol. 1., ed. Henry Beveridge, trans. Christopher Fetherstone (Grand Rapids: Wm. B. Eerdmans, 1957), 120–22.

82. *Commentary Upon the Acts of the Apostles*, 1:120.

83. *Institutes* 4.15.19, 1319; cf. 4.10.12, 1190.

84. *Institutes* 4.10.14, 1192.

85. *Institutes* 4.15.19, 1319.

86. *Institutes* 4.15.19, 1320.

87. *Institutes* 4.15.19, 1319.

Church and over time became part of a whole system of rules and rituals, which served only to burden the conscience and obfuscate grace. While the former covenant had numerous signs or sacraments, God has given the church these two: baptism and the Eucharist. These are the two Jesus himself authorized after his resurrection, and they "excel in singular dignity."[88]

Other ceremonies—whether penance, ordination, marriage, or extreme unction—are not sacraments in this sense. Nor is confirmation, though it is a custom that Calvin warmly approves. For those baptized in infancy, there is value in having a ceremony "at the end of childhood or at the beginning of adolescence" in which confirmands are presented by their parents to make a confession of their faith before the church, in a solemn ceremony with a simple laying on of hands.[89] Instruction in the faith should certainly precede confirmation.[90]

Good teaching is needed for people to grasp the connection between baptism and God's promises. This teaching will increase faith more than undue attention to the ceremony itself. Should baptism be done by sprinkling or immersion? At times, Calvin calls the water an "outward sprinkling,"[91] but he also makes a slight case for immersion:

> Whether the person being baptized should be wholly immersed, and whether thrice or once, whether he should only be sprinkled with water—these details are of no importance, but ought to be optional to churches according to the diversity of countries. Yet the word "baptize" means to immerse, and it is clear that the rite of immersion was observed in the ancient church.[92]

The following excerpt from Calvin's *Institutes of the Christian Religion* reviews the benefits of baptism:

BAPTISM

(Baptism [is] a sign of our forgiveness, of our participation in Christ's death and resurrection and also in his blessings, 1–6)

1. The meaning of baptism

Baptism is the sign of the initiation by which we are received into the society of the church, in order that, engrafted in Christ, we may be reckoned among God's children. Now baptism was given to us by God for these ends (which I have taught to be common

88. *Institutes* 4.19.3, 1451.
89. *Institutes* 4.19.4, 1452.
90. *Institutes* 4.19.4, 1451.
91. *Institutes* 4.16.2, 1325.
92. *Institutes* 4.16.19, 1320.

to all sacraments): first, to serve our faith before him; secondly, to serve our confession before men. We shall treat in order the reasons for each aspect of its institution. Baptism brings three things to our faith which we must deal with individually. The first thing that the Lord sets out for us is that baptism should be a token and proof of our cleansing; or (the better to explain what I mean) it is like a sealed document to confirm to us that all our sins are so abolished, remitted, and effaced that they can never come to his sight, be recalled, or charged against us. For he wills that all who believe be baptized for the remission of sins [Matt. 28:19; Acts 2.38]. . . .

112. Its virtue not in water without the Word

. . . For Paul did not mean to signify that our cleansing and salvation are accomplished by water, or that water contains in itself the power to cleanse, regenerate, and renew; nor that here is the cause of salvation, but only that in this sacrament are received the knowledge and certainty of such gifts. This the words themselves explain clearly enough. For Paul joins together the Word of life and the baptism of water, as if he said: "Through the gospel a message of our cleansing and sanctification is brought to us; through such baptism the message is sealed." And Peter immediately adds that this baptism is not a removal of filth from the flesh but a good conscience before God [1 Pet. 3:21], which is represented by means of water from the resemblance to cleansing and washing. Who therefore, may say that we are cleansed by this water which attests with certainty that Christ's blood is our true and only laver? Thus, the surest argument to refute the self-deception of those who attribute everything to the power of the water can be sought in the meaning of baptism itself, which draws us away, not only from the visible element which meets our eyes, but from all other means, that it may fasten our minds upon Christ alone. . . .

115. Baptism as token of mortification and renewal in Christ

Baptism also brings another benefit, for it shows us our mortification in Christ, and new life in him. Indeed (as the apostle says), "we have been baptized into his death," "buried with him into death, . . . that we may walk in newness of life" [Rom. 6:3–4]. By these words he not only exhorts us to follow Christ as if he had said that we are admonished through baptism to die to our desires by an example of his resurrection. But he also takes hold of something far higher, namely, that through baptism Christ makes us sharers in his death, that we may be engrafted in it [Rom. 6:5]. And, just as the twig draws substance and nourishment from the root to which it is grafted, so those who receive baptism with right faith truly feel the effective working of Christ's death in the mortification of their flesh, together with the working of his resurrection in the vivification of the Spirit [Rom. 6:8]. From this, Paul takes occasion for exhortation: if we are Christians, we ought to be dead to sin and alive to righteousness [Rom. 6:11]. He uses this same argument in another place; we were circumcised and put off the old man after we were buried in Christ through baptism [Col. 2:11–12]. And in this sense, in the passage which I have previously quoted, he called it the washing of regeneration and of renewal [Titus 3:5]. Thus, the free pardon of sins and the imputation of righteousness are first promised us, and then the grace of the Holy Spirit to reform us to newness of life.

6. Baptism as token of our union in Christ

Lastly, our faith receives from baptism the advantage of its sure testimony to us that we are not only ingrafted into the death and life of Christ, but so united to Christ himself that we become sharers in all his blessings. For he dedicated and sanctified baptism in his own body [Matt. 3:13] in order that he might have it in common with us as the firmest bond of the union and fellowship which he has deigned to form with us. Hence, Paul proves that we are children of God from the fact that we put on Christ in baptism [Gal. 3:26–27]. Thus we see that the fulfillment of baptism is in Christ, whom also for this reason we call the proper object of baptism. Consequently, it is not strange that the apostles are reported to have baptized in his name [Acts 8:16; 19:5], although they had also been bidden to baptize in the name of the Father and of the Spirit [Matt. 28:19]. For all the gifts of God proffered in baptism are found in Christ alone. Yet this cannot take place unless he who baptizes in Christ invokes also the names of the Father and the Spirit. For we are cleansed by his blood because of our merciful Father, wishing to receive us into grace in accordance with his incomparable kindness, has set this Mediator among us to gain favor for us in his sight. But we obtain regeneration by Christ's death and resurrection only if we are sanctified by the Spirit and imbued with a new and spiritual nature. For this reason we obtain and, so to speak, clearly discern in the Father the cause, in the Son the matter, and in the Spirit the effect, of our purgation and our regeneration. So John first baptized, so later did the apostles, "with a baptism of repentance unto forgiveness of sins" [Matt. 3:6, 11; Luke 3:16; John 3:23; 4:1; Acts 2:38, 41]—meaning by the word "repentance" such regeneration; and by "forgiveness of sins," cleansing.[93]

---

93. *Institutes* 4.15.1–6, 1303–8.

6

John Wesley

Baptism Is, and Is Not, the New Birth

Jesus answered, "Very truly, I tell you, no one can enter the kingdom of God without being born of water and Spirit. . . . Do not be
astonished that I said to you, 'You must be born from above.'"
                                                              John 3:5, 7

A PASSION FOR AUTHENTIC CHRISTIANITY

Many young people, it is said, are searching for authenticity. Instead of Christianity that is shallow or phony, they want the real thing—genuine, bona fide
examples of people living their faith. Counterexamples abound, and it may be
easier to define authenticity by what it is not.

It is not nominal Christianity, or Sunday-only Christianity. It is not what
Bonhoeffer called "cheap grace," a pseudo-gospel that preaches "forgiveness
without repentance," and "baptism without the discipline of the community."[1]
It is not what some chagrined pastors call "easy believism," a complacent attitude that says in effect, "I'm born again and going to heaven when I die, so
who cares how I live today?"

By contrast, authenticity says that if there has been a new birth there needs
to be a new life. It says baptism summons people to a life of ongoing discipleship, pursued with God-given passion. This new life often goes against the

---

1. Dietrich Bonhoeffer, *Works*, vol. 4, ed. Geffrey B. Kelly and John D. Godsey, trans.
Barbara Green and Reinhard Krauss (Minneapolis: Augsburg Fortress, 2001), 44.

stream of surrounding society as well as the grain of fallen humanity. Thus authentic Christianity may entail facing external pressures and inner temptations that are severe.

If this way of life can be hard, it can also easily catch fire when it sparks the imagination of people who long for a real experience of God. This desire must be among the various factors that contributed to the remarkable rise of Methodism in England and America during the eighteenth and early nineteenth centuries. At one point Methodism was probably the fastest-growing Christian movement of the modern era, and it set the stage for Pentecostalism, which has been the fastest-growing ever.

John Wesley (1703–1791) was the founder of Methodism, though he remained an Anglican priest who taught loyalty to the Anglican Church. But as an Anglican he sought "genuine fruits of the Spirit of God."[2] He preached faith—a "living faith," not a "dead faith."[3] He preached love—a "love not only ever burning in your hearts, but flaming out in all your actions and conversations, and making your whole life one 'labor of love,' one continued obedience to those commands, 'Be ye merciful, as God is merciful'; 'Be ye holy, as I the Lord am holy.'"[4]

If *authenticity* is a recent watchword, then *holiness* was the biblical word Wesley often used. To be holy is to be marked, set apart, devoted to God; to be authentic is to be genuine, true, recognizable as real. The two conditions are complementary, even if not identical, for in this context both refer to a passionate faith that penetrates deeply and radiates into daily life.

While coming of age at Oxford, Wesley and some friends began their quest for the authentic Christian life. He and a group of like-minded souls came together as the Holy Club in 1730–1731. Then they acquired the name Methodists due to their methodical manner of living, which included practices of Bible study and prayer. For them holiness meant clear, deep changes, both in beliefs and behaviors.

Wesley's pursuit of holiness involved a regimen of spiritual disciplines at which many people today, young or old, might recoil. As a minor example, for a period of time he decided to eat only bread, to see "whether life might not be as well sustained by one sort as by a variety of food." He found he was "never more vigorous and healthy."[5] The goal of such practices was not just

---

2. John Wesley, *Works*, vol. 1, ed. Albert Outler (Nashville: Abingdon Press, 1984), Sermon 8, 237. Subsequent citations of sermons and journal entries refer to numbered volumes from this edition.

3. *Works*, vol. 1, Sermon 18, 421–22.

4. *Works*, vol. 1, Sermon 18, 428.

5. *Works*, vol. 18, Journal 1 (March 7–April 5, 1736), 155.

to be an ascetic but to remove distractions from a life of wholehearted service to Christ.

Welsey spoke of the "almost Christian" versus the "altogether Christian," to portray the contrast between shallow, nominal faith versus authentic, life-transforming faith. The "almost Christian" is someone who, like King Agrippa in the book of Acts, listens to Christian teaching and may even try to live an honest, sincere life, but basically this person is a heathen. The "altogether Christian" is the person whose entire life is defined by faith in Christ and whose heart is full of evident love for God and neighbor.

The almost Christian and the altogether Christian are two very different people, though they can also be the same person over the course of a lifetime. The authentic Christian life is a lifelong endeavor, marked by moments of transformation. Young people often have the most passion for this pursuit, but it is not just for the young. Wesley's own passion hardly seemed to wane. Not only on Sundays but throughout the week he would preach two or three sermons on a given day, often more. "When I am called to do more . . . I find strength according to my need," he wrote in his journal.[6] All told, it is estimated he delivered over forty thousand sermons. Throughout his life, even at eighty-seven, he was rising at four in the morning and preaching at five. Mobs of people gathered, indoors or out, to listen intently or else scoff violently. On numerous occasions, rocks and sundry objects were hurled at him, especially during his early years. Often the failure of these objects to hit their target convinced listeners that the speaker had God's favor.

Wesley's life was all action as well as talk. In the winter of his eighty-second year, he could be seen, as one biographer relates, "trudging all day through London streets ankle deep in melting snow begging £200 so that he could add clothes to his annual provision of food and fuel for the poor."[7] He might easily have supplied that amount himself, for eventually his published writings produced a fine income (the equivalent of $160,000 a year), except he gave this money away almost as soon as it came in. He once responded to critics who accused him of seeking financial gain, "If I leave behind me 10 pounds . . . you and all mankind bear witness against me that 'I lived and died a thief and a robber.'"[8]

Personal habits aside, there was also systemic change, social and economic, that took place in the towns where Wesley preached and started Methodist societies. There was not only more help for the poor, but less

6. *Works*, vol. 22, Journal 14 (April 18–29, 1766), 38.

7. Stephen Tomkins, *John Wesley: A Biography* (Grand Rapids: Wm. B. Eerdmans, 2003), 191.

8. *Works*, vol. 11, ed. Gerald R. Cragg (1975), 87–88.

poverty, as the gospel and lifestyle he preached gave the "lower classes" new hope and energy.

No one would claim that Wesley's life was normal or balanced, nor did he ever claim to be sinless, though he did teach, controversially, that it is possible for a person to become sinless and perfect in love (since Jesus, who said, "be ye perfect," would not command what is not possible). If anything, however, his biography raises the question of whether an authentic Christian life can *ever* be normal by the standards of a surrounding society. His sermons, essays, and daily journal also raise questions about baptism, a word we have only now mentioned in this chapter. For as a first question, one may wonder whether baptism is vital or peripheral to Wesley's theology.

I think it is vital, because Wesley connects baptism, both positively and negatively, to being born again. When considering Wesley's view of baptism, the relationship between baptism and the new birth is certainly the central issue.

Wesley was a prominent parent of modern evangelical theology, the touchstone of which is regeneration—a believer becoming born again by the Spirit of God. Is baptism the same thing as this new birth? A short if insufficient answer is this: For all infants, it is. For most adults, it is not. Thus baptism is, and is not, the new birth.

Some "paradoxes" are simply contradictions, and some scholars write that Wesley contradicts himself here. He was trying, they say, to remain a good Anglican while starting an evangelical movement, and the tension between these two motives can be seen in his strange theology of baptism. But whatever his motives, it is possible to see Wesley's position on baptism as being coherent, not contradictory.

The starting point for finding this consistency is to note how Wesley wants to ground all his views in Scripture. In studying Scripture, he looks at Church tradition, both ancient and Anglican. He looks at experience, both his own and others. He wants to know: What does Scripture say about baptism? And what does baptism say about living an authentic Christian life?

THE CONNECTION—AND CONTRAST— BETWEEN BAPTISM AND NEW BIRTH

In being both sacramental and evangelical, Wesley's voice may speak to rising generations today. Yet there is no skirting the apparent discrepancy between two statements he makes. The first comes from a confirmation manual written by his father Samuel, an Anglican priest. Samuel defended infant baptism and depicted it as new birth. John makes these views his own by publishing in 1758, under his own name, an abridged version of his father's essay. He states:

By baptism, we who were "by nature children of wrath" are made the children of God. And *this regeneration which our Church in so many places ascribes to baptism* is more than barely being admitted into the Church. . . . Being "grafted into the body of Christ's Church [through infant baptism], we are made children of God by adoption and grace."[9]

Here the connection between baptism and regeneration is clear.

Two years later, in 1760, Wesley penned a sermon entitled "The New Birth" that seems to paint a quite different picture. "Without holiness," he quotes from Hebrews, "no one can see God" (Heb. 12:14). To see God, one must be holy, and to become holy one must be born again. The new birth is essential to seeing God in heaven or being "happy even in this world." Then he states, "Baptism is not the new birth: they are not one and the same thing." Appealing to Church authority, just as in the previous essay, he reinforces the point: "Nothing therefore is plainer than that, according to the Church of England, baptism is not the new birth."[10]

The 1760 sermon and 1758 essay do seem at odds. Yet ultimately we can say that Wesley's position is consistent. These two works are like two panels of the same painting—a painting with deep contrasts, to be sure. If we adopt this idea of contrast-yet-consistency, we can point to six specific contrasts in Wesley's view of baptism. Together they illumine how baptism and the new birth are connected but not identical. Together they also show his ongoing concern for authentic Christian living.

First, as just noted, there is a contrast between infants and adults. The contrast here is not in the ability to make a covenant. Both infants and adults can enter the baptismal covenant.[11] But adults can break it. They can live in ways opposite to their baptism. Growing up, we grow in our capacity to respond to God or else reject God's grace. We can accept the new birth given in baptism and live it out, or else reject it and lose out.

Second, there is a contrast between causality and identity. Baptism can, by God's grace, contribute to *causing* the new birth without itself *being* the new birth. Wesley says that the Church "ascribes" the new birth to baptism. Elsewhere he says the new birth is "ordinarily annexed to baptism."[12] These are statements of causality, not identity.

9. "On Baptism," in *John Wesley*, ed. Albert Outler (New York: Oxford University Press, 1964), 322; italics added.

10. *Works*, vol. 2, Sermon 45, 195, 196, 197; italics added.

11. "On Baptism," 324.

12. *Works*, vol. 1, Sermon 18, 417. Does the phrase "ordinarily annexed to baptism" mean that ordinarily the new birth is joined to baptism, or that people ordinarily, but

Wesley, like Augustine and Calvin before him, distinguishes the *signum* and *res*, the sign and the thing.[13] God uses the sign of baptism to cause the reality of the new birth for infants. Since the sign and the reality coincide, we can say that for infants baptism *is* what God *causes* it to be. But the distinction between identity and causality still pertains, and it becomes important in the case of adults. Adults have free will to cause a split between the sign and the reality; they can contravene the very thing (God's grace) that baptism signifies and infuses into infants.[14]

In the 1758 essay, where Wesley unites baptism and the new birth, he also clears a space for this adult freedom. He says that baptism saves us, "if we live answerable thereto."[15] Now the flip side: in the 1760 sermon, where he distinguishes baptism and new birth, he also clears a space for infant regeneration: "It is certain, our Church supposes that all who are baptized in their infancy are at the same time born again."[16]

Wesley agrees with this Church doctrine. We "cannot comprehend how this work can be wrought in infants," anymore than we can know how God regenerates older people through evangelical conversion.[17] In both cases it is God's doing. Yet the point Wesley emphasizes is this: in both cases the fruit of what people do in their subsequent lives makes it clear whether their spiritual regeneration is still a present reality. What matters is not just having a valid baptism, but living an authentic, holy life.

Third, there is a contrast between being "born of water" and being "born of the Spirit." Like many theologians, ancient or Anglican, Wesley reads Jesus' words in John 3:5–8 as referring to baptism. But within these words, he draws a distinction between being baptized in water (a human act that is visible, involving the body) and being given new birth (a divine act that is invisible, involving the soul and spirit). Wesley says, "A man may possibly be 'born of water,' and yet not be 'born of the Spirit.'"[18] Here he is speaking about adults and also about the difference between outward sign and inward grace.

---

wrongly, associate them? I have chosen the first option, based on Wesley's overall writing about baptism and because in another sermon published the same year the phrase "annexed to" refers to something God does (1748; Sermon 17, 408).

13. *Works*, vol. 2, Sermon 45, 196. If this distinction between sign and thing is a "Western" way to see baptism, in other respects Wesley also reflects Eastern Orthodox views. For example, he sees baptism as a summons to human synergy or cooperation with God's energies.

14. *Works*, vol. 2, Sermon 45, 196; "On Baptism," 323.

15. "On Baptism," 323.

16. *Works*, vol. 2, Sermon 45, 197.

17. *Works*, vol. 2, Sermon 45, 197.

18. *Works*, vol. 2, Sermon 45, 197.

Wesley was not the first to suggest that there can be a baptismal "birth" without a spiritual rebirth. Gregory of Nyssa in the fourth century made a very similar point. Gregory wrote that the grace of baptism draws people into moral improvement—to authentic change. If someone claims to be a child of God, says Gregory, then we should be able to detect a family resemblance to the Parent. We should be able to recognize this person "by the same marks whereby we recognize God." Let us suppose I claim to be God's adopted child, born again in baptism, but this new birth does not change my "moral condition." On the contrary, people know me as someone who treats others unjustly and accuses them falsely, someone who is greedy for gain and "lives in luxury at the cost of men's calamities." In that case, Gregory sounds a stern warning:

> But if, when the bath has been applied to the body, the soul has not cleansed itself from the stains of its passions and affections, but the life after initiation keeps on a level with the uninitiate life, then, though it may be a bold thing to say, yet I will say it and will not shrink; in these cases the water is but water, for the gift of the Holy Ghost in no ways appears in him who is thus baptismally born.[19]

Gregory and Wesley agree: It is possible for a person to be born of the water but not of the Spirit. Being born of the Spirit entails living an authentic Christian life. Wesley, just like Gregory, is concerned about the "marks" and "fruit" of a person's life subsequent to baptism.

Fourth, therefore, there is a contrast between doctrinal concepts and plain evidence. It is important to have both. We need sound doctrine. But being a child of God is not all about winning battles of doctrine against other people. It entails winning the battle over sin in our own lives. The apostle John puts it bluntly when he says that children of the devil sin, whereas children of God do not—they practice righteousness (1 John 3:7–10). Wesley quotes these verses, adding: "By this plain mark (the committing or not committing sin) are they distinguished from each other."[20] His sermon is entitled "The Marks of the New Birth." Wesley is not urging us to go around inspecting others to see whether they are marked sinners, but to examine ourselves to see whether, even if we have been baptized, we need to be born again and truly become children of God.

Now we come to a critical juncture. Wesley's hearers may reject this exhortation because the logic of their doctrine runs like this: (1) The new birth comes about through baptism. (2) Baptism can happen only once. (3) Thus the

---

19. Gregory of Nyssa, "The Great Catechism," in *Nicene and Post-Nicene Fathers of the Christian Church*, vol. 5, trans. Philip Schaff and Henry Wace (New York: Christian Literature Company, 1893), 508.

20. *Works*, vol. 1, Sermon 18, 421.

new birth can happen only once and only through baptism. (4) Thus too, a baptized person is always born again and always a child of God.

Wesley agrees with the premises (1 and 2), but not the conclusions (3 and 4). The first statement is scriptural; John 3 connects water and new birth, while Titus 3 refers to the "washing of rebirth."[21] The second statement is traditional and logical; baptism is analogous to Christ's death and resurrection, which happened only once. But Wesley challenges the third and fourth statements by reasoning from the plain evidence of experience. A baptized person is not automatically and always a child of God. If I live my daily life as a child of the devil, I am clearly not born again at the present time, even though I was baptized as an infant. Thus if new birth happens *only through* baptism, I have no hope and am "consigned to hell," since a person must be a child of God to enter heaven.[22] Likewise, if new birth can happen *only once*, I have no hope, since I did indeed receive new birth once through infant baptism.

In short, our concepts about Christianity must be held accountable to what it means to live out the Christian life. Doctrinal concepts are based on Scripture, but plain evidence drives us to examine the full range of Scripture, and then sometimes to expand our concepts. In this case, it may at first seem strange to think of having more than one new birth—of a person becoming born again *again*, as it were (first through baptism, later through a "quickening" by God's Spirit).[23] But it is stranger still to think a person could have a new birth yet no new life; or to think a society of people could ignore God's justice and holiness just because a baptismal ritual gave them false assurance that all is well between them and God.

Fifth, there is a contrast between the past and present. The past, whether Church tradition or our personal histories, gives vital reference points. The past matters in so many ways. But we live or die, stand or fall in the present hour. And the present hour is where the Spirit of Christ stands ready to give us faith, hope, and love. Wesley's biggest question about the new birth is present and personal—"whether at this hour (answer to God and not to man!) you are thus a child of God or no!"[24] He asks this question with insistence:

> The question is not what you was made in baptism (do not evade!) but what you are now. Is the Spirit of adoption now in your heart? To your own heart let the appeal be made. I ask not whether you *was* born of water and the Spirit. But *are* you *now* the temple of the Holy Ghost which dwelleth in you? [1 Cor. 6:19]. . . .

21. "On Baptism," 322.
22. *Works*, vol. 1, Sermon 18, 429.
23. *Works*, vol. 2, Sermon 45, 193.
24. *Works*, vol. 1, Sermon 18, 428.

> Say not then in your heart, I *was once* baptized, therefore I *am now* a child of God. . . .
> "Verily, verily, I say unto you, ye also must be born again." "Except" ye also "be born again, ye cannot see the kingdom of God" [John 3:3]. Lean no more on the staff of that broken reed [Isa. 36:6], that ye *were* born again in baptism. Who denies that ye were then made "children of God, and heirs of the kingdom of God" [Rom. 8:16–17]? But notwithstanding this, ye are now children of the devil; therefore ye must be born again. And let not Satan put it into your heart to cavil at a word, when a thing is clear. Ye have heard what are the marks of the children of God; all ye who have them not on your souls, baptized or unbaptized, must needs receive them, or without doubt ye will perish everlastingly. [Wesley is concluding his sermon here, having already described the "marks"—the authentic faith, hope, and love—that characterize God's children.] And if ye have been baptized your only hope is this: that those who were made the children of God by baptism, but are now children of the devil, may yet again receive "power to become the sons of God" [John 1:12]; that they may receive again what they have lost, even the "Spirit of adoption, crying in their hearts, Abba, Father" [Rom. 8:15]![25]

What concerns Wesley most is the present hour. The past may have been a time of baptismal regeneration—or sinful degeneration. But the present hour is the time for repentance and hope in Christ. The Christian life is a kind of ongoing baptism or continual altar call.

Sixth, in light of all the contrasts just named, there is the central contrast between baptism and new birth. In his preaching on baptism, Wesley shifts the center of gravity to new birth, even as he shifts it from past to present, from abstract ideas to plain evidence, and from water to Spirit. Yet contrast here is not contradiction. In fact the goal is continuity—bringing all of these pairs into better harmony. In a more perfect world, everyone born of water would be born of the Spirit. Every new birth would then issue in a new life. Every baptized infant would thus grow to become altogether a Christian, with every moment as pure and holy as the hour of baptism. In short, everyone baptized would be regenerated for life.

HOW WESLEY SEES THE NEW BIRTH

However, the world is not perfect. There is sin—original, personal, social, and generational—with which to contend. Wesley writes often of sin. Human sin is so large that only God's grace is greater, hence the human need for new birth by God's Spirit.

25. *Works*, vol. 1, Sermon 18, 428–30.

In the relationship between baptism and new birth, the new birth comes to the foreground and has conceptual priority in Wesley's thinking. God's action also has priority over human action. Whether regeneration takes place through infant baptism or believer's conversion, it is God's doing. The work of God comes before human works. Yet God's action also summons a human reaction. The fruits of the new birth are fruits of the Spirit, but they fully involve human "tempers, thoughts, words, and actions."[26]

Wesley describes the person born of God as one "who by faith perceives the continual actings of God upon his spirit, and by a kind of spiritual re-action returns the grace he receives, in unceasing love, and praise, and prayer."[27] Later in the same sermon, he expands this description of the synergy between God and humanity. He describes the new life that follows the new birth this way:

> It immediately and necessarily implies the continual inspiration of God's Holy Spirit: God's breathing into the soul, and the soul's breathing back what it first receives from God. . . . He first loves us, and manifests himself unto us. While we are yet afar off, he calls us to himself, and shines upon our hearts. But if we do not then love him who first loved us; if we will not hearken to his voice; if we turn our eye away from him, and will not attend to the light which he pours upon us: [then] his Spirit will not always strive; he will gradually withdraw, and leave us to the darkness of our own hearts. He will not continue to breathe into our soul unless our soul breathes toward him again; unless our love, and prayer, and thanksgiving return to him, a sacrifice wherewith he is well pleased.[28]

Thus divine love and human responsibility are both important. We can start at the beginning, as Wesley does, with the creation of the world. "God is love" (1 John 4:8, 16), and God created humanity to be "full of love." This love was originally the "sole principle" of every human thought, word, and action.[29]

But humanity, while made in God's image, was "not made immutable." We were "created able to stand, and yet liable to fall." When the first humans did fall, by exercising their will in "flat rebellion" against God, they became separated from God. They "lost both the knowledge and the love of God." They became "unholy as well as unhappy." Essentially, they died. They "died to God, the most dreadful of all deaths."[30]

This death answers the question of why it is needful for every person born

26. *Works*, vol. 2, Sermon 45, 188; cf. 194.
27. *Works*, vol. 1, Sermon 19, 435–36.
28. *Works*, vol. 1, Sermon 19, 442.
29. *Works*, vol. 2, Sermon 45, 188.
30. *Works*, vol. 2, Sermon 45, 189.

on earth to be born again. Every descendant of Adam "comes into the world spiritually dead, dead to God, wholly 'dead in sin' [Eph. 2:5; Col. 2:13]."[31] The image of God is one of total "righteousness and holiness" (Eph. 4:24), but every person "born into the world now bears the image of the devil, in pride and self-will; the image of the beast, in sensual appetites and desires. This then is the foundation of the new birth—the entire corruption of our nature. Hence it is that being 'born in sin' we 'must be born again' [John 3:7]."[32]

If natural corruption at birth is *why* everyone needs to have a supernatural rebirth, then *how* the new birth happens is God's doing.[33] Justification is what God does *for* us, while regeneration is what God does *in* us. Justification takes away sin's guilt, while regeneration takes away its power. Both justification and regeneration are acts of God, which people receive through faith in Jesus Christ, and both are received "in the one and the same moment."[34]

The exact length of this moment is never an issue, but Wesley does note that the new birth is an event: "A child is born of a woman in a moment, or at least a very short time. . . . In like manner a child is born of God in a short time, if not in a moment."[35] Since this new birth is something God does, we cannot tell "the precise manner how it is done," but we can say how it matters to our daily living.[36]

In answering this question, Wesley begins historically. Around the time of Jesus, he says, new converts to Judaism were baptized, after which they were said to be "born again." Wesley refers us to Jesus' conversation with Nicodemus. Jesus tells Nicodemus that as "a teacher of Israel" (John 3:10), he ought to have made the connection between water and being born again, though Jesus is using the phrase "in a stronger sense." In the Christian context, the new birth means that someone who has been a "child of the devil" becomes "adopted into the family of God."[37]

The analogy to physical birth is particularly instructive. A child in the womb has eyes but does not see. The child is alive but dead to the world. However, once the child is born the natural senses begin opening up in relation to natural objects, and understanding starts to grow. So it is with the new birth. A once-born person has eyes but does not see in a spiritual sense. Though a living person, he or she "is a dead Christian." However, once a person is born

31. *Works*, vol. 2, Sermon 45, 190.
32. *Works*, vol. 2, Sermon 45, 191.
33. *Works*, vol. 2, Sermon 45, 191.
34. *Works*, vol. 1, Sermon 19, 431–32.
35. *Works*, vol. 2, Sermon 45, 198.
36. *Works*, vol. 2, Sermon 45, 191.
37. *Works*, vol. 2, Sermon 45, 191.

of the Spirit "there is a total change," whereby the spiritual senses come alive; "the eyes of understanding are opened" (Eph. 1:18), and the spiritual ears are "now capable of hearing the inward voice of God." This voice says, "Be of good cheer, thy sins are forgiven thee" (Matt. 9:2). It says, "Go and sin no more" (John 8:11).[38]

For Methodists, the name Aldersgate and the date of May 24, 1738, are famous as the time and place where Wesley heard this voice with his own spiritual senses. He records what happened that evening in London:

> I went very unwillingly to a society in Aldersgate-Street, where one was reading Luther's preface to the Epistle to the Romans. About a quarter before nine, while he was describing the change which God works in the heart through faith in Christ, I felt my heart strangely warmed. I felt I did trust in Christ, Christ alone for salvation: And an assurance was given me, that he had taken away *my* sins, even *mine*, and saved *me* from the law of sin and death.[39]

With this salvation there was still spiritual struggle. Upon returning home from the meeting Wesley found he "was much buffeted with temptations; but cried out, and they fled away."[40] The temptations came back, not with enough force to defeat him, but sometimes to discourage him. Once when writing to his brother Charles he even doubted whether in sixty years he had ever truly loved God.[41]

During such times of attack, is it best to "remember your baptism"? Or is it better to forget your baptism and cry out to God? A ritual of remembering baptism was one of the most popular devotional practices in Wesley's day, but it was not one Wesley advocated. In general, it is hard to say whether a ritual manifests true or false piety, since so much depends on the disposition of the heart. But in calling people to repentance and rebirth, Wesley does not advise a ritual or remembering baptism but says with irony that, were it not a sin to lie, people should deny their baptism ever took place:

> But perhaps the sinner himself, to whom in real charity we say, "You must be born again," has been taught to say, "I defy your new doctrine; I need not be born again. I was born again when I was baptized. What! Would you have me deny my baptism?" I answer,

---

38. *Works*, vol. 2, Sermon 45, 192.
39. *Works*, vol. 18, Journal, May 24, 1738, 249–50.
40. *Works*, vol. 18, Journal, May 24, 1738, 250.
41. *The Letters of John Wesley* (8 vols.), ed. John Telford (London: Epworth Press, 1931), June 27, 1766.

first, there is nothing under heaven which can excuse a lie. Otherwise I should say to an open sinner, "If you have been baptized, do not own it." For how highly does this aggravate your guilt! How will it increase your damnation! Was you devoted to God at eight days old, and have you been all these years devoting yourself to the devil?

I answer, secondly, you have already denied your baptism; and that in the most effectual manner. You have denied it a thousand and a thousand times; and you do so still day by day. For in your baptism you renounced the devil and all his works. Whenever therefore you give place to him again, whenever you do any of the works of the devil, then you deny your baptism.

I answer, thirdly, be you baptized or unbaptized, you must be born again. Otherwise it is not possible you should be inwardly holy: and without inward as well as outward holiness you cannot be happy even in this world; much less in the world to come.[42]

Wesley goes on to say that even if you think you lead a good and moral life, still you must be born again, "if you have not already experienced this inward work of God."[43]

Here we come to a place of ambiguity. Does Wesley believe that infant baptism and its regeneration are sufficient, provided people live holy lives from infancy through all their adult years? Or is he saying that everyone, whether baptized as infants or not, must have a new birth whereby one is conscious of the "inward work of God" that brings forth authentic faith, love, and hope?[44] Perhaps this ambiguity is a Gordian knot, and easily cut through. Even if Wesley sees the first option as a theoretical possibility, the reality of postbaptismal sin makes the second option the only secure course for nearly everyone.

HOW THE WESLEYS (FATHER AND SON) SEE BAPTISM

Given the reality of sin, to desire a felt assurance of God's forgiveness is not to denigrate infant baptism or deny its many benefits. To see these benefits, we return to "A Short Discourse of Baptism," the manual that Samuel Wesley, John's father, published in 1700. John made the discourse shorter still and published it under his own name in 1758.

As bare essentials, Christian baptism requires (1) the application of water, (2) the invocation of the name of the Trinity, and (3) an episcopal administrator. The first is obvious, the second is Christ's command (in Matt. 28:19), and

42. *Works*, vol. 2, Sermon 45, 199–200.
43. *Works*, vol. 2, Sermon 45, 201.
44. *Works*, vol. 1, Sermon 18, 417–30.

the third derives from the way authority has passed from Christ to the apostles to their successors, down to the present day.[45]

As basic questions, we may inquire further into the *what*, *why*, *when*, and *who* of baptism.

What is baptism? Says Wesley, "It is the initiatory sacrament which enters us into covenant with God." He calls baptism "a sign, seal, pledge and means of grace." Just as circumcision "was a sign and seal of God's covenant, so is this."[46]

Baptism may be done "by 'washing,' 'dipping' or 'sprinkling' the person."[47] ("Dipping" refers to immersion.) When serving as a missionary to the colony of Georgia in the 1730s, Wesley insisted on baptizing infants by trine immersion.[48] He was following the rubric of the first Prayer Book of Edward VI (1549), which allowed sprinkling "only if the child be weak."[49] The Church of England had changed this rule by the end of the sixteenth century, to permit water being poured over the child, but Wesley kept to the earlier pattern.

In a journal entry of 1736, he records how an infant named Mary Welch was immersed, "according to the custom of the first church and the rule of the Church of England." He notes, "The child was ill then, but recovered from that hour."[50] Nevertheless, Wesley caught flak from some parents who did not want their infants, even healthy ones, being immersed.[51] By 1758 he himself had modified his position to embrace washing and sprinkling as well as immersion.

He defends a variety of practices by reasoning from Scripture. While John the Baptist baptized "where there was much water" (John 3:23), the "much" here could refer to breadth rather than depth, "since a narrow place would not have been sufficient for so great a multitude." Thus we do not know for a fact that Jesus himself was baptized by immersion. So too when the eunuch was baptized by Philip, "they both went down to the water" (Acts 8:38), but the going down may refer to the chariot; it "implies no determinate depth of water."[52]

Further, the word *baptize* in Scripture can refer to washing or sprinkling or immersion. When the Hebrews "were all baptized in the cloud and the sea" (1

---

45. "On Baptism," 318.

46. "On Baptism," 319.

47. "On Baptism," 319.

48. For example, see *Works*, vol. 18, ed. W. Reginald Ward and Richard P. Heitzenrater (1988), Journal 1 (February 22, 1736), 360.

49. G. Hartford and M. Stevenson, *The Prayer Book Dictionary* (London, 1925), 79; quoted in Bernard George Holland, *Baptism in Early Methodism* (London: Epworth Press, 1970), 157.

50. *Works*, vol. 18, Journal 1 (Feruary 21, 1736), 150.

51. *Works*, vol. 18, Journal 1 (May 5, 1736), 157, (August 16), 190.

52. "On Baptism," 319.

Cor. 10:2), they were sprinkled "by drops of the sea water and refreshing dews from the cloud."[53] When the Pharisees "baptized" pots and cups (Mark 7:4), they washed them and they did not necessarily immerse them, since Jesus said they would "cleanse the outside only" (Matt. 23:25).

In short, the quantity of baptismal water is not what matters. But whether by sprinkling, pouring, or immersion, *why is baptism done?* Wesley names five benefits.

- Baptism washes away the guilt of original sin. Both the ancient church teachers and the Ninth Article of the Anglican Church say "that we are all born under the guilt of Adam's sin and that all sin deserves eternal misery." Baptism washes this guilt by applying to us "the merits of Christ's life and death." When Ephesians says that Christ gave himself for the church, "in order to make her holy by cleansing her with the washing of water by the word" (5:26), this washing refers to baptism, "the ordinary instrument of our justification."[54]
- By baptism we enter into covenant with God. God, who made a covenant with Abraham and his physical descendants, also promised to make a new covenant with "the spiritual Israel"—to "give them a new heart and a new spirit, to sprinkle clean water upon them," notes Wesley, quoting Ezekiel 36.[55] Baptismal water is a "figure" of this new covenant, and baptism itself is the entryway to the new covenant, as circumcision was to the old.
- By baptism we become members of Christ: "As many of you were baptized into Christ have clothed yourselves with Christ" (Gal. 3:27). By baptism we also become members of the church, for "in the one Spirit we were all baptized into one body" (1 Cor. 12:13). Union with Christ means receiving all the influence of his grace. Union with the Church means receiving all the promises and privileges Christ gave to it.[56]
- By baptism we become children of God. Here Wesley, following the Book of Common Prayer, states explicitly that baptism brings about the new birth. When Jesus tells Nicodemus that a person must be born again of water and the Spirit (John 3:5), the water refers to baptism. Likewise Paul calls baptism "the washing of rebirth" (Titus 3:5). The power of baptism is not the outward washing but the inward grace that God adds to it. God infuses baptism with grace, which is "not wholly taken away unless we quench the Holy Spirit of God by long-continued wickedness."[57]
- By baptism we become "heirs of the kingdom of heaven," because God adopts us as children. As "joint heirs with Christ" (Rom. 8:17) we receive the title to the coming kingdom, and even in this life we receive the "earnest" or first installment of this inheritance.

53. "On Baptism," 320.
54. "On Baptism," 320, 321.
55. "On Baptism," 322.
56. "On Baptism," 322.
57. "On Baptism," 323.

Having covered the what and why of baptism, the Wesleys turn to a *when* question: *For how long did Christ intend baptism to remain in the church?* The answer is, "always." Circumcision lasted as long as the covenant of the law. Baptism, "which came in its room," will last as long as the gospel covenant. "In the ordinary way, there is no other means of entering into the Church or into heaven."[58]

The comparison with circumcision shows the necessity of baptism. God gave people circumcision as the seal of his covenant with them. Of course the inward circumcision of the heart mattered more than the outward circumcision of the flesh. Nevertheless, God commanded the outward to be done and even said that any male who did not receive it was to be cut off from the people (Gen. 17:14)—because, notes Wesley, that person "had despised . . . God's everlasting covenant by despising the seal of it." It is the same with baptism: "In all ages, the outward baptism is a means of the *inward*, as outward circumcision was of the circumcision of the heart."[59]

Thus baptism is the means of salvation. Wesley sums up the benefits of baptism by quoting 1 Peter 3:21: "Baptism doth now save us." Yet he also clarifies: "*Baptism doth now save us* if we live answerable thereto—if we repent, believe, and obey the gospel."[60] The divine action is meant to summon a human response.

What if this response does not occur? Here we return to the previous dilemma. On the one side, as it were, Scripture ties the new birth to baptism. On the other side, it ties the new birth to repentance, faith, and living a new life. But what if there is a tug-of-war between the two sides? In other words, what if there has been baptism on the one side, but no authentic faith or holiness to show for it—has there been a new birth or not? Wesley, as we have seen, somewhat splits the difference. He says that many people *were* born again in baptism but they are not so now. They stand in need of regeneration once more. Thus in splitting the difference he gives clear priority to living out faith with authenticity.

Infants, however, have no such problem, because they have not had time either to "live answerable thereto" or fail to do so. Baptism benefits them greatly. Thus we will want to know the reasons for infant baptism and answer any objections against it.

---

58. "On Baptism," 319, 323.
59. "On Baptism," 323.
60. "On Baptism," 323.

WESLEY'S DEFENSE OF INFANT BAPTISM

The "grand question," says Wesley, is this: "Who are the proper subjects of baptisms?"[61] The answer is infants, according to Scripture, reason, and the practice of the early church. These five facts about infants become five good reasons for baptizing them.

Infants are guilty of original sin, because they are descended from Adam. It is true that Christ, the second Adam, "has found a remedy for this disease." But we receive this remedy through the "ordinary means God hath appointed"— namely, baptism. Put another way, infants need to be washed in order to be saved. Christ supplies this washing, and it is applied to infants through baptism. Can God save unbaptized infants? Of course, for God is not bound to baptism. But we are, since God has given and commanded it. There may be extraordinary cases in which people cannot receive baptism, but "extraordinary cases do not make void a standing rule."[62]

Infants are capable of making a covenant. In Deuteronomy 29, the Lord summons all the people, including the "little children," to be in covenant with him. They entered into the covenant before they could perform all its obligations, but there is no doubt they were able to enter into it, for "God would never have made a covenant with 'little ones' if they had not been capable of it."[63]

Infants ought to "come to Christ." In the Gospels, Jesus rebukes adults who hinder infants from coming to him. Today, how can infants come to Jesus except through the Church, and how can they enter the Church except through baptism? Under the old covenant, infants were admitted through circumcision, "and can we suppose they are in a worse condition under the gospel than they were under the law?"[64]

Infants were baptized by the apostles. How can we know that? First, the apostles were Jewish and already familiar with the practice of baptizing infants, because ancient sources tell us that converts to Judaism, "even whole families together, parents and children," were baptized. Second, the apostles were Christians, and it is recorded in Acts and 1 Corinthians that they baptized whole families, which would have included children. Says Wesley, "Three thousand were baptized by the apostles in one day and five thousand in another. And can it be reasonably supposed that there were no children among such vast numbers?"[65]

61. "On Baptism," 324.
62. "On Baptism," 324.
63. "On Baptism," 324.
64. "On Baptism," 326.
65. "On Baptism," 327.

Infants have been baptized by "the Christian Church in all places and in all ages." Augustine in the West and Origen in the East both say the practice of baptizing infants began with the apostles themselves. And "it has been the practice of all regular churches ever since."[66]

Wesley notes that in the ancient church every baptized person, whether infant or adult, had two or more people who served as sponsors and witnesses. These sponsors undertook to be "a kind of spiritual parents to the baptized . . . and were expected to supply whatever spiritual helps were wanting, either through the death or neglect of natural parents."[67] Through instruction and example, they were to guide young people into the new life that follows the new birth, the authentic Christian life of the "altogether Christian."

66. "On Baptism," 328.
67. "On Baptism," 332.

7

Karl Barth

Baptism Is Prayer

And baptism . . . now saves you—not as a removal of dirt from the body, but as an appeal to God for a good conscience, through the resurrection of Jesus Christ.

1 Pet. 3:21

THE FREEDOM TO BE FAITHFUL

Liberty. Freedom. Liberation.

These familiar words point to deep desires. Defining documents of the United States—from Jefferson's Declaration of Independence, to Lincoln's Emancipation Proclamation, to King's "I Have a Dream" speech—all start by speaking about human freedom. Around the world, the cry for freedom goes forth whenever people have sought to establish democracy, end apartheid, or challenge exploitation. The cry is global, but also often deeply personal. People struggling with addictions or other demons also long to be free.

The Bible speaks of the "glorious liberty" of God's children (Rom. 8:21, RSV), and this idea reverberates through the eight-thousand-plus pages of the *Church Dogmatics* of Karl Barth (1886–1968). It was, said Markus Barth, the central theme of his father's life and work.[1]

---

1. The "liberty of God's children" is his enduring theme and recurring question. See Markus Barth, "A Biographical Note," sound recording (Los Angeles: Pacifica Tape Library, 1962). Cf. Karl Barth, *Church Dogmatics* (Edinburgh: T. & T. Clark, 1936–1977), IV/4, 154. Subsequent references to *Church Dogmatics*, vol. IV, part 4 are given as page numbers in parentheses in the text.

Certainly freedom is central to Barth's view of baptism. The kind of freedom he cares most about is the freedom that enables a person to turn to God and be faithful to God. Put another way, he is concerned with the freedom that enables a person to become a Christian—to be transformed so utterly that it makes perfect sense to speak of this person as having "a very different humanity," with a new nature, an inner change, a wonderful new birth, a dying and resurrection (11). God is the One who liberates a person for this freedom, but water baptism is the first step, and free step, of human response (72, 90). As the first step of the Christian life, baptism "is a model for all the steps that follow" (201). It is a step of conversion. It is taken in faith and obedience and hope (212).

Barth's view of baptism is a clear corrective to any notion of freedom that says it means simply being able to do whatever I want. Look, it's a free country, someone may say. But if we look at the human condition we find people in bondage to "self-will and anxiety" (136; cf. 142). True freedom means a person makes the transition from self-will to obeying God, and from anxiety to hoping in God (136, 138, 142). Again, baptism is the turning point in this transition.

When this true freedom arrives, then people are no longer free to follow the old path of a "false pretended freedom" (142). This path is closed. What lies open instead is a new life of faithfulness to God. And God too—God first—is free. God's "free election" calls a person to this new life (132). In fact, with "free generosity" God chooses all people (142). (This in essence is Barth's view of divine election.)

Thus God is free to act, people are free to respond, and good teaching on baptism must honor both sides of this relationality. They are not one and the same; they are as distinct as Spirit baptism and water baptism. In brief, baptism with the Holy Spirit is God's free action, accomplished in the history of Jesus Christ. Baptism with water is the free response of the candidate and community, in which this history becomes their history and Christ's liberty becomes their liberty.

Barth rejects any theology of baptism that fails to recognize both sides—humanity's "free work on the one side and God's free work on the other" (88). At the time of the French Revolution people were sometimes baptized into "liberty, equality and fraternity," and at the turn of the twentieth century, people at the Bremen cathedral were sometimes baptized into "the true, the beautiful and the good." But these baptisms "were very definitely not Christian baptisms" (92). They portray the new life one-sidedly as human endeavors, eclipsing God's freedom.

By the same token and more controversially, Barth concludes that good theology cannot endorse infant baptism because it squeezes human freedom out of the picture. Candidates for baptism ought to make a responsible decision; they ought to choose freely the freedom that God is offering them. They should not be "objects of an event which storms past them" (132). When candidates freely request water baptism from the community, this action honors "the work and sway of the free Holy Spirit, who calls to freedom and who creates freedom" in people. Barth goes so far as to say that the Holy Spirit "constantly suffers violence from infant baptism" (192).

These words are part of the final fragment of *Church Dogmatics*. Sensing his mortality, Barth says, "I am thus about to make a poor exit," for though he was the most influential theologian of the twentieth century, he predicts his views on baptism will leave him in "theological and ecclesiastical isolation." But he also says that "the day will come when justice will be done to me in this matter," and he asks readers not to take his opposition to infant baptism out of context (xii). It needs to be seen in light of the fact that for most of his life Barth supported the practice, before the biblical scholarship of his son Markus prompted a change of mind.

Further, his opposition needs to be seen in light of his positive statement that all Christian ethics are based on baptism. For ethics are essentially humanity's "free and active answer . . . to the divine work and word of grace," and water baptism is essentially the first ethical decision that sets the pattern for all the others. Done in community, it becomes the prototype for all good works. Thus "the doctrine of baptism (as God's own work: baptism with the Holy Ghost, and also as man's liturgical work: baptism with water)" is the "foundation of the Christian life" (ix).

For water baptism to be what God intends, namely, the foundational act of human freedom, churches that practice infant baptism will need to start practicing "responsible baptism" instead. Barth calls for "long overdue reform at this small but practically decisive point" so that the Church can become a "missionary and mature rather than immature Church" (xi).

Barth gives a multilayered description of this "responsible baptism"; especially he speaks of it as "conversion." But ultimately, in the final words of the final fragment of a systematic theology numbering more than six million words, Barth decides that "baptism is prayer" (210). In prayer, divine and human action meet—freely.

HOW IS IT POSSIBLE TO BE A CHRISTIAN?

While Barth ends by saying that baptism is prayer, he starts by asking a large and basic question: How does a person become a Christian? What makes the "event of the Christian life" possible? God is faithful, but people as a rule are not, so how can there be "such a thing as genuine human faithfulness in relation to God's own faithfulness"? Put another way, how does the kingdom of

God become an actual reality in someone's life, entering the sphere of "being, life, thought, will and action" (3–4)?

To answer the question thus posed, Barth first decides to "set aside three views which have become classical in the history of Christian theology." As he puts it, a popular Roman Catholic view of the Christian life says God infuses people with supernatural powers. A "theological existentialist" (often liberal Protestant) view proposes that God spurs people on to fulfill their natural moral impulses. Meanwhile a typical Lutheran or Reformed position says that God judges a person graciously, though the person remains essentially a sinner (4–5).

There is some truth in all three. Faithfulness to God must include fulfillment of natural powers; it may well entail receiving supernatural ones, but still people are imperfect, hence the need for gracious judgment. However, these answers all describe the situation of someone who has already turned to God (for infusion, influence, or mercy), whereas the question posed a moment ago is more basic: How does a person become *free in the first place* to turn to God and enter a covenant with God? The "decisive point" here is the change whereby people are free to be and do what they could not before—namely, "be faithful to God" (5–6).

The Bible uses various images to speak of this great change. Barth finds four main motifs. Becoming a Christian is described as putting on new apparel (such as a wedding garment, white robe, or spiritual armor); as receiving new birth; as having a new, circumcised heart; and as dying and resurrection (6–10). The last may be the most definitive, yet all these images reinforce how the change that takes place is a "divine change." It is a "mystery and miracle" that only God could accomplish. And yet again this divine change involves people who make a "free decision" to enter into "free partnership with God" (6). How is this possible? Really this question of *how* is ultimately a question of *who*. Who possibly could be freely faithful to God?

Jesus Christ is the one Person who is "faithful to God as God is faithful to him," the one free person in the world. Yet this faithfulness, his faithfulness, is sufficient for all, since he is "the Representative of all" and "the Liberator of all" (13, 25). He is "the One elected from eternity to be the Head and Saviour of all." Because the life of faithfulness that he lived was lived for all, therefore "the change which took place in His history took place for all. In it the turning of all from unfaithfulness to faithfulness took place. In this history of His the Christian life became an event as the life of all." While the history of Jesus Christ is an event that applies to all, Christians are people who know and affirm that their "own history took place along with the history of Jesus Christ" (13).

Clearly Barth has in mind a special understanding of "history." If I say that my history took place before I was born, or that my personal history is more properly defined by the history of another Person, these claims easily fly in the face of empirical evidence and individual identity. That could be a good thing too, since the empirical world and individual identity are both bound by sin and are thus false starting points.

To start in the right place, with Jesus Christ, we need to use different words to speak of history. Earlier in *Church Dogmatics* Barth speaks of *Historie* (ordinary history) as separate from *Geschichte* (suprahistory), and likewise in *The Epistle to the Romans* he distinguishes "so-called history" from "real history." "So-called history" is phenomenal, temporally structured, and known naturally through empirical sciences. It is the history to which most English-speaking people refer when using that word. But "real history" refers to the kingdom of God and to God's activity in Jesus Christ.[2] We have a biblical way to describe *this* history: it is called the "baptism with the Holy Spirit." To see why, let us consider the connection between Christ's history and ours.

DIVINE ACTION: BAPTISM WITH THE HOLY SPIRIT

The history of Jesus Christ shows how faithfulness to God "is not only possible but actual." But what, one could ask, has that got to do with me?—"What has the freedom of His life as very Son of God and Son of Man to do with my necessary liberation to be a child of God?" (17, 18).

For his freedom to liberate us, his history must occur within us, not just outside us. There must be a "genuine intercourse" between God and humanity, "two different partners." Though quite different, the activity of each partner is vital. We must not "conjure away the mystery" of this intercourse by making the Christian life something that God does with people as mere passive appendages, or by making it something that people do with Jesus merely as an example of human potential (18–20). The Bible says reconciliation between God and humanity is an event God causes in Christ, yet the command to "be reconciled to God" (2 Cor. 5:20) is not superfluous; it summons a real response. So there is movement both from above to below, and from below to above.

From the standpoint of God's movement toward humanity, the resurrection of Jesus Christ is decisive. Death threatens every personal history, but in

---

2. Between the two histories there is division, though less than in Rudolf Bultmann's separation of *Heilsgeschichte* from ordinary history; rather, as Barth says in *The Epistle to the Romans*, kingdom history interpenetrates empirical history in order to transform it.

the resurrection the "temporal, spatial and personal life" of Christ triumphs over death. This event has cosmic significance. It becomes a proclamation to all, a pledge and promise to all whereby Jesus says, "What I was and did, I was for you and did for you." This event becomes a power available to all: "The history of Jesus Christ has shown it has indwelling power by the fact that Jesus Christ is risen from the dead" (24–25).

From the standpoint of humanity's movement toward God, the work of the Holy Spirit is decisive. By the Holy Spirit a person receives the "freedom, ability, willingness and readiness" to be open, rather than closed, to this proclamation and power. "The work of the Holy Spirit . . . does not entail the paralysing dismissal or absence of the human spirit, mind, knowledge and will"; instead, the Holy Spirit bears witness to the human spirit, so that a person moved by the Spirit can cry, "Abba, Father" to God. By the Spirit, the revelation of Jesus Christ reaches people so they can freely run to God, instead of running away (27–28).

The term *baptism with the Holy Spirit* brings together these two related acts of God—the resurrection by which God changes human history and the revelation by which God changes human hearts. The term refers to both; it encompasses the divine change that grounds the Christian life and the power that propels it. The power of people to be faithful to God "is the power of their baptism with the Holy Ghost" (30).

Can we find biblical evidence to support this understanding of Spirit baptism? In general, the word *baptism* denotes an act of cleansing (its noun form is a New Testament neologism), but many passages (e.g., 1 Cor. 12:13; John 1:33; Acts 1:5; 11:16; 19:2) make a sharp distinction between Spirit baptism and water baptism. John the Baptist tells people that Jesus will give a greater baptism, in other words, a greater "cleansing." Indeed, at Pentecost this "divine cleansing and reorientation" starts to occur, empowering people to become "public witnesses of Jesus" (cf. Acts 1:8). And witnessing is no isolated or narrow activity: "In fact the ministry of witness forms the meaning and scope of the whole of the Christian life" (30). Witnessing entails conversion to Christ, it involves repentance and forgiveness of sins—and these are the concrete meanings Peter at Pentecost associates with baptism (Acts 2:38; see also Mark 1:4).

We find therefore a clear connection between Spirit baptism and witnessing (Acts 1:5, 8) and then in turn between witnessing and the entire sweep of Christian living. Says Barth, "We thus regard it as legitimate to understand by the baptism with the Holy Ghost . . . the divine preparation of [people] for the Christian life in its totality." He reinforces this idea: "The term 'baptism of the Spirit'" is a very appropriate "slogan for" and "epitome of the divine change which founds the whole Christian life" (31).

For its part, water baptism epitomizes the human change—the decision, obedience, and hope to which Spirit baptism summons people. Thus baptism, in a word, is the answer to "the problem of the Christian beginning" (31). From the divine side, the Christian life begins with Spirit baptism; from the human side, with water baptism.

The last fragment of *Church Dogmatics* is divided into two sections, entitled "Baptism with the Holy Spirit" and "Baptism with Water." Barth sums up Spirit baptism in five points. First, Spirit baptism is the self-impartation of Jesus Christ, who alone makes people into Christians. Only God can baptize with the Spirit; no human person can, or even the Church as a whole. Spirit baptism calls for water baptism, but water baptism does not cause Spirit baptism (31–33).

Second, Spirit baptism is a form of grace. Water baptism is not. Nor is water baptism a "sacrament," but Spirit baptism is "a sacramental happening in the current sense of the term," since it is "divinely effective, divinely causative, divinely creative" (34). Ultimately there is one sacrament, Jesus Christ; the one mystery is his history and humanity's inclusion in it.[3] But since Spirit baptism refers directly to this mystery, we can rightly say that it brings about the new heart, the new birth, and the liberation and empowering of humanity. Furthermore, Spirit baptism accomplishes these things "realistically, not just . . . figuratively"; indeed, it accomplishes these things with such "reality and perfection" that they "cannot be negated or even diminished by the brokenness of [human] disobedience, however severe." The change that Spirit baptism brings about in people is real and permanent; it is "not just enlightenment from without, but a lighting up from within" (34–35).

Third, Spirit baptism liberates a person for gratitude and obedience. God wills for this human response to be free, which brings us to the problem of *ethics* and *ethos*—the human actions and attitude that rightly correspond to God's grace (35). This problem concerns the second section of Barth's discourse, to which we will turn momentarily.

Fourth, Spirit baptism is "the beginning of the new Christian life . . . in a distinctive fellow-humanity." We could call it the start of the church, except people often think of the church as merely a "religious society," whereas Spirit baptism commences a wholly new way of being in community. It frees

---

3. Barth writes of water baptism that it "responds to a mystery, the sacrament of the history of Jesus Christ, of His resurrection, of the outpouring of the Holy Spirit. It is not itself, however, a mystery or sacrament" (102). In a conversation with pastors, Barth said, "There is only *one* sacrament—the one who has himself risen from the dead" (David A. Davis, "Signs from a Weary God," sermon given on December 19, 2004, at Nassau Presbyterian Church, Princeton, NJ; available at www.nassauchurch.org).

humanity from all isolation; in being joined to Jesus, people enter "the circle around him" (Mark 3:34) (36–37).

Fifth, Spirit baptism is a real beginning, not a perfect finish. As a radical inception into the Christian life it calls for ongoing "radical conversion." The people of God are pilgrim people who pray to God, "thy kingdom come." They are "constantly chasing this perfection" of God's kingdom at the same time they await constantly its coming (38–40).

HUMAN ACTION: BAPTISM WITH WATER

If Spirit baptism is the "objective" foundation of the Christian life, then water baptism is its "subjective" foundation. The two need "to be correlated as well as distinguished" (41; cf. 72, 134). To sense their close correlation yet clear distinction, we might think of how the Council of Chalcedon in 451 described the two natures of Jesus Christ (the divine and human) as a "union without confusion." As George Hunsinger writes of Barth, "It is probably safe to say that no one in the history of theology ever possessed a more deeply imbued Chalcedonian imagination."[4]

Thus after contemplating the fully divine action of Spirit baptism, Barth turns to the fully human action of water baptism, "the Yes of a heart truly liberated by grace." If someone begins to believe—"even if only in the quantity, though also the quality, of a grain of mustard-seed, even if only, though seriously, with the petition: 'Lord, help thou mine unbelief' (Mk. 9:24)"—then one will want to do something irrevocable. To establish that I have a new life, with a clear before and after, I will want to take a step that can never be reversed, a step "which neither need nor can be repeated." Baptism with water is this "immediate first step." Awakened to faith, a person "freely asks to be baptised." As a definition: "Christian baptism is the first form of the human decision which in the foundation of the Christian life corresponds to the divine change" (42–44).

While over the centuries theologians have had many ideas about water baptism, Barth wants to hold his notions accountable to the "data which can be taken from the New Testament with relative exegetical certainty" (44). Interestingly, though the New Testament everywhere portrays water baptism as a given fact of Christian life, nowhere does it dictate how baptism

---

4. George Hunsinger, *How to Read Karl Barth* (New York: Oxford University Press, 1991), 85. Barth does not explicitly name the Chalcedonian pattern in *CD* IV/4, but he does allude to it: "Each of the elements [Spirit baptism and water baptism] . . . will be misunderstood if it is either separated from or, instead of being distinguished, mixed together or confused with the other" (41).

should be done. In fact, nowhere, "with one significant exception," is baptism even the major theme in the New Testament. Usually the writers refer to baptism briefly and allusively in order to reinforce an ethical aspect of the Christian message (47).

Clearly baptism in the New Testament is a bodily washing with water, and at the Jordan it "possibly, or even probably, took the form of immersion, though this is not absolutely certain." Since three thousand were baptized on one day of Pentecost (Acts 2:41), we surmise that baptism "might equally well have taken the form of affusion or sprinkling" (45). One procedural point is clear: a person does not baptize herself or himself. No one can pretend to be a "bold individual left to arrange things with God," for water baptism is done by the community, which recognizes a person's faith; and in principle any member of the community can administer it if circumstances require (49–50).

In turning from *how* to *why* the first Christians were baptized, we come to the one place in the New Testament where baptism *is* the central theme, namely "the account of the activity of John the Baptist with which the record of the history of Jesus Christ opens in all four Gospels" (47). This baptism of Jesus ought to be our continual reference point for grasping what baptism is to us. Specifically now, "we shall have to speak of (I) the basis, (II) the goal and (III) the meaning of Christian baptism" (50).

THE BASIS OF WATER BAPTISM

Barth asks why baptism is "not superfluous, but necessary." One straightforward answer is to say that Christ commands it. He "sets the command to baptise alongside (and even before) the command to teach" in his final appearance to the disciples in Matthew 28:18–20 (50–51). But this appearance, like every Easter happening, is best seen as a powerful working out of what has already been accomplished in Christ's life and death. So the command to baptize the nations takes us back to the Jordan and to "the beginning of the history of Jesus Christ" (53).[5] His ministry starts with his baptism; here we discover "the true basis of Christian baptism" (52).

If Spirit baptism brings together related acts of God (the resurrection that changes history and the revelation that changes hearts), then Jesus' baptism at the Jordan brings together Spirit baptism with water baptism. His baptism "is in a sense the point of intersection of the divine change and the

5. Barth says "all the Evangelists (implicitly even the fourth)" regarded Christ's baptism as the start of his history (53). Cf. Acts 10:37–38.

human decision." There at the Jordan, Spirit baptism, "the epitome of the divine change," meets water baptism, "the first concrete step of human decision." They meet without mingling; there is union without confusion. The two, "though plainly distinct, are directly one and the same" (53).

Since John baptized people who came confessing their sins, we might wonder why Jesus needed to be baptized. Barth finds three reasons (54–68):

- His baptism is an act of submission to God—of free, concrete, and unconditional obedience to the lordship of God.
- It is an act of solidarity with sinners—of free, concrete, and unequivocal fellowship with people who had fallen victim to God's judgment and who could put their hope only in God's "free remission of their sins" (54).
- It is an act of service to God and to people—by which Jesus begins to do God's work, which he alone could do for humanity, and humanity's work, which he alone could do for God.

These points warrant further notice. Submitting to the will of God, Jesus enters his office as Messiah, Savior, and Mediator not by an arbitrary or self-designed act but by an act that is given to him because he is a member of his people: "Himself an Israelite, He heard with all Israel (Lk. 3:2) the Word of God which had come to John." Rabbi John announced "a new and directly imminent act of God which will radically change the situation of Israel and the Israelite. Jesus accepts this announcement. He submits in advance to what God is about to do" (54–55).

Hence Jesus obeys the call to conversion issued to God's people. John offered baptism to those who repented, "confessing their sins" (Matt. 3:6), and like the others Jesus confessed his sins. "*His* sins?" Barth asks—the notion is startling. But the alternative is worse. If we do not say that Jesus confessed his own sins, then "we say at root that this was just a theatrical show." In effect, we "deny the totality of His self-giving to men, and therewith the totality of His self-giving to God" (59).

But Jesus' baptism was not just a theatrical show. He does not shrink from full solidarity with humanity; he takes the sins of all into himself, making a genuine confession before baptism. To press the idea further, we can say paradoxically that the sinlessness of Jesus was demonstrated by the fact that he did not refuse any aspect of baptism, including a true confession of his own sins—the sins of the world that became his own (58).

We can see more clearly how Jesus' baptism is the basis for all Christian baptism if we picture ourselves as the first Christians, for whom this event is no historical curiosity but the beginning of the gospel (Mark 1:1), the start of his earthly ministry and of our new life. To integrate our lives more fully with his, we begin as he did, with the same concrete act by which he began.

This train of thought, so easily imagined, is not spelled out anywhere in the New Testament, perhaps because it was so self-evident to the New Testament community (68).

THE GOAL OF WATER BAPTISM

The goal of baptism ought to correspond to this basis. For John and those he baptized, the goal of water baptism was to prepare for "the coming kingdom, the coming judgment, the coming grace of God"—that is, the coming baptizer with the Holy Spirit (70). This was the goal for Jesus as well, though he himself was this coming Baptizer.

Now it would be strange if today's Christian baptism were somehow better or stronger than the baptism that Jesus received. Instead of trying to inflate water baptism into a supernatural event, we should allow it to have its proper dignity as a human act, the value of which lies not so much in what we do, what we say, or how we administer it, but rather in the way that "it points forward, away from itself and beyond itself, to its fulfillment in the future baptism with the Holy Spirit." In short, "the goal of [water] baptism is . . . baptism with the Holy Spirit" (71, 72). We note, therefore, that Spirit baptism is both the basis *and* the goal of water baptism.

The human act of water baptism is certainly different from the divine act of Spirit baptism; but is John's water baptism very different from post-Pentecost water baptism? No, says Barth. Essentially these two are "one and the same baptism," though they do differ in terms of intensity and proximity to the kingdom of God (86). Barth finds six points of comparison. First, in both John's baptism and Christian baptism, God's kingdom is inbreaking, but after Pentecost the demand for attention to this reign grows more serious, more sharp, and also more comforting (75–76).

Second, both John's baptism and Christian baptism anticipate an outpouring and imparting of the Holy Spirit, but after Pentecost this expectation is greatly met, so subsequent baptism becomes a petition for the Spirit to come once more in power (76–77).

Third, both John's baptism and Christian baptism emphasize repentance and coming judgment, but after the Cross the demand for repentance is stronger because God's judgment and mercy are both clearer. The mystery is revealed that people have become "the murderers of their Judge and therewith the executioner of the judgment which He allowed to fall on Him in their place!" In allowing and willing the Judge to be judged in their place, God frees people from their sins. In taking away the sins of the world, God also takes away "any liberty for further sin, or compulsion thereto" (78, 79).

Fourth, as just implied, both John's baptism and Christian baptism have in view the forgiveness of sins, but after "the promise became fulfillment," the emphasis shifted. Sin became no less serious, but forgiveness became more vivid and joyous. The Ethiopian eunuch baptized by Philip "went on his way rejoicing" (Acts 8:39), a reaction we do not read happening to those baptized by John (82).

Fifth, both John's baptism and Christian baptism proclaim a new fellowship for the people of God; however, Christian baptism actually *establishes* this fellowship, so that those who are baptized become brothers and sisters "in the Lord" (83).

Sixth, both John's baptism and Christian baptism convey that this new fellowship unites Jews and Gentiles, but after Pentecost this union becomes a reality. John's baptism simply hints at it when, for example, he says that God is able from stones to raise up children to Abraham (Matt. 3:9 and Luke 3:8) (84).

It was said the goal of water baptism is Spirit baptism, but it is equally true to say the goal is Jesus Christ, since Spirit baptism is how the history of Jesus Christ becomes our own personal history. When the Bible speaks of baptizing people "into Christ" (Gal. 3:27, Rom. 6:3), or "into the name of Jesus Christ" (Acts 2:38), it declares the energetic movement toward the goal. A person is baptized *into* Jesus.

For centuries churches have used the solemn Trinitarian form, "*in* the name of the Father and of the Son and of the Holy Spirit" (found in Matt. 28:19). The problem here is not in lengthening the names—there is "no theological need to disturb ecumenical custom"—but in shortening the prepositions, from *into* to *in*. The phrase "*in* the name" implies that the minister is baptizing by God's commission, which is true enough; but the biblical phrase *eis to onoma* is better translated "*into* the name," for this preposition makes it clear that baptism is "unequivocally . . . a movement into Jesus Christ, into the washing of [humanity] accomplished in Him" (92).

WHY WATER BAPTISM IS NOT A SACRAMENT

Thus concerning its basis, baptism is not a step that takes place through the will of other people (such as parents) but instead is "an act of free obedience to the command of Jesus Christ." Concerning its goal, baptism "is not a step in the dark" but a movement into Christ. Concerning its meaning, baptism is not a work of God but a human work done in community. If we claim water baptism is some "immanent divine work," says Barth, then "the presumed better becomes the enemy of the good, and one misses the meaning" (101). Instead, water baptism "is the human action whose meaning is obedience to Jesus Christ and hope in Him." Though there may still be consensus among Roman Catholic, Lutheran, and Reformed churches that water baptism is a sacrament or divine action, "this consensus needs to be demythologized" (105).

Of course we can rightly say that God causes *everything*—God is the *auctor primarius*, the principal author, in back of every "creaturely occurrence" and especially acts occurring within the community that bears witness to Jesus Christ (105). But this general sense of God's "omnicausality" should not detract from the fact that God intends water baptism to be a free human act: "Our objection to the sacramental interpretation of baptism is directed against this conjuring away of the free man whom God liberates and summons to his own free and responsible action" (22, 106).

Some people will agree that the external work of water baptism is not a divine act, then go on to speak of an internal work God does, taking the form of "experiences, inspirations, illuminations, exaltations or raptures," which they identify as being "the baptism of the Spirit." Barth contradicts this view as well, for here again the focus on human freedom and obedience is lost through an "exclusive interest in a divine factor." Those who focus on Spirit baptism in this manner may denigrate or even omit the outer, human work of water baptism and thus thwart its meaning—the "ethical meaning of baptism" as humanity's free answer to God's grace (106–7).

Before saying more about this ethical meaning, we ought to investigate several places in Scripture where it seems, at least on the surface, that water baptism *is* a divine action or sacrament. A prime example is Acts 22:16, where Ananias tells Paul, "Get up, be baptized, and have your sins washed away, calling on [Jesus'] name." If baptism is the causal instrument of Paul's cleansing from sin, it would be a sacrament. The context, however, makes this interpretation unlikely. Ananias has just told Paul what God has done for him; already he has received grace, and, implicitly, forgiveness has been extended to him through the Righteous One (v. 14). That is why he says, "Why do you delay?" (v. 16). In other words, given the fact that by Jesus your sins are already washed away, you are now liberated to discharge your God-ordained ministry. Notes Barth:

> The guilty Saul, who is nevertheless ordained to be the witness of Jesus, will not pray in vain for the forgiveness of sins to Him, the Just One, who has called him to Himself. His water baptism will not effect this. It is, however, his prayer for it, not merely in words, but in a concrete act (112).

Another sacramental-sounding passage is Ephesians 5:25–26: "Christ loved the church and gave himself up for her, in order to make her holy by cleansing her with the washing of water by the word." Author and readers alike would think of baptism here, but is this passage describing two different processes in which Jesus first gives himself for the beloved church, then sanctifies it by the washing of water with the word? If so, then the washing would be sacramental. But more likely the passage depicts one unified process: Christ sanctifies and cleanses the church precisely *by* loving it and giving himself for it. Washing and the word are ways of speaking about Christ's work, his love and self-sacrifice. (Jesus expresses a parallel idea in John 15:3: "You have already been cleansed by the word that I have spoken to you.") The washing is not a direct reference to water baptism but an allusion to it, reminding readers of their human act, an act that reflects and points to the divinely cleansing work of Christ (113–14).

For a third passage that might seem sacramental but really is not we turn to Titus 3:5, which speaks of "the washing of rebirth and renewal." The context of these words is an ethical admonition to do good works (vv. 1 and 8), and the logic here is that good works are now doable because the loving-kindness of God has appeared to save people from enslavement to the old regime of hatred and unbridled desires (vv. 3–4). God has saved people through the washing and rebirth caused by the Holy Spirit (v. 5). While "washing" again alludes to the act of baptism, it speaks explicitly about the activity of the Holy Spirit. We are saved not by our righteous acts but by God's mercy alone—that is the overall meaning here. If the washing *were* seen as a sacrament, then the verse would be saying in effect: Righteous acts do not save us, but the act of being baptized does. This interpretation would contradict the whole thrust of the passage (114–15).

Galatians 3:26–28 is one passage that does in fact speak directly about baptism: "For in Christ Jesus you are all children of God through faith. As many of you as were baptized into Christ have clothed yourselves with Christ. There is no longer Jew or Greek, there is no longer slave or free, there is no longer male and female; for all of you are one in Christ Jesus." The unity that comes from putting on Christ means that Gentiles do not have to undergo circumcision and become Jews first in order to become Christians. But is Paul saying, You Gentiles don't have to be circumcised, you have to be baptized instead, for water baptism actually accomplishes the putting on of Christ? If that were his meaning, why didn't he say so outright? After all, the whole thrust of the letter points away from ceremonial acts and toward (as Barth notes) "the divine act and revelation in Jesus Christ, faith in Him, and the work of the Holy Ghost." Barth concludes, "It is thus more natural to assume that Gal. 3:27 is looking back to the divine change . . . and that baptism is recalled as the concrete moment in their own life in which they for their part confirmed, recognized and accepted their investing with Christ from above" (116).

A comparison between baptism and circumcision is found in Colossians

2:9–12, which is used to support a sacramental view of baptism, as well as infant baptism. However, the focus here is really faith, not baptism. The idea that water baptism equals "the circumcision of Christ" is hard to accept, given the parallelism between being buried with Christ and being raised with Christ, both of which happen through faith in the power of God who raised Jesus. Further, it would be strange if the "circumcision made without hands" were intended to mean water baptism, which *is* done that way, and stranger still if the whole attack against rituals in this letter were dependent for its decisive point on the idea that the ritual of water baptism is the one that really counts. It seems more likely, therefore, that Colossians 2:12 offers "a reminiscence of baptism," and the same can be said of Romans 6:3–5. In both cases, the reasoning runs like this: Recall your baptism, the concrete act whereby you confirmed what God did to bring about "your liberation from all autonomous attempts at deification or salvation. . . . Hold fast to this!" (119–20).

Champions of a sacramental understanding of baptism have often appealed to John 3:5, where Jesus tells Nicodemus, "No one can enter the kingdom of God without being born of water and the Spirit." Clearly Jesus is speaking about one event, not two, for a moment later he reduces the two terms to one, saying simply that one must be born of the Spirit (vv. 6 and 8). Later on, Jesus refers to the Holy Spirit as "living water" (4:10; also 7:38), so perhaps Jesus is telling Nicodemus that one must be born by this water of the Spirit. Besides "water and the Spirit," there are many other pairs in the Fourth Gospel, such as "resurrection and life" (11:25) or "believe and know" (6:69), where the latter term receives the greater emphasis and explains the former (120–21).

By this kind of investigation, Barth concludes that no passage of Scripture certainly ascribes a sacramental meaning to water baptism, and many passages certainly do not. In some cases "water" is an image for the activity of Jesus or the Holy Spirit, while in other cases water baptism is best understood as being a confirmation of this divine activity. In sum, baptism is not a sacrament; its meaning "is to be sought in its character as a true and genuine human action which responds to the divine act and word" (128).

THE MEANING OF RESPONSIBLE BAPTISM

The glory of water baptism, then, lies not in some hidden act of God but in its being a very visible act of humanity. It is a very human act too, only "rough and approximate" in the way it responds to and reflects the total cleansing and renewal that take place in Christ's death and the Spirit's outpouring (130, 140). Yet because it is concrete, public, and communal (unlike an inner conviction), baptism has a certain "precision and comprehensive validity." Its social character, the relationship between candidate and community, is indispensable. If there are sponsors, their purpose should be to underscore and intensify this relationship, not supplant it (130–31).

But baptism is not solely or even mainly a social action. Its purpose, in a word, is *conversion* (136, 152). And conversion, Barth makes clear, is not "an intellectual, ethical, or religious change of mind," or even that plus a change of behavior, attitude, or activity (139). All these things can and should follow, but first and foremost baptism means conversion *to God*. As soon as one knowingly says "God," as soon as one decides to "let God be God" (and to let God be *my* God), that changes everything, starting with the person I am (139–42). If baptism means conversion, then conversion in turn means that a person is "bound and liberated, claimed, consoled, cheered and ruled" by Jesus Christ (150; cf. 154). It is Christ who accomplishes this liberation—in his "history which . . . heals everything"—but water baptism is the "concrete confirmation of [one's] conversion" (150, 147). It is the act by which one renounces "the way of self-will and anxiety" and embraces "the way of obedience and hope" (141–42). Conversion, obedience, and hope are thus the crux of its meaning (147).

Barth describes "the freedom of those who are bound by and in and to Jesus Christ" (154). Here is a central paradox of the Christian faith: to gain true liberty one must give up illusory autonomy. Thus, while there must be freedom *for* baptism, there can be no freedom *from* it; there can be no evading this plain command. Some "eternal obstacle" might prevent or delay a person from being baptized—for example, if a person cannot find a "true Christian community," or if the community for some reason refuses to baptize a person. But such situations are "highly abnormal" (156–57).

As a free response to God, baptism is also a "responsible human act" (153). The community for its part is responsible to teach the candidates. In line with Augustine's guidance for instructing catechumens, good teaching will consist in "imparting to them a material and intelligible *narratio* of the great acts of God which is orientated to their future baptism." Particular attention should be given to "the decisive story of the baptism of Jesus (preferably according to Matt. 3:13f.)" (152, 153). Such instruction will aim to teach candidates about their adopted history; its purpose is not to test their moral, religious, or intellectual worthiness (152). The candidates for their part are responsible for making a "wholly free, conscious and voluntary decision" (163). Baptism is their renunciation and pledge, whereby they confirm "God's No" and "God's Yes" to humanity—God's No to "an old corrupt humanity," and God's Yes to "the new humanity that has come on the scene in Jesus Christ" (158). Baptism presupposes "human beings who are capable of thought and action and who may be summoned as such to conversion, obedience, hope, and the decision of faith" (166). For this reason, the Church should not practice infant baptism.

WHY BARTH OPPOSES INFANT BAPTISM

While infant baptism "might well have been practised relatively early, possibly even in the New Testament churches, as many investigators believe," it became the general rule only from the era of Constantine, with its "closely knit unity of people, society, state, kingdom and church, the unity into which everyone, hardly born and without being asked for his consent, was integrated at once in infant baptism." This practice guaranteed continuity to the Church, but would not the Church today have greater vibrancy if it had to exist, as in the first days, "as a small and unassuming group of aliens, though also, freed of much ballast, as a mobile brotherhood" (168)?

At any rate, the doctrine that defends infant baptism stems mainly from the Reformation, and as the premier Reformed theologian of the twentieth century, Barth undertakes to refute it. His line of reasoning runs like this: For a doctrine of infant baptism to be theologically sound, it must do X; instead, proponents of infant baptism do Y.

First, for example, proponents would need to show how infant baptism is anchored in the basis, goal, and meaning of baptism itself (179). Instead, the Reformers' doctrines of infant baptism seem to arise as a "supplement or appendix." Calvin's exposition of baptism itself, with its emphasis on faith, does not prepare us for his "forcible defense of infant baptism" (169, 170). Luther connects the two better, but together they seem at odds with the main themes of his theology, such as justification by faith alone and the freedom of the Christian person (169).

Second, proponents of infant baptism ought to be able to present and support their case calmly, but Barth finds that on this subject Reformation writers are often "tense and irritable." Third, their logic should be consistent; premises introduced at the start should remain in force throughout. But the leading Reformers (except Zwingli) give inconsistent arguments (171). Luther and Calvin start from the clear premise that the baptized person must have faith, then cloud that idea with conjecture about the alien, secret, vicarious, or miraculous ways that infants might receive faith.

Fourth, most simply, a sound doctrine of infant baptism would need to prove what it sets out to prove, not something else. Instead, proponents of infant baptism offer indisputable truths that fail to address the dispute at hand. All things are possible with God. What God commands is always good and meaningful. God's covenant of grace embraces children. God's promises are the horizon within which every child lives, even from the womb. Jesus promised all children access to himself. It is a high privilege to be born into a Christian home (175–76). Notes Barth:

> All these things are clear and true, if not self-evident. . . . But none of them demand that these children can and should be baptized. These things prove neither the legitimacy nor the necessity of infant baptism. . . . They simply show that little children have before them a way on which they later might come, rather than be brought, to faith and obedience, to knowledge and confession, and hence to a desire for baptism, and to baptism itself as their own renunciation and pledge. (176)

After stating how doctrines of infant baptism do not in general meet these four criteria for cogency, Barth goes on to address many of the specific arguments, scriptural and theological, that come into play. Some people point out, for example, that the New Testament does not expressly prohibit infant baptism. In response, Barth says, while this fact could imply that the practice was commonly accepted, it could equally well mean "that in the New Testament period no one even considered baptism of this kind." Many passages in Acts (2:37–38; 8:12, 38; 10:44–45; 16:14–15, 32–33; and 22:16) depict persons or groups being baptized after they receive the word of God. Even in cases where whole households are baptized, the sequence is the same: "preaching—faith—baptism" (179, 180).

Appeal is often made to Acts 2:39, where Peter says, "The promise is for you, and for your children. . . ." But we must read these words in context, not as proof-text. Peter is speaking to those who have heard his sermon and been "cut to the heart." He is telling them to repent and be baptized, that they may receive the Holy Spirit. He is saying the promise of the Holy Spirit is for their children "and for all who are far away, everyone whom the Lord our God calls to him." Future generations and other nations will in time have the opportunity to hear the summons to conversion and respond the way Peter's listeners did that day. Rather than being a defense of infant baptism, this train of thought says baptism is an act of repentance and faith (184).

In short, "the personal faith of the candidate is indispensable to baptism." At the same time, Barth is no champion of rugged individualism. "There is no doubt," he says, "that we all live by the faith of others which is directed to us and which intercedes for us: by the faith of our neighbours, of the congregation around us, of the whole universal Christian Church of every age and place." But this faith never becomes a "vicarious faith" by which infants may be baptized. The only true form of vicarious faith is that which comes from Jesus Christ, the "author of our faith" (Heb. 12:2). His faith, however, "empowers us for our own faith"; by his faith we are "liberated to believe for ourselves" (186).

Recognizing the need for personal faith, churches that practice infant baptism will often have a rite of confirmation, in which a person, usually of adolescent age, renews or ratifies the baptismal covenant; indeed, says Barth, "infant baptism cries out for this kind of supplementation." But what if, in confirmation, "there is again no express desire or confession on the part of the supposedly Christian young person?" (188). At the very least, a church that practices infant baptism should not treat confirmation lightly. It should be undertaken in freedom and sincerity, and not because it "automatically falls due at a specific age or stage." Still, if there is infant baptism, a rite of confirmation is very much preferable to rebaptism. The latter Barth rejects outright. While rebaptism evinces a "worthy concern," it is wrong "even when for the time being Christians are those who have been customarily baptized in infancy." From a theological standpoint, infant baptism "is highly doubtful and questionable. . . . Nevertheless, one cannot say it is invalid" (189).

Barth addresses other, more subsidiary, arguments used to defend infant baptism. He says, "The strongest—I myself used it for some decades—is that infant baptism is so remarkably vivid a depiction of the free and omnipotent grace of God which is independent of all human thought and will, faith and unbelief" (189). But if we think about it, the minister pouring water over the infant may be less a picture of God's sovereign grace than it is of grace being set in motion by the minister and thus made to work automatically. Furthermore, Barth notes, some churches are inconsistent. If they baptize infants, they should by the same logic admit them to the Lord's Supper (190).

Some have pointed out, as Luther did, that God has not withheld the Holy Spirit from people baptized in infancy, or from the Church that practiced infant baptism for centuries. However, this fact may be a sign of God's patience rather than God's pleasure. Says Barth: "Wretched Church if through its transgressions the Holy Spirit refused to acknowledge its ministry or to make its ministry fruitful!" (190). Yes, the Church has not been destroyed by infant baptism—"any more than by corrupt preaching or so many other corruptions"—but it would be wrong to assume "that this practice will not harm it in the future." History shows that God is greatly patient, but certain "judgments and disasters" are unavoidable when people are too-long obstinate (194).

Another argument for infant baptism, found in the Heidelberg Catechism, is somewhat more subtle because it makes a distinction between divine action and human action, and in this way starts to resemble Barth's own reasoning. It is said that baptism (here *water* baptism) is how God acts to offer a promise and pledge of the Holy Spirit. This promise is given to infants, apart from their faith; the human act of faith can come later. Barth responds by noting that God's promise is already given not just to infants but to all people, and not just apart from faith but apart from water. He asks, "To what extent does this promise and pledge, which is real and valid in itself . . . , stand in need of any actualization, representation, or depiction (through baptism)? What is really needed is not a supplementing of this promise, which has long since been secure and in force, but rather that [people] should come who are ready to hear and grasp the promise" (191). Water baptism, then, is how people grasp God's promise.

Yet another defense of infant baptism raises the dangers of requiring the "free decision and confession of the candidate." What if candidates come with "imaginary or hypocritical conversions"? What if churches become "Pharisaical sects" with legalistic requirements (192)? These risks are real; in some sense everything done in the Church and in theology is dangerous. The dangers here are best faced through teaching and preaching that instructs candidates before baptism, without setting up undue barriers. Such instruction should take to heart Luther's point that while faith brings us to baptism, we are not saved by our human ability to have faith. It is true that people may try to turn faith into a kind of work, but the best way to avoid confusing faith and works is by "sound evangelical proclamation and instruction," not by baptizing people before they are "even capable of distinguishing the things which might be confused" (193). Furthermore, the dangers of practicing responsible baptism are far less than the danger of people evading responsibility by appealing to infant baptism.

Barth mentions in passing how some people have defended infant baptism on the grounds that pious parents need to know their children are within the sphere of God's covenantal love. But surely these parents can see that Jesus' words "Let the little children come to me" (Mark 10:14) apply to their child too. If they insist on baptism, their need may stem more from "superstition rather than faith" (193). Still others promote infant baptism as a time when parents and people in the congregation pledge to nurture children in the faith; however, a service of infant presentation or dedication is the better way to make this commitment, if a specific rite is needed.

Barth concludes his case against infant baptism by saying, "Enough of this tiresome matter! Theology can and should do no more than advise the Church" (194). And the Church, he says, would do well to seek and listen to such advice.

BAPTISM IS PRAYER

We return now to the view that water baptism is "the first step of the Christian life," that it is "a free and responsible human act," and that the person responsible for choosing baptism is also responding to what God has done and is doing in Jesus Christ and through the Holy Spirit (205). We return to the fact that *obedience* and *hope* are the meaning of baptism. Yet now one final thing needs to be said: The meaning of baptism is also to be found "in the act of prayer" (210). We can see why prayer is so central to baptism if we probe the aspect of hope, specifically noting three things.

First, the hope of baptism must be hope in Jesus Christ. Christians are baptized people who have been given "a new birth into a living hope" (1 Pet. 1:3). As this verse goes on to say, the basis for hope is not their baptism but the power of the resurrection of Jesus Christ (197). Romans 6 makes a similar point, and Barth concludes: "The persistent power of baptism for the life of Christians consists in the confession of the persistent power of the death and resurrection of Jesus Christ" (196).

The "object and content" of baptismal hope is Jesus Christ, because anything less leads to despair (197). We have said, for example, that baptism is the first step of the new life, and it must be followed by other steps. But when we look at these other steps, do we see a clear trajectory toward God, a steady walk of unwavering obedience? No, too often we seem to find a continuation of our old life, "as though nothing had happened." Too easily we appraise our situation as a "a flagrant or secret . . . failure, a creeping or drastic declension." It is as if we take one good step in baptism, then live a life that contradicts it. Upon further reflection the despair deepens: who is to say even the first step of baptism was earnest and true? Evidence could well suggest that it too "suffered from the same radical frailty as that which followed" (204, 205). But this we recall and therefore we have hope: Jesus Christ is on this path, walking toward us. The hope of baptism is not hope in our goodness subsequent to baptism, or hope in the inner goodness of the act itself; it is hope in Jesus Christ. It must be hope in Jesus Christ, or there is no hope at all (206–7).

Second, however, this hope must not be a passive hope. We cannot be idle and inactive, with a complacent attitude that says Jesus Christ will make everything turn out well. We cannot treat Jesus with "the same assurance and familiarity as we do a bank account" (209). There is a real relationship in which he too has freedom. How then can we act?

Third, prayer is a kind of active hope, and baptism is a kind of prayer. Our "saving deed of hope" in Jesus Christ consists in the fact that the baptismal candidates and the baptizing community "pray together that He will answer and be responsible for them, i.e., for the whole ocean of mistakes both after and already in baptism." Prayer with hope in Jesus Christ "is an act, the most vigorous act that [a person] can do" (208–9).

Barth gives this point emphasis: "The act of prayer [is] the meaning of baptism?" Yes, it is, as we see in Luke's account of Jesus' baptism: "Now when all the people were baptized, and when Jesus also had been baptized and was praying, the heaven was opened" (Luke 3:21). Here "His baptism is materially defined as His prayer. Can Christian baptism be anything other or better? Why should it not finally seek to be this both humbly and boldly?" (210).

Luke's account of Paul's baptism makes a similar connection. As Barth relates, Ananias (in Acts 22:16) "tells him to get up, to gird himself for a resolute act. This act consists in being baptized, and the meaning of this act is that he should call on the name of Jesus. . . . Why should not Christian baptism have its true meaning quite simply and powerfully in this calling on His name?" (210).

A final verse of Scripture that "undoubtedly points in the same direction" is 1 Peter 3:21, which describes baptism as "the request to God for a good conscience through the resurrection of Jesus Christ" (Barth's translation). Notes Barth: If this is not a definition of the meaning of baptism, it is a description not unlike a definition. . . . Quite apart from the important passages in Luke, it justifies us in bringing our whole doctrine of baptism to a climax in what is expressly stated here, namely, that baptism is a prayer to God" (211). Barth's last word on the subject of baptism is his exposition of this verse.

The reference to baptism in 1 Peter 3:21 is part of an ethical admonition. "The ethics of 1 Peter," says Barth, "can be summed up in three sentences" (211). Christians are to do good, shunning the evil around them. They are to be witnesses of their Lord. They are to bear the sufferings inflicted on them by the heathen. The basis for these ethics is Jesus Christ (3:18). They can live this way because he has defeated the power of sin, he has suffered in the flesh, and he has first been a witness:

> Christ went and made a proclamation to the spirits in prison, who in former times did not obey, when God waited patiently in the days of Noah, during the building of the ark, in which a few, that is, eight persons, were saved through water. And baptism, which this prefigured, now saves you—not as a removal of dirt from the body, but as an appeal to God for a good conscience, through the resurrection of Jesus Christ. (1 Pet. 3:19–21)

The message of salvation that Christ preached to the primeval generation of Noah consisted in the command to build an ark. Here Christians have a clear picture of their own relation to the heathen world around them: "Their position is just the same as that of righteous Noah." Like Noah they can build an "ark." Like Noah they can be saved, not without judgment, but through judgment: "As the building of the ark saved the eight souls, baptism saves them as their own human act, namely, the act of their faith and obedience" (211, 212).

We must be careful with what is being said here. We cannot say that water baptism equals salvation, regeneration, or endowment with the Holy Spirit. These acts are what God does. But water baptism corresponds to God's action; it is a request and prayer for God to act, very much in keeping with the scriptural exhortation that "whoever calls upon the name of the Lord will be saved." Says Barth, "Baptism is a calling on the name of the Lord. It is not just accompanied by *epiclesis* [a prayer of the Holy Spirit to descend]; in itself and as such it is *epiclesis*" (212). Specifically the prayer here is for a good conscience, a "being in harmony with God," which is precisely what Christians need to live a life of well-doing and witness in the world.

In the following quotation from the final pages of Barth's *Church Dogmatics*, he describes the peace that can prevail amid the surging waters of chaos and perdition that surround the Christian—and the hope that attends this act of prayer, this step of baptism, this first step of the Christian life that becomes the model for every step that follows.

> The final thing to be said is that the meaning of the act of baptism consists in this prayer. As the baptising community and those whom it baptises make this prayer together, they look into their future after baptism, very conscious that it will all be a dark and cloudy future. They know the hazards of the way they will tread. They realise that they are no match for them. But the very act which they venture in obedience to God's command, the act of baptism as such, is the overcoming of all worry about this future and hence the act of the most calm, assured and cheerful hope in which they take this first step of the Christian life, just because and to the degree that it is prayer directed to the God who waits for them there in the person of Jesus Christ, and who has already come to them from thence in His person. Because and to the degree that it is prayer to this God, it is an act which conforms to Him in all its humanity, and the participants do neither too little nor too much, but precisely that which gives due honour to Him with whom they have to do, and which is also appropriate and salutary for them in their relationship with Him. Where there is prayer, man's relationship to God is corrected and it is in order. Because and to the degree that baptism is prayer, the participants act in this order. They are free both from any calculating manipulation of God's grace and also from any uncertainty as to its being given. They let God be God, but they let Him be their God, who has called them and to whom they may call in return, who hears them and is heard as they may hear Him, and, hearing, obey Him. Because and to the degree that baptism is prayer, it is at once a very humble and a very bold action, free from all illusions and profoundly sober, yet bold and heaven-storming. As prayer to God which raises no claim, as pure seeking, knocking, asking: Come, Lord Jesus! *Veni Creator Spiritus!* It is unequivocal obedience to God, an unequivocal answer to His justifying and sanctifying work and word. It justifies Him unequivocally. In spite of all the threats in respect of its future, in spite of the doubts which throng in upon it as a fallible work of man, it is well done and without reproach, a saving action (because it actively recognises and honours the Saviour in His grace and freedom alike). As and because it is prayer, it can and should be ventured with childlikeness, without hesitation, confidently, as a genuine act of hope in Jesus Christ. (209–10)

8

Aimee Semple McPherson

Baptism Is Power

John baptized with water, but you will be baptized with the Holy Spirit not many days from now. . . . You will receive power when the Holy Spirit has come upon you; and you will be my witnesses in Jerusalem, and in all Judea and Samaria, and to the ends of the earth.

Acts 1:5, 8

POWER AND IMPOTENCE

We live in an age of great power and impotence. Perhaps that has always been the human condition, but in the last century certain ironies have grown more acute. Money is power, and immense wealth has been created, yet we seem impotent over market forces that leave much of the world impoverished. Technology is power, and we can control so many things, except blindness to the things that matter most. The field of medicine makes powerful advances, yet the onslaught of disease still outpaces our human ingenuity. Information is power, yet a surfeit of information might even be a contributing factor in moral paralysis.

In the intellectual world, amid an array of concepts and competing truth claims, power has become a kind of common denominator. We ask of ideas as well as situations: Who gains or loses power here? Yet with all this attention to power and desire for empowerment, with all the increase and surplus of power being generated—power of all types—there remains the undeniable reality of human weakness.

Baptism is power, said Aimee Semple McPherson (1890–1944). The baptism she meant is not of water but of the Holy Spirit, so the power is not human but divine. When Jesus was baptized in the Jordan, the Holy Spirit descended on him in power, and before Jesus ascended to heaven, he told believers to wait in Jerusalem. You will receive power, he said, when the Holy Spirit has come upon you. So the eleven apostles gathered with the women and Mary the mother of Jesus, to pray. Seven days later, on Pentecost, it happened. The Holy Spirit entered the place where they were praying, with a rush of violent wind and tongues as of fire. They were filled with the Holy Spirit and began to speak in other languages.

The same baptism happens today, in places around the world where the human heart is a clean and empty vessel, and at times when believers in Jesus are willing to tarry in prayer. It happens today because Jesus Christ is the same yesterday, today, and forever (Heb. 13:8).

Jesus himself is the Baptizer with the Holy Spirit.[1] He is also the Only Savior, the Great Physician, and the Soon-Coming King.[2] These four truths are like four ropes, which stressed equally keep in balance the doctrine of the Foursquare Gospel Church.[3] This Pentecostal denomination grew out of the ministry God gave to Sister Aimee, a ministry set in motion in 1908 when as a teenager living in Ontario, Canada, she was baptized in the Spirit.[4]

Her ministry took her around the world, and in time publicity and controversy followed Aimee wherever she went, growing most intense after she settled in Los Angeles. As the events of her personal life became topics of rumor, report, and investigation, she responded to the media by using it (including the successful radio station her ministry owned), which fueled her critics' accusations that she was "grasping for power and profit" of an earthly sort.[5]

But the controversy for which Aimee herself had the most passion was theological. Against both many modernists and fundamentalists she maintained

1. Aimee Semple McPherson, *The Holy Spirit* (Los Angeles: Challpin Publishing Co., 1931), 10.

2. *Holy Spirit*, 193.

3. *Holy Spirit*, 205. Edith Blumhofer thinks it possible, but not certain, that McPherson derived her Foursquare Gospel from the "Fourfold Gospel" of Albert B. Simpson, founder of the Christian and Missionary Alliance Church, who proclaimed that Christ is Savior, Sanctifier, Healer, and coming King. See Blumhofer, *Aimee Semple McPherson: Everybody's Sister* (Grand Rapids: Wm. B. Eerdmans, 1993), 191; also Stephen J. Land, *Pentecostal Spirituality: A Passion for the Kingdom* (Sheffield, UK: Sheffield Academic Press, 1994), 65.

4. Aimee Semple McPherson, *This Is That* (Los Angeles: FourSquare Publications, 1996), 45. Cf. Aimee Semple McPherson, *The Story of My Life* (Waco, TX: Word Books, 1973), 22–30.

5. Blumhofer, *Aimee Semple McPherson*, 21.

that the events recorded in Acts ought to be a blueprint for the church today. The baptism of the Spirit, and all the ensuing supernatural gifts such as divine healing and speaking in tongues, are for now. Jesus did not rescind his promise, and the Spirit did not run out of power. She made this proclamation at a time when Pentecostalism was not so popular, when it was not yet recognized as the fastest-growing expression of Christianity, and when it did not have, as it does today, about half a billion adherents around the world.

In response to charges of fanaticism, Aimee stressed balanced teaching. While the gift of tongues is the initial evidence that one has in fact been baptized in the Spirit, the enduring evidence is the fruit of the Spirit, especially love. Likewise, the power of Spirit baptism is manifest in ecstatic expressions and sanctified emotions, but the power is given for a further purpose: so that people can serve the Lord, doing God's work with God's power; so that sinners may be saved and broken lives be healed; so that the gospel may go forth and the world be transformed in expectant waiting for Jesus to come again.

This view of baptism was not original to Aimee Semple McPherson. As she labored to point out, it came from Scripture, and more recently in history its roots could be found in the Wesleyan revivals of the eighteenth century, the Holiness movements of the nineteenth century, and the outpouring of the Spirit in the area of Azusa Street, Los Angeles, in 1906. Some scholars see Pentecostalism as an integration of Wesleyan and African American spirituality.[6] At any rate, Aimee's teaching was preceded by that of William Seymour and other pastors of the Azusa Street revival, and by that of Robert Semple, an evangelist who came to her town from Ireland when she was seventeen. Through his revival preaching she learned about the necessity of being born again and the possibility of being baptized with the Holy Ghost. Aimee and Robert were married, and went to China as missionaries, where he died. She had two other marriages after that and kept the last name of her second husband, Harold McPherson, though many always knew her as Aimee and church members often called her Sister (the appellation Edith Blumhofer uses in a recent biography).

If Aimee's message was not unique, neither were her methods, but she honed them as few if any had done before. Her famous "illustrated sermons" included one where she dressed in a police uniform and stood beside a motorcycle to warn people about speeding down the wrong avenue of life. "Stop!" she called as police sirens filled the auditorium. "You're speeding to ruin!"[7]

6. Land, *Pentecostal Spirituality*, 35.
7. Aimee Semple McPherson, *In the Service of the King: The Story of My Life* (New York: Boni & Liveright, 1927), 238.

The sermon was inspired not only by the speeding ticket she received while driving in the hills of Los Angeles earlier that week but also by the innovative sermons of Evangeline Booth of the Salvation Army, the church where her mother was active when Aimee was a child.[8] Popular methods cloaked a message that treated sin with gravity, salvation with urgency, and that held out tangible hope of righteousness, peace, and joy in the Holy Spirit.

Other Pentecostals have followed in Aimee's wake, and some have taken different routes. The baptism of the Holy Spirit has meant not only a sanctification of emotions but of intellect, and today many Pentecostal theologians have gained a respected hearing in academic circles; some of these voices will be noted in this chapter, albeit briefly. Pentecostals today who are not seeking media publicity but theological integrity and depth may feel that Aimee is not the ideal representative to choose for this chapter. At the same time it seems clear that the substance of her teaching, in all its power and simplicity, is consistent with what is heard in many Pentecostal churches today.

Aimee's personal life was rather more complex. No doubt the same could be said of other writers covered in this book, but the questionable sides of Aimee's life were projected, as on a movie screen, for all to see. Was she right or wrong to remarry while her second spouse was still living, something she had previously preached against? In her autobiography she conveys that she was wrong, but lonely.[9] Was her kidnapping genuine or staged? She remained adamant to her death that it was real, not a hoax, and a grand jury investigation cleared her of all charges (raising the possibility that the Los Angeles district attorney had been the one seeking publicity). Was her death itself the result of serious kidney disease, or an overdose of sedatives? The coroner's jury said it was both but that the overdose was accidental. Since one of the first effects of the sedative was forgetfulness, as Dr. Mary Ruth Odlt testified, Aimee probably forgot how many pills she had taken.[10]

We could ask other sorts of questions. To what extent was the scrutiny of her life due to her celebrity, and to what extent was her celebrity due to her being a woman? A woman evangelist was not unheard of, but Aimee was heard more widely than any before and was respected highly by many—for her stamina to persist and practical creativity, and for her evident love of Jesus and love of neighbor.[11] With it all, she would be the first to admit she had weaknesses, not because she was a woman but because she was human. Here is where the events

---

8. Blumhofer, *Aimee Semple McPherson*, 6; 50–52, 260–61.
9. *Story of My Life*, 234, 239.
10. Blumhofer, *Aimee Semple McPherson*, 379.
11. Ibid., 21.

of her life just adumbrated connect to the topic of baptism. The Pentecostal message is that God fills human vessels that are empty and holy; the Pentecostal lived experience is that these vessels are also often earthy jars of clay.

Here too the irony of great power and impotence becomes reversed. God uses the foolish and weak things to expose the pretensions of the wise and mighty (1 Cor. 1:27). God uses the poor to liberate the rich, the broken to heal the sick, and the overlooked to open blind eyes. In human weakness clinging to divine strength there is power to turn the world upside down. Spirit baptism bestows this power.

In one of several sermons entitled "The Baptism of the Holy Spirit," Sister Aimee imagines a dialogue with Peter on the day of Pentecost. Peter is asked: Are you not afraid of this great mob of people? Are you not aware that as a disciple of Jesus you may be carried to the whipping post, may be beaten and stoned to death? Peter, I thought you were a timid man, ashamed to be known as one of them?

But God has poured out God's Spirit on this flesh, Peter has been baptized in the Spirit, so he is able to say (as Aimee says): "'Oh, no, I will never be ashamed to be called one of the despised, persecuted, peculiar few any more. The Holy Ghost has come to abide in this life of mine, and the words that I speak I speak not of myself; the works that I do I do not of myself, but the Holy Spirit who has come to dwell within me, He speaks the words; He does the works.'"[12]

Thus Aimee's words become as Peter's words, and Peter's words are those of the Holy Spirit, which in turn echo the words of Jesus. Such intimate relationality—between people and between God and humanity—characterizes Spirit baptism.

THE REAL AND PRESSING ISSUES

Over the centuries much ink has been spent and blood spilled over the question of infant versus believer's baptism. But a fresh reading of the New Testament confronts us with a very different distinction—that of water versus Spirit baptism. John the Baptist makes this distinction at the start of all four Gospels, saying he baptizes with water whereas the One who comes after him will baptize with the Spirit. Jesus reiterates this distinction between water baptism and Spirit baptism at the start of Acts (1:5).

---

12. "The Baptism of the Holy Spirit," in *American Sermons: The Pilgrims to Martin Luther King, Jr.*, ed. Michael Warner (New York: Library of America, 1999), 758.

In distinguishing the two, are we saying that water baptism and Spirit baptism can never come together? No, the point is rather that we need to attend more to Spirit baptism and not assume that a person who has been baptized with water has automatically been baptized with the Spirit. The baptism of the Holy Spirit is an event, and one ought to know whether or not it has taken place. When Jesus was baptized in the Jordan, he was filled with the Spirit; he knew it and it was evident to John, who bore witness. Was this event necessary for Jesus to be divine? No, Jesus is divine from birth and from eternity, but in his full humanity he suffered weakness, and in his humanity he lived "a life of Spirit-filled ministry and supernatural power," and he made this life available to his followers.[13]

The first Christians saw clearly the distinction between water baptism and Spirit baptism:

- In Acts 8, the Samaritan believers are baptized with water, but the Holy Spirit does not fall upon them until Peter and John are sent to lay hands on them.
- In Acts 10, the Holy Spirit does fall on Cornelius and his household as Peter is proclaiming "how God anointed Jesus of Nazareth with the Holy Spirit and with power" (10:38); subsequently they are baptized with water.
- In Acts 19, the believers in Ephesus are baptized with water ("into John's baptism" of repentance) but "have not even heard that there is a Holy Spirit" (19:2). When Paul tells them there is, they are baptized again in the name of the Lord Jesus and begin to speak in tongues. Cornelius and his household also speak in tongues when they receive the Spirit (10:46), and the same could be said of the Samaritan believers, for clearly Simon the sorcerer sees something that leads him to implore Peter, "Give me also this power" (8:19).

So in one case Spirit baptism comes before water baptism, in two cases water baptism comes first, and in all three cases speaking in tongues follows Spirit baptism.

From the narrative descriptions in Acts we can extrapolate normative patterns.[14] In stating these patterns, Pentecostals of the early twentieth century could become sharply divided, but Aimee seeks to unify. She finds common ground among Trinitarian Pentecostals and at the same time reaches out to a wider population who is thirsty for a real experience of God. One thing she makes clear: the Christian life is marked by decisive events. Yes, it has an

13. *Holy Spirit*, 19.
14. *Holy Spirit*, 155: "The book of Acts is essentially a 'book of patterns.'"

aspect of being ongoing and gradual as well, but the eventfulness of the
Gospel should not be minimized. The birth, death, and resurrection of Jesus
are events with a clear before and after; so too in the life of the believer are
the new birth, the burial in water baptism, and the receiving of resurrection
power through Spirit baptism.

This quality was noted by revival, Holiness, and Pentecostal preachers
alike, though they often disagreed over the number and sequence of events.
For example, Pentecostals who came from a Wesleyan background might
speak of three critical experiences—the new birth, then sanctification, then
Spirit baptism—whereas those who came from Baptist backgrounds would
be more inclined to see sanctification as a gradual process following regeneration and thus would speak of two main events, namely, the new birth and
Spirit baptism. Robert Semple's teacher, Charles Durham, had been Baptist
before becoming Pentecostal, and he held this latter view. Aimee leaned this
way as well, however her teaching on baptism does not stress this or any
other scheme.

Instead she focuses continually on what is central to the life of Jesus and
upon what happens when Jesus is in the center of her life. Her teaching is often
autobiographical; in this way she can show just what Spirit baptism is and is
not. It is embodied and palpable; it is not just an abstract theory.[15] It is "sane,
practical, level-headed." It is "*Not* a wild fire excitement that runs to fanaticism, emotionalism, or side issues that cause the recipient to fight and argue
and boast more as to the manner in which the Holy Ghost enters into His temple than of the real, practical power and soul-winning efficiency, which His
dear incoming brings."[16] Whether one calls her view mysticism or pragma-
tism, or both, it helps to hear how she describes Jesus and the Holy Spirit coming into her life.

AIMEE'S AUTOBIOGRAPHICAL ACCOUNT

"You must be born again!" declared Robert Semple to the congregation in
which Aimee, age seventeen, sat listening. Then he "began to talk of the baptism of the Holy Ghost" and its "living, vital power." Suddenly, in the midst
of his sermon, he "closed his eyes and with radiant face began to speak in a language that was not his own." The Spirit-prompted utterance spoke to her
heart. It was, she says, "like the voice of God thundering into my soul awful

15. *This Is That*, 713.
16. *This Is That*, 713.

words of conviction and condemnation. Though the message was spoken in tongues, it seemed that God was saying to me, 'You are a poor, lost, miserable, hell-deserving sinner!'"[17]

Resolution to her crisis came three days later. While driving her horse through the snow on a December afternoon in 1907, she "could hold out no longer."

> "God, be merciful to me, a sinner!" I cried, and the woodland to the left rang with my voice. The sun burst through the clouds. A great peace fell over me. It was as though the warm crimson blood of Calvary was poured over my being. Great tears were splashing down upon my gloved hands as I held the reins.[18]

Her father predicted her transformation would not last more than two weeks, but it did. She was "supremely happy" in her relationship with Jesus: "I took to him my every problem, and he shared my every joy." Then came a nagging thought: "'The whole thing is too one-sided!' I cried. 'You are doing all the giving; I all the receiving. . . . Lord, what can I do in return for thee?'"[19]

Her joy of salvation had inspired a desire to serve. As Cheryl Bridges Johns notes, "For Pentecostals, the experience of the baptism of the Holy Spirit is for the purpose of empowering a believer's life for service."[20] For Aimee, who had not yet received this baptism, the next step was a longing to preach, to share with others the message that brought her such gladness. When told that "women do not preach," she found counterexamples of women's leadership in Scripture. Deborah "led forth her gleaming armies"; the woman at the well "preached the first salvation sermon and led an entire city to Christ"; moreover, "a woman had delivered the first Easter message and none other than the Master had so commissioned her."[21] Her father gave added evidence, pointing out that Paul was taught by a woman and man, Priscilla and Aquila. Paul also spoke of women who prophesied, and when he told the Corinthian women to keep silent he was probably referring to their interrupting services by calling out questions.

For Aimee, the repeated question was this: "But where, where's the door to service!" She felt herself to be "lowly" and "isolated," yet through Bible study she discovered how "the baptism of the Holy Ghost . . . galvanized the

17. *Story of My Life*, 23.
18. *Story of My Life*, 24.
19. *Story of My Life*, 25.
20. Cheryl Bridges Johns, *Pentecostal Formation: A Pedagogy among the Oppressed* (Sheffield, UK: Sheffield Academic Press, 1993), 94.
21. *Story of My Life*, 26.

mediocre and transformed them into evangelists of power." She wondered, "Is this selfsame power for men and women of today?"[22] Acts 2:39 assured her it was. "The promise is for you, for your children, and for all who are far away, everyone whom the Lord our God calls."

"Earnestly," she says, "I began to seek this power," even cutting school in the afternoon to do so: "'Just where have you been, my lady?' inquired my mother. 'At prayer meeting,' I replied miserably."[23] The local preacher warned that in "seeking this so-called power" she might become "possessed with an evil spirit." At last her mother issued an ultimatum: "If you skip school and attend another of these services, I shall insist upon your remaining at home entirely!" (28–29). But that same day a blizzard swept through the area, stranding her close to the house where Pentecostals lived, and where she had been going to pray. She describes what happened next:

From Monday until Saturday I prayed. Rising at any hour I awakened, I would slip out of bed, wrap the covers about me, and kneel, beseeching the Power above me to empty me of self and fill me with the Power promised from above. On that last morning the air was still frosty. . . . The blizzard had continued throughout the entire week. Drifts were piled so high about the doors that even the sound of snow shovels had ceased until the frost-nipping, ear-piercing winds would die down. Trains had ceased to run. Snow plows could not get through. Even telephone wires were down.

Shivering, but determined, I bowed my knees beside the big leather Morris chair and stormed the gates of prayer. I felt as though I had been battering my way through a thick stone wall that was now as thin as tissue paper. "Lord," I cried, "I'll never eat or sleep again until you fill me with this promised Spirit of power!"

"I am more willing to give than you are to receive," said my open Bible.

"Forgive me!" I murmured. "The waiting is on my part, not on thine." And then the glory fell. My tightly closed eyes envisioned the Man of Galilee, bleeding, dying, thorn-crowned on Golgotha's Tree. Tears streamed down my face. I found my trembling lips singing:

Let me love Thee, Savior,
Take my life forever,
Nothing but Thy service,
My soul shall satisfy.

"Glory, glory to Jesus!" I repeated over and over. Then my lips began to quiver and I began to speak in other tongues like those of the ancient Upper Room. Ripples, waves, billows, oceans, cloudbursts of blessing flooded my being. My form slipped to the floor and lay there submerged beneath the downpour. A little puddle of tears wet the carpet.

22. *Story of My Life*, 27.
23. *Story of My Life*, 28.

I shook as though I were holding the negative and positive handles of the electric battery in the school laboratory.

"This settles it," I declared. "From this moment on my life is thine and thine alone. Honor or dishonor, weal or woe, pain or pleasure—naught shall move or change me from the sunshine of thy love and the footstep of thy service."[24]

Edith Blumhofer confirms most of this account, though she adjusts the timetable, figuring Aimee started on Friday, January 31, 1908; on Saturday she "came through" to the baptism with the Holy Spirit, and on Sunday she "went down" under the power (after which a chagrined family acquaintance left the service to phone her mother).[25]

We can move from these snapshots of experience to a more systematic reflection by asking, as a journalist might, about the *who, what, why, when,* and *how* of Spirit baptism.

WHAT IS SPIRIT BAPTISM?

Jesus, who baptizes with the Spirit, calls this baptism "the promise of my Father" (Luke 24:49 KJV). The Spirit proceeds from the Father through the Son; this trinitarian understanding is implicit in McPherson's teaching. She states, "There are three in the Godhead: Father, Son and Holy Spirit. The Holy Spirit is more than an influence; He is the third Person of the Godhead. Jesus Christ never referred to the Spirit as 'it,' but as 'He.'"[26] Spirit baptism, therefore, is a *who* before it is a *what*. The baptism of the Spirit is the gift of God himself; a doctrine of *theosis* seems implicit in McPherson's teaching. She calls the Christian life the "divine life." This life honors the distinctness of the three Persons in the Godhead.

Different branches came from these early Pentecostal roots. Some scholars surmise that Oneness Pentecostals adopted their modalist views in part because they feared tritheism. More recently, trinitarian Pentecostal theologians have sought to develop the connection between baptism and *theosis*. Steven Land, for example, finds in Pentecostalism a "fivefold gospel"—essentially the four tenets named by McPherson, plus "sanctification" as a "definite work of grace"—that is simultaneously christocentric and pneumatic; hence it

---

24. *Story of My Life*, 30–31.
25. Blumhofer, *Aimee Semple McPherson*, 65–66.
26. *Holy Spirit*, 182–83; cf. Land, *Pentecostal Spirituality*, 60.

issues in "a soteriology which emphasizes salvation as participation in the divine life more than removal of guilt.[27] Likewise, Frank Macchia holds that Spirit baptism is essentially "participation in God."[28]

Aimee conveys some of these ideas in common language. What is Spirit baptism? It is the "glorious baptism of Power."[29] But we are never to lose sight of the fact that the power comes from God; we cannot separate the gift from the Giver. "Power . . . is the believer's possession only in a derivative and relational sense."[30] These words are Land's, but they concur with McPherson's. In her book *The Holy Spirit*, she starts by showing how this power, "the quickening power of the Holy Spirit," makes a tangible difference when it really is the believer's possession. She personally has needed this power to deliver an average of fifteen addresses each week and to shepherd a ministry with eighteen thousand members.[31] However, she moves quickly from autobiography to the life of Jesus in order to explicate the "relational" nature of this power.

She reviews Christ's life—how he healed diseases, overturned money tables, fed people in soul and body, and "pointed the way to living vital relationship with God the Father"—then asks, "By what power had all these miracles been accomplished?" She traces the answer to the banks of the Jordan, where Jesus was baptized and where he was "motivated, actuated, enveloped by the power of the Holy Spirit sent down from the Father upon Him."[32] As Luke writes, "Jesus returned in the power of the Spirit into Galilee" (Luke 4:14 KJV).

Thus the gospel of Jesus is not just words but acts; not just theories but facts. Jesus does not just point out affliction but shows the way to health. There is an integration of words and works, evident when Jesus says, "The words that I speak unto you, I speak not of myself; but He that dwelleth in me, He doeth the works" (John 14:10).[33] The relationality of the Godhead is also evident here: the Father dwells in the Son through the Spirit. Though Jesus himself is God, he empties himself of divinity, in order to live the divine life tenderly enveloped and completely wrapped up in the Holy Spirit: "He, conceived of the Spirit, baptized with the Spirit, led by the Spirit, wrought His matchless works by the power of the Spirit."[34]

27. Land, *Pentecostal Spirituality*, 18, 23; cf. 30, 70.

28. Frank D. Macchia, *Baptized in the Spirit: A Global Pentecostal Theology* (Grand Rapids: Zondervan, 2006), 117; cf. 41, 45, 97, 104, 154.

29. *Holy Spirit*, 162.

30. Land, *Pentecostal Spirituality*, 157.

31. *Holy Spirit*, 8–9.

32. *Holy Spirit*, 19, 20.

33. As quoted three times in *Holy Spirit*, 20, 24, 27.

34. *Holy Spirit*, 26.

Jesus also says something amazing. He tells his followers that they will do the same works he did—and even greater works (John 14:12). As Aimee says, "There was, then, to be no cessation of the power; but—oh, staggering thought!—rather an increase thereof!"[35] To do these works, to have this power, they must wait. After the "ascending Christ" comes the "descending Holy Spirit."[36] Only then is the mantle of power, which fell on Jesus at the Jordan, passed to believers who are to carry on his work. As Elijah needed to be caught up before Elisha could receive his mantle, so Jesus had to ascend before his Spirit could be outpoured. Without this outpouring they could go nowhere and do nothing. That is why Jesus tells them to tarry in Jerusalem (Luke 24:49) and why he says they need to be baptized, but not with water: "For John truly baptized with water, but ye shall be baptized with the Holy Ghost not many days from hence." These words, which Aimee quotes to contemporary listeners, convey clearly that water baptism is not the same as Spirit baptism, and they highlight the need for Spirit baptism. "Ye shall receive power, after that the Holy Ghost is come upon you and ye shall be witnesses unto me," Jesus goes on to say.[37]

Though not the same as Spirit baptism, water baptism is still important. The Ephesian believers in Acts 19 lacked power and needed to receive the Holy Spirit,[38] but first there is a baptismal service wherein they "are buried in a watery grave."[39] Water baptism corresponds to the death of Jesus. Scripture does not explicate exactly how, nor does Aimee try to do so. But there is clearly no circumventing water baptism. In fact, Aimee at one point reports that "during each of the eight summers and winters that the Temple [the building for her ministry] has been opened, we have registered an average of ten thousand converts at our altars; and baptized an average of three thousand in water by immersion."[40] For some candidates, it was not the first time. Blumhofer notes that Aimee's daughter "Roberta was baptized at least twice, and it is uncertain how many times Sister submitted to immersion."[41]

There are photographs of an outdoor service in which Aimee and her children were baptized by an African American pastor. In an era of segregation,

---

35. *Holy Spirit*, 35.
36. *Holy Spirit*, 264.
37. *Holy Spirit*, 47.
38. *Holy Spirit*, 151.
39. Aimee Semple McPherson, "Baptism of the Holy Spirit," in *American Sermons: The Pilgrims to Martin Luther King, Jr.*, ed. Michael Warner (New York: Library Classics, 1999), 760.
40. *Holy Spirit*, 100.
41. Blumhofer, *Aimee Semple McPherson*, 123.

these baptisms were said to give tangible evidence that the color line had been washed away in the blood of Jesus. They also reinforce how water baptism is to be understood as an ordinance—obeying a specific command of Jesus. By contrast, Spirit baptism is a crisis and, like regeneration, it radically changes a person so that ever after one is never the same.[42]

While Aimee draws together strands from John and Luke to show how baptism is power, more recently Macchia has sought to unify Luke and Paul in order to show that "the substance of Spirit baptism" is "an outpouring of divine love."[43] Here the central verse is Romans 5:5: "God has poured out his love into our hearts by the Holy Spirit."[44] Macchia finds this theme in early Pentecostal teachings; moreover, he notes that while love can be seen as a continual abiding in God's presence, "growth in love does have its dramatic moments of filling, ecstasy, and power."[45]

WHY IS SPIRIT BAPTISM GIVEN?

While observers may note how Spirit baptism inspires ecstasy in worship, its ongoing purpose is energy for service. These two aims are not competing but complementary. "Thank God for the mountain top experience!" says Aimee. "Without it we would be unfitted for service in the valley."[46]

Pastors may sense the need for such an experience when, surveying their ministry, they see "the lack of power, the indifference and absence of young people, the cold materialism and unbelief of those that remain and the lack of revival fires."[47] The pastor's predicament reflects the temper of the times: "These are days of coldness and perplexity; days of atheism and unbelief; days of modernism, higher criticism and pantheism; days when the world is surging in from every side and battling the outposts of the church, and men have a name that they live but are dead. The baptism of the Holy Spirit is needed today as never before!" (174).

It may be that this baptism is also being received as never before. The countercurrent to modern trends is strong, and looking at church attendance one would have to say that the "the most popular religion in the world today is the

42. Land, *Pentecostal Spirituality*, 117.

43. Macchia, *Baptized in the Spirit*, 17. Cf. 15, 18, 35, 60, 63, 81, 212, 243.

44. Ibid., 257.

45. Ibid., 82.

46. *Holy Spirit*, 188. Subsequent references to this work are given as page numbers in parentheses in the text.

47. *This Is That*, 712.

old time religion. The religion with blood, warmth, fire and glory; the religion with animation, spirit, joy, and zest . . . ; a revival punctured with nights and days of prayer and permeated with enthusiastic praise is in as great, if not greater, demand today than ever before in the history of the world" (101–2). This demand is not just a human desire or form of escapism, but rather it is consistent with God's nature: "Our God is a consuming fire, and He would not have those who worship Him cold or luke-warm, but aflame with His love. He would kindle our prayers, our testimonies, our songs, our messages until they blaze with Holy Fire and heavenly zeal" (116).

Thus *ecstasy* can denote two different things. It can mean a loss of control, a flight into euphoria that removes one from reality. But these symptoms do not characterize true Spirit baptism; here *ecstasy*, in keeping with the literal meaning of the word, is to stand outside—to stand outside the ego-constricted self and to stand in God's presence, thus to be filled with God's Spirit. When God's love is poured into the human heart it brings intense joy and delight that cannot be contained. A person in this latter condition, judged by outside appearances, may even look drunk, as the Spirit-filled believers were accused of being at Pentecost. Their bodies were like vessels into which God poured the new wine of the Spirit: "Descending from the Upper Room hilariously happy, they noised abroad that thing which the Lord had done. There seemed to be no stopping the effervescent bubbling over of that experience!" (239).

To have "thrilling emotions" is perfectly proper for the person who has been baptized with the Spirit (31). Still, from Pentecost until today, the charge of reckless fanaticism has followed Spirit-filled believers. McPherson recognizes there are valid concerns as well as invalid criticisms. Perhaps to offset the coldness and neglect with which churches have historically treated Spirit baptism, some Pentecostals have "over-emphasized manifestations." They may have "zeal without knowledge." They may be like Peter on the Mount of Transfiguration, "so charmed and delighted with the ecstatic blessing and soul-surging glory of the sacred spot that he desired to remain and build" (186–87).

Aimee describes what happens when people live only for the next spiritual high: "The result is an increased feasting upon the ecstatic and the fleshly manifestations. A meeting has lost its charm for them unless there is a great abundance of spiritual emotion" (207). Here to be "ecstatic" is not a good thing; here the Spirit-led drive has been thwarted by a more self-centered desire to escape the world or to live in suspended animation. By contrast, Spirit baptism draws you out of the world, and out of yourself, in order to fire you back into the world with a greater velocity to love and serve God. Steven Land describes healthy ecstasy this way:

> The ecstasy of Pentecostals is not a possession or loss of self-control. It is a relinquishment of control in trust that believes that the kingdom-like salvation is a gift of God that has nothing to do with self-willed and technique-manipulated progress but has everything to do with the power of God who raised Jesus and sends the Spirit with witness and wonders into the community of hope.[48]

In teaching about this power, Aimee strove for balance and so drew criticism from both sides. Some Pentecostals accused her of quenching the Spirit because she maintained order in worship meetings. Many mainline Christians accused her of emotionalism. She responded to the former by stating that Spirit baptism is "Power under control" (200). She challenged the latter not to issue blanket criticisms. If Mary, "whose complete sanctification made her worthy to be the Mother of our Lord," both needed and humbly received this baptism on Pentecost, then "surely there is no excuse for you and me. Surely we need it too" (64). Yes, many said, surely we need the Holy Spirit, but why all the fanaticism, excitement, and manifestations? These we can do without. Aimee replied that such things were experienced by the one hundred and twenty on the day of Pentecost, including the blessed women and apostles; it would be wise not to call *them* fanatics or accuse them of being overemotional—"that is, at least until we can accomplish as much or more good in the church, or acquire as many genuine conversions to the Faith of the Son as they" (99).

Here we see clearly that the power is given for the purpose of service, especially bringing people to Christ in these last days (244). "We all know," says Aimee, "that we need more power by which to accomplish this great task of soul winning!" (195). Essentially we are in the position of Elisha who, after he was commissioned, must have cried out, "If I have been chosen to do my master's work, I must have my master's power!" (249; cf. 243).

WHEN IS SPIRIT BAPTISM GIVEN?
HOW IS IT RECEIVED?

Spirit baptism is for today. Jesus is the great I am, not the great I was.[49] Likewise the baptism he gives is present tense, and so are the gifts of the Spirit, including tongues, prophecy, and healing. Some dispensationalists would say that the age of miracles has passed, but if we are reckoning dispensations we must frame the matter this way: The Old Testament records the dispensation

---

48. Land, *Pentecostal Spirituality*, 177.
49. *This Is That*, 704.

of the Father, the New Testament the life of Jesus Christ upon the earth, and then came the Church age—the dispensation of the Holy Spirit—in which we are now living (153). Some dispensationalists (such as followers of C. I. Scofield) would say that eras cannot be overlapping, but these dispensations of the Father, Son, and Holy Spirit are indeed interpenetrating.[50]

Peter makes it clear that Spirit baptism is for the present age when in Acts 2:39 he tells those who have witnessed its manifestations, "This promise is . . . to all that are afar off, even as many as the Lord our God shall call." Today, far from Peter's day, people come to church hungry to receive this promise afresh, but too often their preachers offer instead a "canned product called 'self-effort' and 'human substitutes'" (92, 95).

While there is no invariable sequence or formula by which a person receives the baptism of the Holy Spirit, we can outline certain principles. Peter tells the listeners on Pentecost to "repent and be baptized" in order to receive the gift of the Holy Spirit. To repent is to be converted and have one's sins blotted out. To be baptized in water shows "the world the separation from the old life; the burial of the past, and the birth of the new." Aimee concludes, "It is plain that one must first accept the Christ before being filled with the Spirit" (90).

Second, Spirit baptism is given to those who are "cleansed and consecrated" (90). Here we should choose words carefully. One does not earn Spirit baptism. "It is not a case of our worthiness, but His; not our merits, but the merits of the precious atoning Blood." At the same time, in colloquial terms, we may say that God does not fill with the Spirit those who are too full of themselves. "All He asks is a clean, empty vessel, that He may fill it and make it meet for the Master's use" (63). The division of responsibility can be stated this way: "Yours it is to be clean and empty, surrendered and ready! His it is to take you up, fill you with His Spirit and pour you out again as full pitchers of Living Waters" (45).

McPherson returns often to this idea of being "empty" to express the condition of human readiness. As a real-life parable, she describes sailing to China as a missionary. One day, she says, "our ship lay in a dead calm on the Indian Ocean. . . . A peculiar hush held in the atmosphere. . . . It was as though sea and sky were breathlessly waiting, listening for some distant sound. . . . So still was the air that breathing was difficult." The dead quiet was shattered by voices from the ship's bridge.

> Sailors were ordered to lash deck chairs and make fast the forward cargo. Then, to my amazement, all passengers were instructed to leave the deck and go below. . . .

50. Land, *Pentecostal Spirituality*, 79.

Upon the distant horizon, I saw a black wall of water suddenly rear itself up. A sound which can be likened but to the screaming of women was heard high overhead. "'O-o-o-o-o!" it wailed, and ran up, up the scale to a shrill shriek.

A steward rapped sharply on the door. There was a strained look upon his face. He closed the porthole, screwed the fastening tightly. . . . I felt the need of speech and asked the inconsequential question:

"What shall we do for air? There was little enough before you closed the windows, but now it will be stifling."

"Don't worry about air!" said he a little grimly. "There will be plenty of it along in a few minutes."

Indeed there was. The wind came, the waters raged, the ship danced upon the sea like a cork, and for four days people stayed below and got horribly sick.

"What is the cause of such a storm?" we asked the captain when he came to the table for the first time in many anxious days.

"A vacuum," he replied. "Whenever there is an empty pocket, such as that through which we sailed, the winds from all directions rush in to fill it."

Aimee connects her ocean adventure to Scripture: "There was an empty place in the Upper Room. The hearts of the hundred and twenty were not only willing, yielded and clean; but they were empty. Because they were emptied of self and self-desire, the rushing, mighty fulness of God's Holy Spirit came in and filled them to overflowing" (112–15).

Other attributes characterized the spiritual atmosphere in that Upper Room before the first Pentecostal baptism: peace, trust, love, obedience, surrender, purity, and unity (71–73). Such qualities in a person and within a community exemplify the readiness and "emptiness" that prepare the way for Spirit baptism.

Thus the Holy Spirit fills those who have both received Jesus and renounced self-will. A third principle is this: Spirit baptism comes in response to prayer. "The revival on the Day of Pentecost was not 'worked up,'" says Aimee. "It was 'prayed down'" (80). She taught this message to those who came to the Angeles Temple, whether for worship meetings or ministerial training. "We have tarrying meetings for the baptism of the Holy Spirit first, and counsel all to be endued with power for service. And power does fall!" (199). She admonishes those who say they cannot take the time to persevere in prayer for God to baptize them. "No time to look unto the Lord for the baptism of Fire? As well might the sail declare, 'I have no time to wait for the wind'" (69).

In the past, mighty servants of God knew this power was necessary for ministry, but in her day she saw how often people resisted praying for the baptism of the Holy Spirit. She recounts her meeting with one pastor:

> I thought of his tiny church, his steadily dwindling congregations, his dry, prepared sermons, his empty altars, his teas and his socials and of the great denomination which he represents. . . . What a blessing it would have been could he have fallen to his knees in such a spirit of prayer and tears as once shook strong men such as Wesley, Finney, Knox, and Cartwright! How one should have rejoiced to have heard him lift his voice in real prayer and praise. (83)

The modern seminary may sometimes foster this resistance to praying for Spirit baptism. Too often the seminary has become a temple of modernism and higher criticism, with a "bloodless, miracle-denying, hypercritical atmosphere." There appears to be power in its imposing façade, but the real power of God is often found elsewhere. Says Aimee, "It is still the humble, yielded, importunate seeker after the Holy Ghost that wields the sceptre of spiritual power," and this power is manifested in ministry that brings people to Christ. Persons can be equipped for such ministry by the right education: "Religious education, when directed by Spirit-filled teachers whose messages are bathed with prayer . . . is a priceless heritage to the student who trains for ministry" (68).

If there is a dearth of spiritual power in the church today, the problem is not in the pews but with the clergy. "It is we—we of the clergy—who have failed God miserably in not tarrying before Him for the power and praying down the rushing, mighty wind upon our particular valley of 'dry bones'!" (111). Aimee sums up the relation between education and prayer this way: "Rather a simple education upon the knees in the closet of prayer before an open, tear-stained Bible and the irresistible power of God's invisible army than all the theological quibblings and analyzings and ponderings in the world, without the broken and contrite spirit with power from on High!" (110).

Though some people mistakenly equate Spirit baptism with speaking in tongues, the foregoing should make clear it is much more than that. Certainly tongues are important. When baptized in the Spirit on Pentecost, all the people spoke in tongues, including the Virgin Mary, "and it is difficult to conceive the Lord giving to her an experience which would be unbecoming for her own heart and lips" (123).

Using Augustinian terms, Aimee calls tongues "the glorious outward sign of the inward work" (123). It would be fair to ask whether tongues are *always* the initial evidence that a person has in fact been baptized with the Holy Spirit. Aimee does not precisely answer this question. The book of Acts gives us the normative pattern that tongues follow Spirit baptism. It does not say this pattern is an inviolable rule. But for the person who asks, so much has to do with motive. Says Aimee, "One would perhaps hesitate to make the statement that none shall receive the Spirit in a different manner than did the disciples and the saints of Bible days. It is, however, a self-evident fact that they who refuse the Bible way, and seek some other door, are certainly a long time without find-ing. Perhaps the Lord must make them willing to receive before He can fill them with the old time power" (122).

Tongues and other gifts come from the Giver who gives only good gifts. The prayer for Spirit baptism is not some wish list of particular things one does or does not want. It is a prayer for God to come and to baptize, for God to come and to breathe. Aimee ends one chapter with a kind of prayer that seems a fitting way to end this one:

Lord Jesus, breathe upon us now! Sweep from our hearts all that would hinder Thy Holy Spirit from having right-of-way! Wash us afresh with Thy Precious Blood! Behold, we place ourselves anew upon Thine Holy Altar! Bind us to the horns thereof with strong cords of love! Descend upon us in flames of fire from out the heavenly altars! Baptize us now with power!

Lord, we give to Thee, no matter what the cost, complete right-of-way in our lives. We do not seek the popular way, nor are we cutting corners. We are not seeking that which will help us to stand high in the opinions of the high priests of the synagogue. We are crying unto you for such old-fashioned, dynamic, Holy Ghost power as will bring men and women unto Thee.

Come, Lord, fill our cup to overflowing! Grant, we pray Thee, that such a wave of hunger shall come o'er this congregation that none of us shall rest ere we have tarried until we have been endued with power from on high, and been sent speeding back to meet the world with the requisite for all its needs! (215–16).

Selected Bibliography

Thomas Aquinas

Aquinas, Thomas. *Summa Theologiae*. Translated by Fathers of the English Dominican Province. Westminster, MD: Christian Classics, 1981.

———. *Summa Theologiae*. London: Blackfriars, 1964–1975.

Coppleston, F. C. *Aquinas*. New York: Penguin Books, 1991.

Davies, Brian, ed. *Aquinas's Summa Theologiae: Critical Essays*. New York: Rowman & Littlefield, 2006.

———. *The Thought of Thomas Aquinas*. New York: Oxford University Press, 1993.

Foster, Kenlem, ed. *The Life of Saint Thomas Aquinas: Biographical Documents*. Baltimore: Helicon Press, 1959.

Gilson, Etienne. *The Spirit of Thomism*. New York: P. J. Kenedy & Sons, 1964.

Grenet, Paul. *Thomism: An Introduction*. Translated by James F. Ross. New York: Harper & Row, 1967.

Healy, Nicholas. *Thomas Aquinas: Theologian of the Christian Life*. Burlington, VT: Ashgate Publishing Company, 2003.

Kenny, Anthony, ed. *Aquinas: A Collection of Critical Essays*. Notre Dame, IN: University of Notre Dame Press, 1976.

Kretzmann, Norman, and Eleonore Stump, eds. *The Cambridge Companion to Aquinas*. New York: Cambridge University Press, 1995.

Maritain, Jacques. *St. Thomas Aquinas*. New York: Meridian Books, 1960.

McInerny, Ralph. *Aquinas*. Malden, MA: Blackwell Publishing, 2004.

Nichols, Aidan. *Discovering Aquinas: An Introduction to His Life, Work, and Influence*. Grand Rapids: Wm. B. Eerdmans, 2002.

O'Meara, Thomas F. *Thomas Aquinas: Theologian*. Notre Dame, IN: University of Notre Dame Press, 1997.

Stump, Eleonore. *Aquinas*. London: Routledge, 2003.

Torrell, Jean-Pierre, O. P. *Aquinas' Summa: Background, Structure, and Reception*. Translated by Benedict M. Guevin, OSB. Washington, DC: Catholic University Press, 2005.

———. *Saint Thomas Aquinas*, Vol. 2, *Spiritual Master*. Translated by Robert Royal. Washington, DC: Catholic University Press, 2003.

Wawrykow, Joseph. *The Westminster Handbook to Thomas Aquinas*. Louisville, KY: Westminster John Knox Press, 2005.

Karl Barth

Barth, Karl. *Church Dogmatics*. Translated and edited by G. W. Bromiley. Edinburgh: T. & T. Clark, 1936–1977.

————. *The Teaching of the Church Regarding Baptism*. Translated by Ernest Payne. London: SCM Press, 1948.

————. *The Word of God and the Word of Man*. Translated by Douglas Horton. New York: Harper, 1957.

Bowden, John. *Karl Barth*. London: SCM Press, 1971.

Busch, Eberhard. *Karl Barth: His Life from Letters and Autobiographical Texts*. Translated by John Bowden. Philadelphia: Fortress Press, 1976.

Hunsinger, George. *How to Read Karl Barth*. New York: Oxford University Press, 1991.

McCormack, Bruce. *Karl Barth's Critically Realistic Dialectical Theology: Its Genesis and Development, 1909–1936*. Oxford: Oxford University Press, 1995.

John Calvin

Bouwsma, William James. *John Calvin*. New York: Oxford University Press, 1988.

Calvin, John. *Commentaries*. Edited by Henry Beveridge. Translated by Christopher Fetherstone. Grand Rapids: Wm. B. Eerdmans, 1957.

————. *The Institutes of the Christian Religion*. 2 vols. Edited by John T. McNeill. Translated by Ford Lewis Battles. Philadelphia: Westminster Press, 1960.

————. *Treatises on the Sacraments: Catechism of the Church of Geneva, Forms of Prayer, and Confessions of Faith*. Translated by Henry Beveridge. Grand Rapids: Reformation Heritage Books, 2002.

Douglass, Jane Dempsey. *Women, Freedom, and Calvin*. Philadelphia: Westminster Press, 1985.

Dowey, Edward A. *The Knowledge of God in Calvin's Theology*. New York: Columbia University Press, 1952.

Hesselink, I. John. *Calvin's First Catechism*. Louisville, KY: Westminster John Knox Press, 1997.

McDonnell, Kilian. *John Calvin, the Church, and the Eucharist*. Princeton, NJ: Princeton University Press, 1967.

McKim, Donald K., ed. *The Cambridge Companion to John Calvin*. New York: Cambridge University Press, 2004.

Muller, Richard A. *The Unaccomodated Calvin*. New York: Oxford University Press, 2000.

Niesel, Wilhelm. *The Theology of Calvin*. Translated by Harold Knight. Grand Rapids: Baker Books, 1980.

Parker, Thomas H. L. *Calvin's New Testament Commentaries*. Grand Rapids: Wm. B. Eerdmans, 1971.

————. *Portrait of Calvin*. Philadelphia: Westminster Press, 1954.

Steinmetz, David Curtis. *Calvin in Context*. New York: Oxford University Press, 1995.

Torrance, Thomas F. *Calvin's Doctrine of Man*. Grand Rapids: Wm. B. Eerdmans, 1977.

Martin Luther

Aland, Kurt. *Four Reformers: Luther, Melanchthon, Calvin, Zwingli*. Translated by James L. Schaaf. Minneapolis: Augsburg Publishing House, 1979.

Bainton, Roland. *Here I Stand: A Life of Martin Luther*. New York, Abingdon-Cokesbury Press, 1950.

Luther, Martin. *The Book of Concord: The Confessions of the Evangelical Lutheran Church*. Translated and edited by Theodore G. Tappert. Philadelphia: Muhlenberg Press, 1959.

————. *Luther's Works*. Edited by Jaroslav Pelikan (vols. 1–30) and Helmut T. Lehman (vols. 31–55). St. Louis: Concordia Publishing House, 1958; Philadelphia: Mulhenberg Press, 1959.

McKim, Donald K., ed. *The Cambridge Companion to Martin Luther.* New York: Cambridge University Press, 2003.

Moe-Lobeda, Cynthia D. *Healing a Broken World: Globalization and God.* Minneapolis: Fortress Press, 2002.

Tillich, Paul. *The Courage to Be.* New Haven, CT: Yale University Press, 1980.

Trigg, Jonathan D. *Baptism in the Theology of Martin Luther.* Leiden: E. J. Brill, 1994.

Wengert, Timothy J. *Harvesting Martin Luther's Reflections on Theology, Ethics, and the Church.* Grand Rapids: Wm. B. Eerdmans, 2003.

Aimee Semple McPherson

Blumhofer, Edith. *Aimee Semple McPherson: Everybody's Sister.* Grand Rapids: Wm. B. Eerdmans, 1993.

Blumhofer, Edith, and Randall Balmer, eds. *Modern Christian Revivals.* Chicago: University of Illinois Press, 1993.

Blumhofer, Edith, Russell Spittler, and Grant Wacker. *Pentecostal Currents in American Protestantism.* Chicago: University of Illinois Press, 1999.

Chan, Simon. *Pentecostal Theology and the Christian Spiritual Tradition.* Sheffield, UK: Sheffield Academic Press, 2000.

Dayton, Donald W. *Theological Roots of Pentecostalism.* Grand Rapids: Francis Asbury Press, 1987.

Faupel, D. William. *The Everlasting Gospel: The Significance of Eschatology in the Development of Pentecostal Thought.* Sheffield, UK: Sheffield Academic Press, 1996.

Jacoben, Douglas. *Thinking in the Spirit: Theologies of the Early Pentecostal Movement.* Bloomington: Indiana University Press, 2003.

Johns, Cheryl Bridges. *Pentecostal Formation: A Pedagogy among the Oppressed.* Sheffield, UK: Sheffield Academic Press, 1993.

Land, Steven J. *Pentecostal Spirituality: A Passion for the Kingdom.* Sheffield, UK: Sheffield Academic Press, 1994.

Macchia, Frank D. *Baptized in the Spirit: A Global Pentecostal Theology.* Grand Rapids: Zondervan, 2006.

McPherson, Aimee Semple. *The Holy Spirit.* Los Angeles: Challpin Publishing Co., 1931.

———. *In the Service of the King: The Story of My Life.* New York: Boni & Liveright, 1927.

———. *The Story of My Life.* Waco, TX: Word Books, 1973.

———. *This Is That.* Los Angeles: FourSquare Publications, 1996.

Wacker, Grant. *Heaven Below: Early Pentecostals and American Culture.* Cambridge, MA: Harvard University Press, 2001.

Warner, Michael, ed. *American Sermons: The Pilgrims to Martin Luther King, Jr.* New York: Library Classics, 1999.

Alexander Schmemann

Fisch, Thomas, ed. *Liturgy and Tradition: Theological Reflections of Alexander Schmemann.* Crestwood, NY: St. Vladimir's Seminary Press, 1990.

Hopko, Thomas. "Two 'Nos' and One 'Yes.'" *St. Vladimir's Theological Quarterly* 28, no. 1 (1984): 45–48.

Kadavil, Mathai. *The World as Sacrament: Sacramentality of Creation from the Perspectives of Leonardo Boff, Alexander Schmemann, and Saint Ephrem.* Dudley, MA: Peeters, 2005.

Meyendorff, John. "A Life Worth Living." *St. Vladimir's Theological Quarterly* 28, no. 1 (1984): 3–10.

Plekon, Michael. "The Church, the Eucharist, and the Kingdom: Towards an Assessment of Alexander Schmemann's Theological Legacy." *St. Vladimir's Theological Quarterly* 40, no. 3 (1996): 119–43.

———. *Living Icons: Persons of Faith in the Eastern Church*. Notre Dame, IN: University of Notre Dame Press, 2002.

Schmemann, Alexander. *The Celebration of Faith: Sermons*. Vol. 1. Trans. by John A. Jillians. Crestwood, NY: St. Vladimir's Seminary Press, 1991.

———. *The Eucharist: Sacrament of the Kingdom*. Crestwood, NY: St. Vladimir's Seminary Press, 1987.

———. *For the Life of the World: Sacraments and Orthodoxy*. Crestwood, NY: St. Vladimir's Seminary Press, 2002.

———. *The Journals of Father Alexander Schmemann, 1973–1983*. Trans. Juliana Schmemann. Crestwood, NY: St. Vladimir's Seminary Press, 2000.

———. "Problems of Orthodoxy in America: The Spiritual Problem." *St. Vladimir's Theological Quarterly* 9, no. 4 (1965).

———. "Russian Theology: 1920–1972: An Introductory Survey." *St. Vladimir's Theological Quarterly* 16 (1972).

———. *Of Water and the Spirit: A Liturgical Study of Baptism*. Crestwood, NY: St. Vladimir's Seminary Press, 1974.

———, ed. *Church, World, Mission: Reflections on Orthodoxy and the West*. Crestwood, NY: St. Vladimir's Seminary Press, 1997.

Scorer, Peter. "Alexander Schmemann (1921–83)." *Sobernost* 6, no. 2 (1984): 64–68.

Slesinki, Robert. "The Theological Legacy of Alexander Schmemann." *Diakonia* 29 (1984–1985): 87–95.

John Wesley

Borgen, Ole E. *John Wesley on the Sacraments*. Zurich: Publishing House of the United Methodist Church, 1972.

Haddal, Ingvar. *John Wesley: A Biography*. New York: Epworth Press, 1961.

Hattersley, Roy. *The Life of John Wesley: A Brand from the Burning*. New York: Doubleday, 2003.

Holland, Bernard George. *Baptism in Early Methodism*. London: Epworth Press, 1970.

Schmidt, Martin. *John Wesley: A Theological Biography*. Translated by Denis Inman. New York: Abingdon Press, 1973.

Smith, Timothy L., ed. *Whitefield and Wesley on the New Birth*. Grand Rapids: Francis Asbury Press, 1986.

Tomkins, Stephen. *John Wesley: A Biography*. Grand Rapids: Wm. B. Eerdmans, 2003.

Wesley, John. *The Works of John Wesley*. 4 vols. Edited by Albert C. Outler. Nashville: Abingdon Press, 1984.

John Howard Yoder

Bender, Ross Thomas. *The People of God: A Mennonite Interpretation of the Free Church Tradition*. Scottdale, PA: Herald Press, 1971.

Dyck, C. J., ed. *The Witness of the Holy Spirit: Proceedings of the Eighth Mennonite World Conference*. Nappannee, IN: Evangel Press, 1968.

Hauerwas, Stanley, Chris K. Huebner, Harry J. Huebner, and Mark Thiessen Nation, eds. *The Wisdom of the Cross: Essays in Honor of John Howard Yoder*. Grand Rapids: Wm. B. Eerdmans, 1999.

Klassen, William, ed. *The New Way of Jesus: Essays Presented to Howard Charles*. Newton, KS: Faith and Life Press, 1980.

LeMaster, Philip. *The Import of Eschatology in John Howard Yoder's Critique of Constantinianism*. San Francisco: Edwin Mellen Research University Press, 1992.

McKim, Donald K., ed. *How Karl Barth Changed My Mind*. Grand Rapids: Wm. B. Eerdmans, 1986.

Stassen, Glen Harold, D. M. Yeager, and John Howard Yoder. *Authentic Transformation: A New Vision of Christ and Culture*. Nashville: Abingdon Press, 1996.

World Council of Churches. *Baptism, Eucharist, and Ministry*. Faith and Order Paper No. 111. Geneva: World Council of Churches Publications, 1982.

Yoder, John Howard. "The Believers' Church Conferences in Historical Perspective." *Mennonite Quarterly Review* 65 (January 1991): 5–19.

———. *Body Politics: Five Practices of the Christian Community before the Watching World*. Scottdale, PA: Herald Press, 2001.

———. *The Ecumenical Movement and the Faithful Church*. Scottdale, PA: Mennonite Publishing House, 1958.

———. *The Politics of Jesus*. Grand Rapids: Wm. B. Eerdmans, 2003.

———. *Preface to Theology: Christology and Theological Method*. Grand Rapids: Brazos Press, 2002.

———. *The Priestly Kingdom*. Notre Dame, IN: University of Notre Dame Press, 1984.

———. "Reinhold Niebuhr and Christian Pacifism." *Mennonite Quarterly Review* 29 (April 1955): 101–17.

———. *The Royal Priesthood: Essays Ecclesiological and Ecumenical*. Edited by Michael G. Cartwright. Scottdale, PA: Herald Press, 1998.

Index